TOWARDS A LIVEABLE AND SUSTAINABLE URBAN ENVIRONMENT

Eco-Cities in East Asia

TOWARDS A LIVEABLE AND SUSTAINABLE URBAN ENVIRONMENT

Eco-Cities in East Asia

editors

Lye Liang Fook
Chen Gang

East Asian Institute, National University of Singapore

World Scientific

NEW JERSEY · LONDON · SINGAPORE · BEIJING · SHANGHAI · HONG KONG · TAIPEI · CHENNAI

Published by

World Scientific Publishing Co. Pte. Ltd.

5 Toh Tuck Link, Singapore 596224

USA office: 27 Warren Street, Suite 401-402, Hackensack, NJ 07601

UK office: 57 Shelton Street, Covent Garden, London WC2H 9HE

British Library Cataloguing-in-Publication Data
A catalogue record for this book is available from the British Library.

TOWARDS A LIVEABLE AND SUSTAINABLE URBAN ENVIRONMENT
Eco-Cities in East Asia

ISBN-13 978-981-4287-76-0
ISBN-10 981-4287-76-8

Typeset by Stallion Press
Email: enquiries@stallionpress.com

Printed in Singapore by World Scientific Printers.

Contents

Acknowledgement

This book is the outcome of a workshop organized by the East Asian Institute (EAI) of the National University of Singapore on 27 February 2009 to share experience on existing practices on eco-cities or eco-friendly projects among scholars and practitioners in the region.

At a broader level, the workshop had intended to lend its voice to the pressing need to devise a more sustainable model of urban living, one that will take into account environmental and social needs while pursuing economic growth.

In particular, we would like to thank Professor John Wong, then Research Director and now Professorial Fellow of EAI, for conceiving the topic of this workshop. Professor John Wong further motivated us to compile the papers submitted at the workshop into a book. He also provided useful ideas that helped us to write the introductory chapter.

We would further like to thank the various contributors for drafting the papers which are compiled in this volume. Our gratitude also extends to the staff from the *World Scientific* for their strong support including editorial, design and coordinating work which has made this publication an enjoyable experience.

Towards Eco-Cities in East Asia

Introduction

The galloping process of industrialisation, urbanisation and globalisation has brought mounting environmental problems including climate change, acid rain, water shortage and pollution, hazardous waste, smog, ozone depletion, loss of bio-diversity and desertification that pose severe challenges to sustainable development of our human society. Environmental considerations are assuming greater importance in the urban planning processes of an increasing number of governments around the world. Cities, now home to half of the world's population, are increasingly at the forefront of our most pressing environmental challenges which require governments, public and private organisations, and individuals to take a fresh perspective at how economic and social activities can best be organised particularly for those living in crowded urban areas.

In some industrialised regions such as the European Union, around 80% of the population there lives in urban areas and the majority of these people live in small to medium-sized towns and cities. In the developing world like China and India, the sheer magnitude of urbanisation driven by massive demographic shifts is unprecedented, with vast implications for human well-being and the environment. In the metropolises where population growth has outpaced the urban capacity to provide sufficient infrastructure and services, the worst environmental problems are at the doorstep. Bearing in mind the fairly-new but serious challenges posed by climate change, people should also be reminded that the world's cities today account for 75% of global energy consumption and 80% of greenhouse gas (GHG) emissions. Although city dwellers in developed countries with the highest per capita levels of consumption in the world are largely responsible for these resource consumption and emissions, major cities in the developing

1

countries especially emerging markets are quickly catching up and becoming wealthier, bringing their consumption levels closer to those of the industrialised world. Due to rapid industrialisation and increased motorised transport, many cities in developing countries are experiencing the world's worst urban air pollution that poses enormous threat to human health. The United Nations Environment Programme (UNEP) estimated in 2008 that urban air pollution causes one million premature deaths each year and costs 2% of the GDP in developed countries and 5% in developing countries.

As a result of these urban growth patterns, cities that occupy less than 3% of the world's land mass witness an ecological footprint that extends far beyond their urban boundaries to the forests, mountains, rivers and ore mines in order to sustain the insatiable needs of the urban population. Consumption of fossil fuels and emissions of GHGs continues to increase, especially for transport, and resources such as metals, water and energy, which should be preserved for future generations, are being excessively exploited. Urban sprawling is eroding large suburbia areas, impairing the overall life quality of more and more people. The need to make cities more resource-efficient and less polluting is hence more urgent than ever.

From Garden City to Eco-City

How to plan and build our cities more sustainably, efficiently and liveably without damaging the ecological surroundings have been a focus of scholars, practitioners and activists for more than a 100 years. As early as 1898, Sir Ebenezer Howard launched the "garden city" movement, aiming to promote the concept of garden cities comprising planned and self-contained communities surrounded by greenbelts as well as carefully balanced areas of residences, industry, and agriculture. Ebenezer Howard's famous book *Tomorrow: a Peaceful Path to Real Reform*, which was first published in 1898 and then re-printed in 1902 as *Garden Cities of To-morrow*, has had profound influence on ecological urban development all over the world and provided indispensable groundwork for the evolution of the "eco-city" concept. In the mid-1970s after the first oil crisis, Urban Ecology, a U.S. Berkeley-based non-profit organisation was established to address the importance of compact urban structure and other city planning approaches in saving energy and resources. This organisation coined the term "eco-city" to address the sustainability of city development. Richard Register, founder of Urban Ecology, argued in his influential book *Ecocities: Building Cities in Balance with Nature* that people have been trying to build cities in balance with nature all along but have continually been led astray.[1] He advocates more density at closer proximity, because when the distance between destinations goes up, so does energy use, waste, and land-use, or "footprint". Urban Ecology organised the first international conference on eco-city that was held in Berkeley, California, in 1990. Up to 2006, five international conferences on this topic had been organised in several countries, namely, Australia, Senegal, Brazil, China and India. Although Urban Ecology defines the eco-city concept as a goal to "rebuild cities in balance with nature", most environmentalists, architects and engineers agree that there is no clear-cut and universal definition, principle, model or content for this notion. In the book *Eco-City Dimensions: Healthy Communities, Healthy Planet*, Mark Roseland listed 10 principles for practitioners to create ecological cities, defining the notion as the most durable kind of settlement that humans are capable of building and a city that provides an acceptable standard of living without depleting the eco-systems or bio-geochemical cycles on which it depends.[2] Today, the main task of working towards a sustainable urban planning is addressed at the United Nations Human Settlements Programme, UN HABITAT. In association with the United Nations Environmental Programme (UNEP), the Sustainable Cities Programme (SCP) has been established to improve urban environmental planning and management, a sister programme to Agenda 21 that aims to manage global issues at a local level.

In the ensuing debate on how to integrate sustainability into city planning, one of the central and foremost issues is the relationship between transportation and urban life. The modern concept of eco-city was set in the context that cities all over the world were being quickly motorised with increasing dependence on the use of private cars. The simultaneous suburbanisation and city sprawling process has made commuters travel much longer distances than before to reach places of exchange such as shops, schools, offices and theatres. Since the establishment of Urban Ecology in 1970s, almost all the eco-city advocators have been talking about compact

---

[1]Register, Richard (2002). *Ecocities: Building Cities in Balance with Nature*. Berkeley: Berkeley Hills Books.
[2]Roseland, Mark (ed.) (1997). *Eco-City Dimensions: Healthy Communities, Healthy Planet*. Gabriola Island, BC: New Society Publishers.

city structure, self-sufficient neighbourhood, strengthened city centre and limitation of private car usage.

David Engwicht was one of those acutely aware of the problem posed by the rapid and increasing allocation of the surface area of cities to motor car usage. In his book *Toward an Eco-City: Calming the Traffic*, David Engwicht discussed how traffic destroys the eco-city, revisiting the fundamental purposes and functions of cities.[3] He argued that the car-dominated way of movement does not facilitate exchange of information, friendship, material goods, culture and knowledge; on the contrary, the wide use of cars in cities inevitably leads to movement space (roads, car parks and train tracks) erosion of exchange space (homes, shops, work places, parks and community halls). According to Engwhicht, this resulted in not only the obliteration of some exchange opportunities but also a vicious cycle in which fewer accessible exchange places require more movement that demands more space be converted from exchange places to movement space. He worked out ten guidelines for re-building the eco-city including building healthy neighbourhoods, optimising exchange efficiency, charging the true costs for access to exchange opportunities and building public facilities, and putting forward four modest proposals, namely, seven year moratorium and revitalisation of neighbourhoods, encouraging exchange-friendly neighbourhood development, city-wide calming and experimental car-free urban villages. Such similar thrusts were also reflected in the works of other urban ecologists such as Richard Register and Mark Roseland, as well as relevant reports by the United Nations and other international organisations. According to the UN HABITAT II Chapter 7 of Article 151, governments in partnership with private sectors, community sectors and other relevant interested parties should "coordinate land-use and transport planning in order to encourage spatial settlement patterns that facilitate access to such basic necessities as workplaces, schools, health care, places of worship, goods and other services, and leisure, thereby reducing the need to travel" and "encourage the use of an optimal combination of modes of transport, including walking, cycling and private and public means of transportation, through appropriate pricing, spatial settlement policies and regulatory measures".

Sustainable transport is just one important aspect that most eco-city projects place emphasis on, while latest research findings have been

---

[3]Engwicht, David (1992). *Towards an Eco-city: Calming the Traffic*, pp. 41–66. Sydney: Envirobook.

increasingly focused on a much more comprehensive picture, which should also include advanced water treatment system, solid waste disposal capacity, wide use of renewable energy and enhancement of bio-diversity. More important is how to translate such well-meaning concepts into practice and balance the environmental protection, economic growth and social harmony in the context of local requirements. Under an eco-city themed project sponsored by European Commission, Philine Gaffron, Ge Huismans and Franz Skala jointly depicted the definition, objectives, planning process and model settlement of eco-cities in *Ecocity Book I: A Better Place to Live*,[4] and subsequently, put forward guidelines and detailed planning techniques and tools to put the concept into practice in *Ecocity Book II: How to Make it Happen*.[5] They advocated that "eco-city guidelines and objectives have to be woven together with local requirements", arguing that "an eco-city should be understood as a single integrated system (holistic approach) and not as a combination or result of many sectoral developments planned in isolation". In their books on eco-city planning, those sectors related to the metabolic and environmental functions of the city (transport, energy and material flows and socio-economic aspects), which conventional planning considers as subsidiary to urban structure, are accorded the same level of importance.

In Ooi Giok Ling's book *Sustainability and Cities: Concept and Assessment*, the author discussed extensively the realisation of sustainable development in cities and the usefulness of quantitative and qualitative indicators to assess and monitor the green effort in cities, using Singapore as a case study.[6] Besides sustainable urban transport, the book also included chapters on urban housing, urban population, management of non-hazardous solid waste and the "neglected agenda" relating to bio-diversity, ecological integrity and public participation. Ooi highlighted the sharp contrast in that Singapore had insisted at the beginning that the cleaning-up would proceed in tandem with economic growth, while the other three emerging markets in East Asia, namely Hong Kong, South Korea and Taiwan had adopted the approach of industrialising first and

---

[4]Gaffron, Philine, Ge Huismans and Franz Skala (2005). *Ecocity Book I: A Better Place to Live*. Vienna: Facultas Verlags-und Buchhandels AG.

[5]Gaffron, Philine, Ge Huismans and Franz Skala (2008). *Ecocity Book II: How to Make It Happen*, Vienna: Facultas Verlags-und Buchhandels AG.

[6]Ooi, Giok Ling (2005). *Sustainability and Cities: Concept and Assessment*, pp. 80–108. Singapore: World Scientific.

then cleaning-up later. Compared with early works on the topic, current research is trying to give a clearer and more detailed and technical solution to implement the eco-city concept rather than just outlining the basic principles.

The growing number of studies on the eco-city concept and practices over the years has underscored the importance of further studying the interaction between urbanisation and sustainable development. Cities are often viewed as the engine of economic growth, but today more and more nations have realised that it is time to alter the traditional emphasis on the single-minded pursuit of higher economic growth with scant regard for environmental protection and social harmony. As the globalisation process deepens and the planet's natural processes transform local problems into transnational and transcontinental issues that demand collective actions, few societies are being left untouched by major environmental problems. As hubs of prosperity, cities have been blamed for causing environmental degradation due to the high-carbon lifestyle and huge amount of waste generated. It is therefore extremely important to understand that one of the most effective solutions to current environmental problems on a global scale lie in the way we plan and build our cities.

Contributions of This Book

The burning issue confronting us today is not whether eco-cities should be built or whether eco-friendly projects should be undertaken but how to ensure that existing cities and new ones that will sprout up will enhance the environment or at least not cause further damage to it. Rather than go for a big-bang, this book advocates a practical and incremental approach to build eco-cities or to simply move closer towards this goal. The steps that are taken should not ignore current realities and challenges. Instead, present realities and challenges ought to be taken on board in planning for eco-cities or eco-friendly projects. This will facilitate a more realistic outcome and gradually encourage more buy-in from existing interests groups long accustomed to the high consumption and high wastage style of living.

It is important to recognise that every government, organisation or individual on this planet, whether in the public or private sectors, can and has a role to play in saving and protecting our environment. In other words, there is a common and shared responsibility for everyone living on this planet. Those who are more capable and have more resources ought to do more. Those who are less able and have less at their disposal should not conveniently eschew playing a role. Having common but differentiated responsibilities should be welcomed.

The concept of "eco-city" originates from the fundamental objective of sustainability and the application of ecological principles to urban planning, design and management. "Sustainability" and in turn "sustainable development" can mean different things to different people, making it challenging to provide a single definition. This book therefore adopts the original and most widely used definition of sustainable development as contained in the 1987 Brundtland Report commissioned by the United Nations General Assembly. The report defines sustainable development as "development that meets the needs of the present without compromising the ability of future generations to meet their own needs".

As an important model of sustainable development, we believe that an eco-city must be economically, environmentally and socially sustainable (see Fig. 1 below). These three essential components must be present in order to be regarded as a sustainable eco-city or an eco-friendly project. First, on the environmental front, the eco-city must be able to protect or, preferably, even enhance the environment. Within the eco-city, there

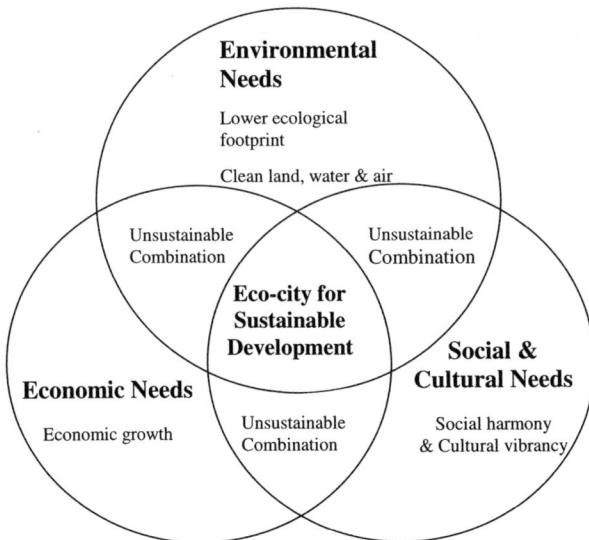

Fig. 1   Eco-city for Sustainable Development

ought to be important aspects or features such as the application of green technologies, environmentally sustainable transportation, rational use of space, green-belts and parks, and cultural and heritage conservation. On the whole, the eco-city should strive towards producing a lower ecological footprint. This would require paying attention not only to what is being practised within the confines of the eco-city itself but also to the impact of building an eco-city beyond the confines of such a city.

Second, on the economic front, the eco-city must be able to contribute to the growth of the economy through attracting investments and generating employment. Economic growth will provide the necessary resources to the government, to organisations and individuals to better protect the environment. More importantly, economic growth will raise the living standards of the people. Over time, with greater prosperity and better living standards, the people will likely become more aware and supportive of efforts to safeguard the environment especially if the environment is regarded as critical to their well-being and quality of life.

Third, on the social and cultural front, the eco-city must be able to meet social considerations including promoting interactions and strengthening the bonds of friendship and even unity among the different ethnic and religious groups of society. An eco-city must not become or be perceived as an enclave for only the rich and powerful but must welcome and be accessible to people from various walks of life. The eco-city should also provide employment for residents living in it so as to maximise convenience for them and minimise travel out of the city. By allowing residents to witness and experience the benefits of living in an eco-city, they will become strong advocates for the norms, values and practices prevalent in such a city. This will foster valuable ground-level support — a key ingredient if the eco-city is to last.

Having discussed the three essential components of an eco-city, it must be unambiguously stated here that this book does not seek to prescribe a single blueprint of sustainability. It would not be prudent to do so as different countries and societies have their unique political, socio-economic, cultural and historical circumstances. Moreover, their capabilities in terms of resources and competitive advantages differ from one to the other. Hence, the model described above is not intended to be a one size that would fit all.

Most importantly, individual countries and societies have to strike a balance among the three essential components of an eco-city. Such a city would not be sustainable if any of the component parts is ignored or neglected. For instance, merely focusing on economic growth and environmental protection would not be viable if the cost involved is too high and the people who are supposed to directly benefit from it are against it. Also, merely concentrating on achieving environmental protection and social and cultural needs without generating economic wealth and gainful employment will be unrealistic. There has to be wealth first before other priorities can be fulfilled. Furthermore, merely emphasising economic growth and social and cultural needs while neglecting the environment will be disastrous in the long run. In pursuit of eco-cities, the three dimensions of harmony or sustainability must be met simultaneously even though the exact mix may differ. Taken together, a project that has a balanced mix of the economic, environmental, and social and cultural needs will be in a good position to reduce the ecological footprint while improving the quality of life for current and future generations.

Besides outlining a model of a sustainable city, the other significant contribution of this book is to provide a snapshot of the development of eco-cities from the Asian perspective. Most books on eco-cities or eco-friendly projects are usually written either from the Western perspective or concentrate on practices in Western countries. A brief survey of the books written on eco-cities or sustainable cities in recent years can generally be divided into three broad categories. The first category includes books that examine the topic of eco-cities or sustainable cities from the broad or strategic perspective. They include aspects such as the significance and rationale, policies and strategies, current debates, salient features, and measurable indicators of building eco-cities or sustainable cities.[7]

The second category of books tends to single out specific aspects or features of eco-cities or sustainable cities for further study. The

---

[7]Kemp, Roger L. (ed.) (2008). *Cities and Growth: A Policy Handbook.* North Carolina: McFarland and Company; Wheeler, Stephen M. and Timothy Beatley (2008). *The Sustainable Urban Development Reader.* New York: Routledge; Wachter Susan M. (2008). *Growing Greener Cities: Urban Sustainability in the 21st Century.* Philadelphia: University of Pennsylvania Press; Fontana-Giusti, Gordana (2008). *Designing Cities for People: Social, Environmental and Psychological Sustainability.* London: Earthscan; Short, Lisa Benton and John Rennie Short (2007). *Cities and Nature.* New York: Routledge; Curwell, Stephen, Mark Deakin and Martin Symes (2005). *Sustainable Urban Development: The Framework and Protocols for Environmental Assessment,* Vol. 1. London: Routledge; Curwell, Stephen, Mark Deakin and Martin Symes (2007). *Sustainable Urban Development: The Environmental Assessment Methods,* Vol. 2. London: Routledge; and, Curwell, Stephen Mark Deakin and Martin Symes (2009). *Sustainable Urban Development: The Toolkit for Assessment,* Vol. 9. London: Routledge.

particulars areas that are being examined may range from the use of green transport and transport-related policies,[8] sources of renewable energy and energy-related policies,[9] land-use and urban policies,[10] urban planning and/or urban design,[11] green houses or green buildings (that are aesthetically compelling as well as environmentally-friendly),[12] rehabilitation of waterways or canals,[13] understanding and implementing sustainable practices at the local levels (as opposed to the national level),[14] the linkage

---

[8]Sucharov, Lance and C. A. Brebbia (ed.) (2000). *Urban Transport VI: Urban Transport and the Environment for the 21st Century.* Boston: Wessex Institute of Technology; Sucharov, Lance and G. Bidini (1997). *Urban Transport III: Urban Transport and the Environment for the 21st Century.* Boston: Computational Mechanics Publications; Newman, Peter and Jeffrey Kenworthy (1999). *Sustainability and Cities: Overcoming Automobile Dependence.* Washington D.C.: Island Press; and, Engwicht, David (1992). *Towards an Eco-City: Calming the Traffic.* Sydney: Envirobook.

[9]Droege, Peter (ed.) (2008). *Urban Energy Transition: From Fossil Fuels to Renewable Power.* Oxford: Elsevier; Mega, Voula (2008). *Sustainable Development, Energy and the City.* New York: Springer; and, Capello, Roberta, Peter Nijkamp and Gerard Pepping (1999). *Sustainable Cities and Energy Policies.* New York: Springer.

[10]Chalifour, Nathalie J, Patricia Kameri-Mbote, Heng Lye Lin and John R. Nolon (ed.) (2007). *Land Use Law for Sustainable Development.* New York: Cambridge University Press; and, Banister, David, Kenneth J. Button and Peter Nijkamp (ed.) (1999). *Environment, Land Use and Urban Policy.* Northampton, Massachusetts: Edward Elgar Publishing.

[11]Cooper, Rachel, Graeme Evans and Christopher Boyko (ed.) (2009). *Designing Sustainable Cities: Decision-Making Tools and Resources for Design.* Ames, Iowa: Wiley-Blackwell; Cliff, Moughtin, Kate McMahon Moughtin and Paola Signoretta (2009). *Urban Design: Health and the Therapeutic Environment.* Amsterdam: Architectural Press; Ratcliffe, John, Michael Stubbs and Miles Keeping (2009). *Urban Planning and Real Estate Development.* Oxford, UK: Routledge; Newman, Peter, Timothy Beatley and Heather Boyer (2009). *Resilient Cities: Responding to Peak Oil and Climate Change.* Washington D.C.: Island Press; Farr, Douglas (2008). *Sustainable Urbanism: Urban Design with Nature.* Hoboken, New Jersey: Wiley; Miller, Donald and Gert de Roo (2004). *Integrating City Planning and Environmental Improvement: Practical Strategies for Sustainable Urban Development.* Brookfield, Victoria: Ashgate Publishing; and, Moughtin, Cliff (1996). *Urban Design: Green Dimensions.* Boston: Butterworth Architecture.

[12]Gallent, Nick and Mark Tewdwr-Jones (2007). *Decent Homes for All: Planning's Evolving Role in Housing Provision.* New York: Routledge; Stang, Alanna and Christopher Hawthorne (2005). *The Green House: New Directions in Sustainable Architecture.* New York: Princeton Architectural Press; and, Yudelson, Jerry (2008). *The Green Building Revolution.* Washington D.C.: Island Press.

[13]Nothmann, Frank (2006). *A Guidebook for Riverside Regeneration: Artery — Transforming Riversides for the Future.* New York: Springer.

[14]Lauren, C. Heberle and Susan M. Opp (2008). *Local Sustainable Urban Development in a Globalized World.* Aldershot, England: Ashgate Publishing; and, Gouldson, Andrew and Peter Roberts (2000). *Integrating Environment and Economy: Strategies for Local and Regional Government.* New York: Routledge.

among tourism, culture and urban renewal,[15] the legal aspects of urban and sustainable development,[16] the integration of agriculture into the urban landscape,[17] to the ethics of architecture.[18]

The third category of books generally focuses on case studies of eco-cities or eco-friendly practices in various countries. In particular, there is a vast literature on the experiences and practices (including achievements and challenges) of building sustainable cities or undertaking eco-friendly projects in the West, which includes the countries in Europe,[19] the U.S.,[20] Canada[21] and Australia.[22] Only some of the more recent ones are highlighted here to provide some flavour and substantiation as they are too numerous to name. The main reason for such voluminous literature is

---

[15]Melanie K. Smith (ed.) (2007). *Tourism, Culture and Regeneration*. Wallingford, CABI Publishing.

[16]Daniel K. Slone, Doris S. Goldstein and Gowder W. Andrew (2008). *A Legal Guide to Urban and Sustainable Development for Planners, Developers and Architects*. Hoboken, New Jersey: Wiley.

[17]Luc J. A. Mougeot (2005). *Agropolis: The Social, Political and Environmental Dimensions of Urban Agriculture*. Ottawa: Earthscan.

[18]Fox Warwick (ed.) (2000). *Ethics and the Built Environment*. London: Routledge.

[19]Clark Peter (ed.) (2006). *The European City and Green Space: London, Stockholm, Helsinki and St. Petersburg, 1850–2000*. Aldershot, England: Ashgate Publishing; Altrock, Uwe (ed.) (2006). *Spatial Planning and Urban Development in the New EU Member States*. Aldershot, England: Ashgate Publishing; Hooper, Alan and John Punter (ed.) (2006). *Capital Cardiff 1975–2020: Regeneration, Competitiveness and the Urban Environment*. Cardiff: University of Wales Press; Hunt, Julian (ed.) (2005). *London's Environment: Prospects for a Sustainable World City*. London: Imperial College Press; Moore, Niamh and Mark Scott (ed.) (2005). *Renewing Urban Communities: Environment, Citizenship and Sustainability in Ireland*. Aldershot, England: Ashgate Publishing; Holmes, Chris (2005). *A New Vision for Housing*. New York: Routledge; C. A. Fletcher and T. Spencer (ed.) (2005). *Flooding and Environmental Challenges for Venice and Its Lagoon*. Cambridge: Cambridge University Press; Chris Couch (2003). *City of Change and Challenge: Urban Planning and Regeneration in Liverpool*. Aldershot, England: Ashgate Publishing; and, Ravetz, Joe and Peter Roberts (2000). *City-Region 2020: Integrated Planning for a Sustainable Environment*. London: Earthscan.

[20]John M. Levy (2009). *Contemporary Urban Planning*. New Jersey: Pearson Prentice Hall; Christopher B. Leinberger (2008). *The Option of Urbanism: Investing in a New American Dream*. Washington D.C: Island Press; Douglas R. Porter (2008). *Managing Growth in America's Communities*. Washington D.C.: Island Press; and, Rob J. Krueger and David Gibbs (2007). *The Sustainable Development Paradox: Urban Political Economy in the United States and Europe*. New York: Guilford Press.

[21]Ferrara, Luigi and Emily Visser (ed.) (2008). *Canada Innovates: Sustainable Building*. Toronto: Key Porter Books; and, Patrick M. Condon, *Sustainability by Design: A Vision for a Region of 4 Million*. Vancouver, B.C.: Design Center for Sustainability.

[22]Beatley, Timothy and Peter Newman (2008). *Green Urbanism Down Under: Learning from Sustainable Communities in Australia*. Washington D.C.: Island Press.

most probably due to the fact that many of the developed countries in the West, which have attained a certain standard of economic growth, have become more aware of the negative impact of unbridled economic activities on the environment. Hence, one of the key focuses of policy-makers, non-governmental organisations, academics and even individuals is to ensure quality growth, i.e., growth that balances the requirements of the environment and other considerations such as social and cultural needs. Even businesses see value in internalising green practices and green standards in their operations to stay competitive in the long run. Their products can become more appealing to consumers which will in turn increase their profit margin.

To be sure, Western authors have also looked at eco-cities or eco-friendly projects in Asia, but these seemed to be generally written within the context of their examination of eco-cities or eco-friendly projects in the developing world which also includes some countries of Asia. For example, in *Designing Sustainable Cities in the Developing World*, Roger Zetter and Georgia Butina Watson examine various case studies in the developing world that included Mexico, South Africa, Brazil, Saudi Arabia, Bethlehem-Palestine and Bijapur (India).[23] India is the only Asian country included in the study. In *Compact Cities: Sustainable Urban Forms for Developing Countries*, Mike Jenks and Rod Burgess discuss compact cities in the context of developing countries that included Colombia, Brazil, Egypt, Chile, South Africa, China (covering case studies on mainland China, Hong Kong and Taiwan), India and Thailand.[24] In these studies, Asia is not seen on its own merits alone, but as part of the developing world.

Increasingly, however, there appears to be greater interest by scholars (that increasingly includes Asian authors either working alone or in collaboration with Western authors) who look at eco-cities or eco-friendly projects either from the Asian perspective or dwelling on Asian examples.

---

[23]Zetter, Roger and Georgia Butina Watson (ed.) (2008). *Designing Sustainable Cities in the Developing World*. Aldershot, England: Ashgate Publishing.

[24]Jenks, Mike and Rod Burgess (2000). *Compact Cities: Sustainable Urban Forms for Developing Countries*. London: Spon Press; Steven A. Moore examines alternative routes to the sustainable city by conducting in-depth study into three cities, namely Austin (Texas), Curitiba (Brazil) and Frankfurt (Germany). No Asian city is mentioned in his study. See Moore, Steven A. (2007). *Alternative Routes to the Sustainable City*. Lanham: Lexington Books; and, Myers Garth Andrew takes a critical look at the issues of refuse disposal and sustainable development in three cities, namely, Dar es Salaam (Tanzania), Zanzibar (Tanzania) and Lusaka (Zambia). See Myers, Garth Andrew (2005). *Disposable Cities: Garbage Governance and Sustainable Development in Urban Africa*. Aldershot: Ashgate Publishing.

Most of such literature tends to focus either on the strategic significance of building sustainable cities in Asia or on examples (or best practices) in the more prominent developing countries such as mainland China (covering case studies on the mainland and Hong Kong)[25] and India.[26] Such growing interest can be attributed to the large and growing population in the urban areas in these two countries which will have significant environmental implications. In addition, while discussing Asia, it is worth noting that countries like Japan and to some extent South Korea have been at the forefront of building eco-cities and have vast experience and insights to share on this topic.[27] And as pointed out earlier, Singapore is another country that had at a very early stage of its independence realised the importance of incorporating the green agenda into its city planning.[28]

The papers in this collection are intended to enrich the existing literature on this topic from the Asian perspective by highlighting case studies of eco-cities or eco-friendly practices carried out by the important developing countries in Southeast Asia like Indonesia, Malaysia, Thailand and the Philippines in addition to the more well-known ones like China, Japan and Singapore. The purpose is to provide an understanding of

---

[25]Pitts, Adrian and Liao Hanwen (2009). *Sustainable Olympic Design and Urban Development*. New York: Taylor and Francis; Day. Kristen A (ed.) (2005). *China's Environment and the Challenge of Sustainable Development*. Armonk: M.E. Sharpe; and, Schaik, Leon Van (2003). *Ecocells: Landscapes and Masterplans*. Chichester, West Sussex, England: Wiley-Academy.

[26]Prasad, Archana (ed.) (2008). *Environment, Development and Society in Contemporary India: An Introduction*. Delhi: Macmillan; Pachauri Rajendra (2007). *Coping with Climate Change: Is Development in India and the World Sustainable*. Canberra: Research School of Pacific and Asian Studies, Australian National University; Bhatnagar Amitabh (2007). *Successful Experiments in Rural Development/Livelihoods: Sage and Sound Recipes*. Bhopal: Madhya Pradesh Rural Livelihoods Project, State Livelihoods Forum and Zenith Books International; Chattopadhyay, Srikumar, and Franke, Richard W. (2006). *Striving for Sustainability: Environmental Stress and Democratic Initiatives in Kerala*. New Delhi: Concept Publishing; and, Ray, Binayak (1996). *India: Sustainable Development and Good Governance Issues*. New Delhi: Atlantic Publishers.

[27]Sorensen, Andre and Carolin Funck (ed.) (2007). *Living Cities in Japan: Citizens' Movements, Machizukuri and Local Environments*. New York: Routledge; and, Tamagawa, Hidenori (2006). *Sustainable Cities: Japanese Perspectives on Physical and Social Structures*. New York: United Nations University Press.

[28]Wong, Tai-Chee, Belinda Yuen and Charles Goldblum (2008). *Spatial Planning for a Sustainable Singapore*. Netherlands: Springer, in association with the Singapore Institute of Planners; Ooi, Giok Ling (2005). *Sustainability and Cities: Concept and Assessment*. Singapore: World Scientific; and, Ruby, Ilka and Andreas Ruby (ed.) (2008). *Urban Transformation*. Berlin: Ruby Press.

the current state of play in building eco-cities or undertaking eco-friendly projects in these countries. The papers highlight the role of various actors such as governments (including central and local), interests groups, local communities and even individuals in this effort. More importantly, the challenges of embarking on such efforts are mentioned as well as the actions needed to address these challenges. The papers indicate that building eco-cities or undertaking eco-city projects are wrought with difficulties and is a process that has to be constantly monitored and even micro-managed to achieve the desired outcomes. Rather than be discouraged by the harsh realities on the ground, such case studies should provide useful references or pointers to proponents of the green agenda to push even stoically ahead by being aware of the challenges they may encounter on the ground.

The first two chapters mainly focus on the theoretical evolution of the concepts and key ideas of eco-cities, their rationale and the urgency to find a more sustainable way forward. In Chapter 1, Hidefumi IMURA provides a strategic overview of urbanisation in Asia and then discusses the objectives and goals of eco-city in the 21st century as well as the policies and measures to achieve them. He observes that although the term eco-city emerged towards the end of the 1980s, the ideas associated with such a term had existed for years. He argues that the meaning of eco-city has changed in line with the expanding breadth of environmental issues as well as changing priorities in the international and national environment policy. In Chapter 2, William S.W. LIM highlights three critically interdependent perspectives. These are the escalating global climatic crisis and the urgency to find a sustainable way forward; the global financial turmoil and the necessity of a new development model, one that is less resource intensive and generates less waste; and, the uniqueness of Asian cities because of their "chaotic order, pluralistic richness and unintentional complexity". Lim is ardently confident that Asian cities will be able to find their own unique and attractive model of preserving their urban landscape by tastefully combining features of the old and new which is likely to be different from the "universalistic assumptions of Eurocentric modernity".

The other chapters adopt a more specific focus by examining examples of eco-cities or eco-friendly projects being undertaken, their achievements and challenges encountered, and the way forward. In Chapter 3, besides a brief overview of the rationale, key ideas and features of eco-cities, LYE Liang Fook and CHEN Gang highlight three interesting case studies, i.e., the on-going Masdar Eco-city or Masdar Initiative in Abu Dhabi, the failed Huangbaiyu Eco-village in Liaoning in China and the on-going

Sino-Singapore Tianjin Eco-city in China. The purpose of highlighting these three examples is to show three different possible models of building eco-cities or eco-friendly projects. Each has its advantages and challenges. The authors also suggest possible ways of tackling these challenges.

In Chapter 4, POW Choon-Piew and Harvey NEO undertakes a critical review of the literature on eco-city (and related notions of urban sustainability and ecological modernisation). They are of the view that the concept remains somewhat elusive and controversial. To substantiate their point, they dwell at length on Shanghai's Dongtan Eco-city project to highlight the relevance and challenges of translating the eco-city concept in China. This project which had received strong endorsement from the British and Chinese governments and which was touted as China's first sustainable eco-city seemed to have run aground.

In Chapter 5, Rujiroj Anambutr explores policies and projects related to the concept of eco-city in Thailand and focuses on their achievements and challenges. While the author finds that the concept is generally recognised and well received by various levels of society, the implementation is still lagging behind. In particular, he examines the philosophy of sufficiency first propounded by Thailand's revered king (King Rama IX) in 1972 which is Thailand's version of balancing development needs with other considerations. He discusses the successes and challenges of implementing this philosophy and ends on the optimistic note that the concept of eco-city "is still thriving in Thailand".

In Chapter 6, Suraya A. AFIFF observes a tendency for state actors to collaborate with business interests to the total disregard of public or individual interests in the name of implementing eco-friendly projects. By examining the politics behind the use of open green spaces in Jakarta, Bandung and Malang, Suraya shows that city administrations sometimes allow private businesses to gain access to the development of green spaces even though such actions are against planning regulations. She stresses the need to take on board the voices of the less influential so that the benefits of eco-friendly projects can be more evenly distributed and not just confined to the rich and powerful.

In Chapter 7, WANG Tao and SHAO Lei highlights the realities, particularly the challenges of implementing eco-cities in China. While there are a few key ministries and agencies that oversee national programmes related to sustainable urban development, they are not the main actors. In their examination of two projects (one in Nanjing and the other in Xi'an), the authors argue that the local governments actually play key roles in the making and implementation of the urban plans. They suggest ways of improving the present incoherent and fragmented approach to urban sustainable development.

In Chapter 8, Hardev Kaur and Mizan Hitam discuss the various sustainable initiatives undertaken by the Malaysian government as part of a comprehensive approach to address the environmental challenges posed by rapid urbanisation. These initiatives include Local Agenda 21 (a community programme for sustainable development), Putrajaya (a model city for sustainable development)) and low-carbon cities in the Iskandar Development Region in Johor. Despite the challenges encountered in carrying out these initiatives, Kuar argues that the green agenda is here to stay due to the combined efforts by various government agencies and local authorities, and active and effective participation at the neighbourhood level involving various stakeholders.

In Chapter 9, Marife BALLESTEROS observes that while the Philippines government seems to have a clear-cut and convincing strategy for achieving economic growth and environmental protection, the implementation phase of its ecological initiatives can be found wanting. Focusing on the development of the Quezon City Central Business District, Marife highlights the institutional factors that impede the development of the green agenda in the district. They include political considerations at the national and local levels that can significantly distort the incentive systems, the poor enforcement of property rights, and the inefficient land administration and management.

Towards Urgent and Practical Action

This book is compiled against the backdrop of heightened awareness and increasing calls for the international community to do more to fight climate change and global warming before it is too late. At the international level, and most recently at the Group of Eight (G8) Leaders' Meeting with other leaders of emerging economies in L'Aquila (Italy) in July 2009, the leaders recognised the scientific view on the need to keep global temperature rise below two degrees Celsius above pre-industrial levels. They also agreed on a global long-term goal of reducing global emissions by at least 50% by 2050 and, as part of this, on an 80% or more reduction goal for developed countries by 2050. These positive outcomes have laid a good foundation for a viable climate deal that is expected to replace the Kyoto Protocol which will expire in 2012. More, however, needs to be done to establish interim targets for emission cuts in the run-up to 2050 for both developed and developing countries alike.

At the regional level, ASEAN and their regional partners have set sustainable development of cities, energy conservation and emission reduction as among the most important topics on their agenda. At the 10th ASEAN Ministerial Meeting on Haze held in Siem Reap (Cambodia) in March 2003, ASEAN Environment Ministers endorsed the Regional Environmental Sustainability Cities Programme (RESCP) that paved the way for the setting Group on Environmentally Sustainable Cities (AWGESC) with Singapore as the chair to drive the RESCP. At a workshop in Singapore in December 2003, the AWGESC developed the Framework on Environmentally Sustainable Cities that mapped out the vision, principles and scope under the RESCP. It identifies the goals, objectives, strategies and activities/programmes for environmental issues, with Clean Air, Clean Water and Clean Land being the focus areas. Altogether, 24 ASEAN cities including Putrajaya, Bangkok, Quezon, Balikpapan and Singapore have been participating in the RESCP. At the 13th ASEAN Summit in November 2007, the ten member countries signed the *ASEAN Declaration on Environmental Sustainability* in Singapore with commitments made in the three main areas of environmental protection and management, responding to climate change and conservation of natural resources. At the same venue, ASEAN, together with its six regional partners (China, India, Japan, Korea, Australia and New Zealand) at the Third East Asia Summit (EAS), passed the landmark *Singapore Declaration on Climate Change,, Energy and the Environment* that reaffirmed "the need to take an effective approach to the interrelated challenges of climate change, energy security and other environmental and health issues, in the context of sustainable development."

The articles in this book is the result of a workshop organised by the East Asian Institute of the National University of Singapore to foster discussion and share experience on existing practices on eco-cities or eco-friendly projects among scholars and practitioners in the region. Held in Singapore on February 27, 2009, the title of the workshop was *Towards a Liveable and Sustainable Urban Environment: Eco-Cities in East Asia* on February 27, 2009 in Singapore.

The ultimate purpose of this book is to strengthen the call for more action to put into practice the many good ideas, concepts, suggestions and experiences that are already out there. More concerted action by all including countries, non-governmental organisations, businesses and even the individual, can together make a difference in ensuring that the world as we know today will continue to be there for our future generations to enjoy. We all have to do our part now.

CHAPTER 1

Eco-Cities: Re-Examining Concepts and Approaches

Hidefumi IMURA*

The term "eco-city" emerged near the end of the 1980s, but the ideas very similar to the eco-city have been around for many years: "Garden city" or "green city" concept was one of them. The meaning of eco-city has changed, coupled with the expanding breadth of environmental issues, and with changing priorities in national and international environmental policy. During the 1960s and 1970s, the objective of the eco-city was simply to make the air, water, and soil clean again. Now in the 21st century, the realisation of an eco-city requires the integration of multiple environmental objectives such as climatic change mitigation, bio-diversity conservation, and sound material cycles with the objectives of economic growth and liveability in cities. This paper first reviews the urbanisation in Asia and evolution of the concept of and approaches to eco-city in Japan, and then discusses the objectives and goals of the eco-city in the 21st century, as well as the policies and measures to achieve them.

Introduction: Eco-Cities and Sustainable Cities

The term "eco-city" first came into use near the end of the 1980s. It emerged as a result of the evolution of environmental policies in countries around the world, and embraces the objectives and principles for the practical application of national environmental policies at the level of the city — where citizens live and work in their daily lives. The actual concepts behind the eco-city are not new, however. They have been around for many years.

---

*Prof. Hidefumi Imura is a Professor in the Graduate School of Environmental Studies, Nagoya University.

Long before what we today would call "environmental policy", Ebenezer
Howard (1850–1928) was advocating the concept of the "garden city".[1] His
idea was to create cities where people could live in harmony with nature,
away from big-city glamour, and it has many points in common with today's
concept of the eco-city.

Nevertheless, even today there is no clear consensus on the exact definition of an eco-city. The ideas that come to mind when one hears the term
differ from person to person, and community to community. Furthermore,
the meaning has also changed with the times. That change has been coupled
with the expanding breadth of environmental issues, and with changing priorities in policy. It was at the end of the 1960s that environmental policies in
Japan and other industrialised countries stemmed from other areas of policy. During the ensuing 50 years, the meaning of "environment", "ecology",
and "eco" also evolved in the context of changes in economies, societies,
and industries at the national and international levels.[2] These also led to
changes in the priorities for the environmental policies of local governments
and communities that were at the forefront of initiatives, and this meant
changes in the very concept of the eco-city.

During the 1960s and 1970s — when the main priority of national environmental policies was to deal with pollution of the atmosphere and of the
water in rivers, lakes, and seas — the objective of the eco-city was simply to
make the air, water, and soil clean again. Now in the 21st century, as worldwide problems such as global warming have emerged as important issues for
human society; the priority of environmental policy in European countries,
Japan, and many other countries is on global warming countermeasures,
biodiversity conservation, resource circulation, and so on. The realisation
of the eco-city today will require the integration of these multiple environmental objectives with the objectives of economic growth, convenience, and
liveability in cities.

Since the United Nations Conference on Environment and Development
(the "Earth Summit") was held in 1992 in Rio de Janeiro, Brazil, "sustainable development" has become a fundamental principle for environment and
development. Related to this is the concept of a "sustainable city". Today,

---

[1] Joan Roelofs. (1999), "Building and Designing with Nature: Urban Design." In *Sustainable Cities*, D. Satterthwaite (ed.), pp. 234–250. London: Earthscan Publications
Ltd.
[2] Imura Hidefumi and Miranda Schreurs, (eds.) (2005). *Environmental Policies in Japan*,
pp. 15–48. Gloucester: Edward Elgar Publishing Ltd.

it is common to use both sustainable city and eco-city to mean virtually the same thing. [3]

The Evolving Concept of the Eco-City

The Garden City

Anyone tracing the origins of the eco-city concept will come across the "garden city" concept advocated by England's Ebenezer Howard at the end of the 19th century. England at the time was in the throes of economic development, people were concentrated in cities, urban air pollution was worsening, and water quality was deteriorating in the Thames and other rivers. Poor workers lived in deplorable housing districts that steadily expanded. Howard's garden city concept was proposed as a way to address this situation. His idea was to build, apart from large cities like London, cities in which employment and housing were located close together. They would be relatively smaller cities, on the scale of about 30,000 to 50,000 people. Residential areas would be surrounded by parks and treed areas, and there would also be space for agriculture and other pursuits. The priority would be on harmony with nature, as well as self-sufficiency. Howard envisioned that even workers who were not well off would have access to rental and collective housing, and his design sought to create comfortable living environments.

The garden city (or "green city") concept had an impact on urban design in Japan and the West from the turn of the 20th century through to the 1930s. In Japan, the concept influenced urban development along railway lines in the large suburban areas of Tokyo and Osaka.

The garden city concept applies not only to small and medium-sized cities. Megacities with populations exceeding five million people are becoming increasingly common, and some concepts of the garden city apply equally well to them. Modern Singapore, for example, is a large city with many green areas and parks located within the urban region. It is as if this were one huge garden city consisting of a collection of smaller garden cities.

---

[3]Satterwaite David. (1999) "The Key Issues and the Works Included." In *Sustainable Cities*, D. Satterwaite (ed.), pp. 3–21; Newman Peter and Jefferey Kenworthy. (1999). *Sustainability and Cities*, pp. 1–26. London: Earthscan Publications Ltd; and Rees William. (1999). "Achieving Sustainability: Reform or Transformation?". In *Sustainable Cities*, D. Satterthwaite (ed.), pp. 22–52.

Eco-Cities and the Birth of Environmental Policy

After the Second World War, the urban populations of countries like the
United Kingdom, Germany, France, and Japan grew rapidly, requiring the
rapid construction of new towns, and the garden city concept had an enormous impact on their design. From the 1960s onward, countries developed
"eco-cities" in order to respond to problems caused by the rapid growth
of urban populations: housing shortages, deterioration of living conditions,
growing pollution problems, increasing automobile traffic, and disappearing
green space. During the 1960s and 1970s, in response to serious pollution
of the atmosphere, rivers, lakes, and seas, the central themes of eco-cities
shifted to restoring the blue skies, clean waters, and so on.

As the relevant measures achieved a certain degree of success in dealing
with pollution problems, the trend in eco-city design began to incorporate
such things as greenery, nature, resources, and energy efficient use — all in
an integrated way. During the 1980s, the term "ecopolis" came into use in
Germany. In Japan, the concept of the "amenity town" appeared after the
serious environmental problems were resolved to some extent, emphasising
attributes such as urban scenery, comfort, leisure, and relaxation.

The German concept of ecopolis emphasised nature in the form of urban
green zones, and also encouraged the use of natural energy sources such as
solar and wind powered electricity generation and proactive approaches to
environmentally friendly activities such as resource recycling. These developments grew in tandem with the public opposition to nuclear power plants,
triggered in part by the Chernobyl nuclear accident in Ukraine, as well as
the emergence of the issue of global warming, and a surge in the popularity
of the political Green Party in the context of these problems.

Since the Middle Ages, Germany has had a strong tradition in the independence of its cities, so unsurprisingly, an important aspect of eco-city
(ecopolis) design in this country was the emphasis on the uniqueness of
each city. The cities of Freiberg and Heidelberg are good examples of cities
that incorporate these concepts.

Eco-Cities and the Role of Asian Cities in the Realisation of a Low-Carbon Society

After the dawn of the 21st century, the theme that rapidly came to the
fore was the redesign and equipping of cities in order to make "low-carbon
society" a reality.

Through the 20th century, the world's urban population increased
14-fold, from 220 million to 2.8 billion. The concentration of population

in cities has many merits in terms of promoting economic growth by bringing production and consumption closer together, but it has also triggered various other problems such as environmental pollution and urban poverty. Thus, to draw out the merits of urbanisation, it is necessary to have "software" tools such as social systems and programmes that address the problems of urbanisation, as well as "hardware" tools such as the construction, operation and maintenance of houses, buildings and infrastructures.

The United Nations reports that the world population reached a major transition point in 2008 when, for the first time in history, half the world's population — 3.3 billion people — lived in cities. The driving force in recent years has been rapid urbanisation in Asia (especially in the 16 ASEAN+6 countries[4]) as demonstrated in Fig. 1. The urbanisation rate (percentage of population living in cities) in Asia was only 16.8% in 1950, but it grew rapidly amid steady economic development, reaching 38.9% in 2005, and is expected to reach 50% in 2025. The urban populations of China and India are growing rapidly; their combined urban populations in 2025 are predicted to reach 500 million. Asia is also rising among the ranks, already being home to 17 of the world's 25 largest cities.

Energy demand has increased along with economic growth in countries of the world, and the emissions of carbon dioxide — a major cause of global

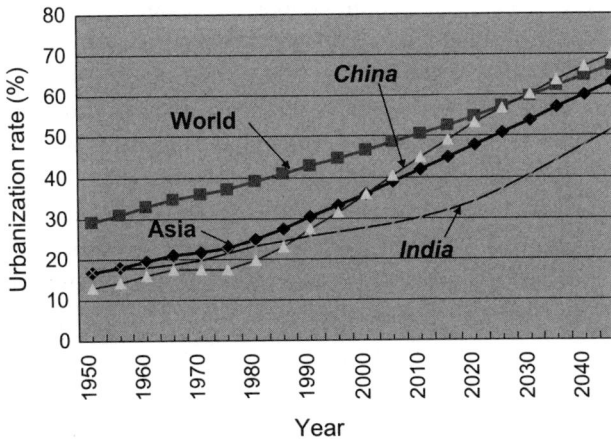

Source: *World Urbanisation Prospects, 2007 Revision* (United Nations, 2007).
Note: Asia in this figure refers to the ASEAN+6 countries.

Fig. 1   Trends in Urbanisation Rates in Asia, the World, China and India.

---

[4]The six countries are China, Japan, South Korea, India, Australia, and New Zealand.

warming — have also increased. This trend is particularly evident in Asia, which continues to experience economic and population growth.

It was in this context that leaders at the G8 Summit of leading economies, held in Hokkaido, Japan, in 2008, agreed to seek international consensus to reduce global greenhouse gas emissions by more than 50% by 2050. The efforts of developed countries alone will not be enough to achieve this target. In view of the predicted economic growth and population expansion in Asia, this region's participation is crucial. Asia is in the process of rapid urbanisation, but infrastructure developments such as housing, roads, public transport systems, water supply and sewerage systems are far behind those in developed countries, so new construction will be necessary. It will be important to incorporate and implement a variety of environmental policies in the context of long-term plans to build urban infrastructure.

Specifically, cities need to articulate policy objectives for aspects such as land use, urban layout, and facilities design that will facilitate low energy consumption; urban green areas and open spaces; harmony with nature; intra-regional recycling of organic material; and resource recycling. Moreover, they need to incorporate these aspects into real measures for urban improvement.

Cities working to address the problem of global warming are demonstrating the very concept of "Think Globally, Act Locally", and such efforts go beyond the traditional paradigm of urban development in which the main emphasis was on creating cities that were prosperous just for their own citizens. This new paradigm is based on the philosophy that cities should contribute to the protection of the global environment by improving themselves. Cities face challenges in doing this, however, because a city's economic and financial conditions will strongly influence the degree of cooperation and consensus obtained from local citizens for these efforts. Thus, the approach to eco-cities should incorporate policies for environment and development and integrate global and local environmental goals as shown in Fig. 2.

Urbanisation in Asia and the Potential for Eco-Cities

Urbanisation and Delayed Infrastructure Development

Asia is often referred to as one whole region, but it contains a diversity of natural and socio-economic conditions. Nevertheless, when compared with

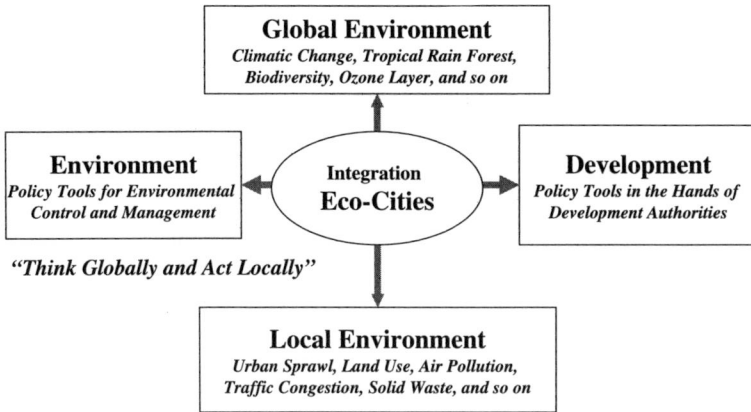

Fig. 2 Integration of Policies in the Concept of Eco-Cities.

the United States and countries in Europe, for example, Asian cities undeniably have certain characteristics in common.

The first feature of Asian cities is their brief history of modern urban construction. Admittedly, some countries have been building cities for millennia — over 3,000 years in the case of China — but it was only the second half of the 20th century that they began building modern urban infrastructure such as subways and other transport systems, or water supply and sewerage systems. Furthermore, Asia has less of a tradition of self-determination by civic bodies operating with relatively little control from state governments — in contrast to certain European cities that were designed with a high degree of autonomy.

Urbanisation in Asia could be described by two characteristics: population migration from the rural areas to the city, and urbanisation outside of the major cities (i.e., the growth of small and medium-sized cities of 500,000 people or less). Correspondingly, countries face challenges in providing enough housing for the population flowing into capitals and other large cities, and in creating enough employment for them. On the other hand, urbanisation outside of the major cities is proceeding without adequate planning. At any rate, infrastructure development is unable to keep pace with population growth.

A major reason for the lag in infrastructure development is the shortage of funds. Rapid economic growth is occurring in tandem with investments in urban environmental infrastructure in Shanghai, Shenzhen, Guangzhou, and other cities along the eastern coast of China. In western inland cities,

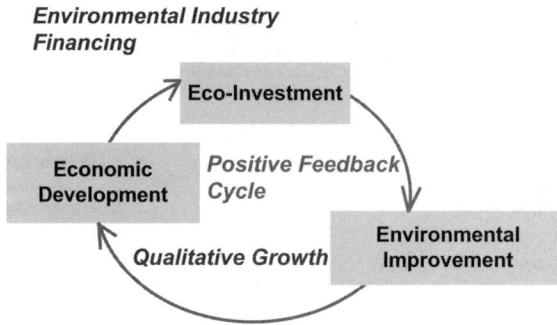

Fig. 3   Positive Feedback Cycle of Eco-Investment and Economic Development.

however, economic growth lags behind other parts of the country, and improvements in urban environmental infrastructure also tend to lag here. Many ASEAN countries achieved remarkable economic growth during and since the 1990s, but investment in environmental infrastructure outside a limited number of capital regions is still lagging as well.

An examination of the situation in Asian cities reveals a strong correlation between economic growth and urban environmental infrastructure. Without economic growth, it is difficult to improve environmental infrastructure. While economic growth results in more consumption of resources and energy, and more pollution, it is also essential to secure funding for environmental investment. Finding the balance between economic growth and environmental investment is one key to the realisation of "sustainable cities" as shown in Fig. 3.

Changes in Urban Economies, and Consumption of Resources and Energy

Urbanisation in Asian countries is occurring together with changes in industrial structure — the growth of service industries. Both production and consumption are concentrated in cities. Urbanisation proceeds together with the economic growth of countries, and there is a tendency for cities to be places where service industries such as commerce and the transport sector concentrate and develop. There is a clear and positive correlation between the proportion of service industries as a proportion of gross domestic product (GDP), and the rate of urbanisation as shown in Fig. 4.

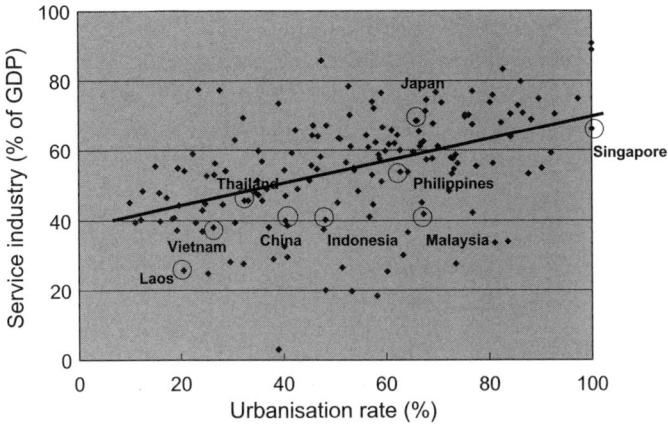

Source: *World Development Indicators* (World Bank). *Annual Report on Trade in Japan* (Tsusho Hakusho, 2008).
Note: Data is for 2005.

Fig. 4   Urbanisation and the Growth of the Service Economy.

The geographical concentration of production and consumption through urbanisation improves productivity by the economies of concentration, and also creates new employment. These positive aspects of urbanisation tend to accelerate the population migration from the country to the city, and which in turn accelerates urbanisation and the growth of production and consumption.

Urbanisation and economic growth are positively correlated: real GDP per capita increases 0.5% for every 1% increase in the urbanisation rate as shown in Fig. 5.[5] An important point worth noting is that the level of real GDP per capita for a given level of urbanisation is higher in Asian countries (with the exception of Indonesia) than the global average. This suggests that Asia can generally utilise the benefits of urbanisation more effectively than elsewhere.

Resource and energy consumption includes a portion related to the productive activities of industry and a portion related to the consumption activities of individuals. An increase in the proportion of service industries is associated with an increase in the consumption activity of

---

[5]Ministry of Economy, Trade and Industry of Japan, *Tsusho Hakusho* (Annual Report on Trade in Japan) 2008, p. 59.

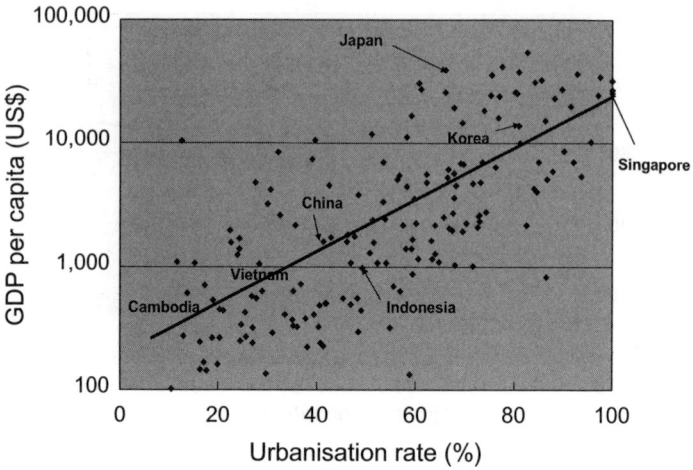

Source: *World Development Indicators* (World Bank). Annual Report on Trade in Japan
(Tsusho Hakusho, 2008).
Note: Data is for 2005.

Fig. 5   Urbanisation and Economic Growth.

individuals — that is, the consumption of resources and energy in the daily
lives of urban dwellers, such as housing (including lighting, air-conditioning,
and cooking, and food and clothes), and automobile use. Furthermore, if
the economy shifts toward service industries, compared to other industries,
the resource and energy consumption growth tends to increase relatively
more for the service industries (wholesale, retail, food, hospitality, finance,
etc.) than for industries like mining and manufacturing.

If we examine sector by sector energy consumption and carbon dioxide
emissions in industrialised countries, the increases in the manufacturing sector are relatively limited, whereas in many cases the increases are larger in
the automobile transport sector and in the non-industrial sector, for example, from electricity and gas consumption for office building and household
air conditioning. The actual situation depends on each country's industrial
structure, but a typical characteristic observed in industrialised countries
is that urban energy consumption is growing dramatically in the building
sector (for office air conditioning and others) and in the transportation
sector.

At present, with the exception of Japan today, the service industry ratio
compared to the urbanisation ratio tends to be lower than the global average
in Asia as illustrated in Fig. 4. But a transformation in industrial structure

is expected to accompany urbanisation in Asia as well. Accordingly, energy is expected to increase dramatically in the commercial and residential sectors, as well as in the transportation sectors of Asian cities.

Environmental Problems Associated with Urbanisation

While the concentration of population in cities brings economic growth through the economies of concentration, on the other hand, in the cities of poor countries in particular, it also presents new issues, such as air pollution, water pollution, and soil contamination, due to increases in emissions of waste and effluent, crowding and electricity shortages due to population density and concentration, and an increase in urban poverty.

To address these issues, cities must make investment into infrastructure, waste treatment facilities, water supply and sewage treatment facilities, roads, power generation facilities, and so on. They must also improve social security and other systems to deal with poverty.

One distinct feature of urbanisation in Asia is the significant increase in income disparities, caused by the fragmentation of urban regions through urban sprawl as result of the population migration from rural areas to the cities.[6] The Gini coefficient measures the relationship between urbanisation and income disparity. In major Asian countries, the Gini coefficient tends to increase along with urbanisation (Fig. 6).

Thus, in Vietnam, Thailand, and other countries where urbanisation is expected to continue, large increases in income disparity are expected. On the other hand, in Asia the Gini coefficient tends to drop after the urbanisation rate reaches 50%. Countries with high levels of both urbanisation and income disparity — China, Malaysia, and the Philippines, etc. — need to correct the disparities through antipoverty measures, more comprehensive social security, and so on.[7]

---

[6]Ibid., p. 60.

[7]This tendency could be seen as a proxy variable of economic development for urbanisation, corresponding to the well-known Kuznets hypothesis, which states that economic development and income inequality, when graphed (X and Y axes, respectively), look like an inverted U. According to the Kuznets hypothesis, income inequality between social classes rises at the early stage of development, but as the economy develops, positive effects from the growth sectors flow to other sectors, resulting in a ripple effect benefiting the economic development of a variety of social classes. Figure 6 depicts the Kuznets hypothesis, replacing "development" with "urbanisation".

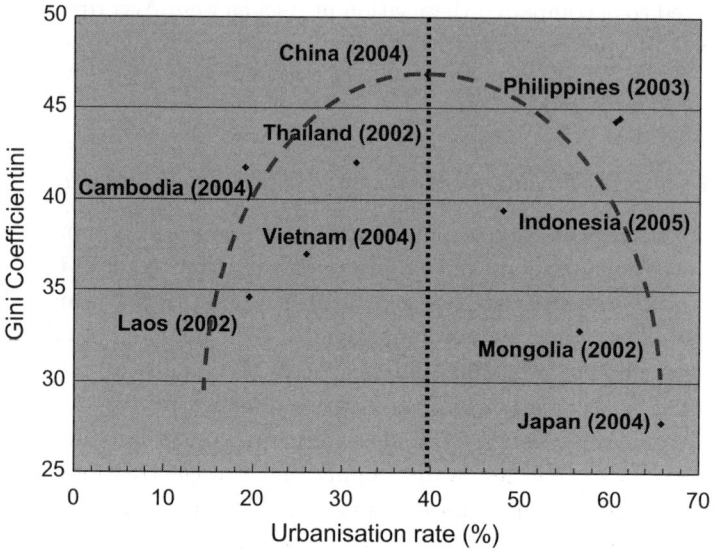

Fig. 6   The Gini Coefficient and Urbanisation in Asia.

Source: World Urbanisation Prospects, the 2006 Revision (United Nations, 2006); World Urbanisation Prospects, the 2007 Revision (United Nations, 2007); Human Development Report 2007/2008 (UNDP); Consumer Survey 2004 (Japan Ministry of Internal Affairs and Communication); WDI (World Bank). Annual Report on Trade in Japan (Tsusho Hakusho, 2008).

Note 1: The year varies by country. Figures in parentheses are t-values.

Note 2: The definition of the Gini coefficient varies by country. For China and Malaysia, it refers to income per capita. For Thailand, Vietnam, Laos, Indonesia, Mongolia and the Philippines, it refers to expenditures per capita. For Japan, it refers to disposable annual income for all households including individuals living alone (disposable income equivalent).

The Eco-City — Economic Activity and Consumption of Resources and Energy

Urban Activities and Resource Circulation

In developed countries today, a majority of the population lives in cities. Developing countries are also urbanising rapidly. The future of the Earth will depend on the future of cities. It is clear that if we are to make our societies on Earth sustainable, we must also make our cities sustainable. Cities are places many people gather to live and engage in economic activities. They take in vast amounts of resources to sustain those activities and then discharge into the environment (atmosphere, water, soil) vast amounts

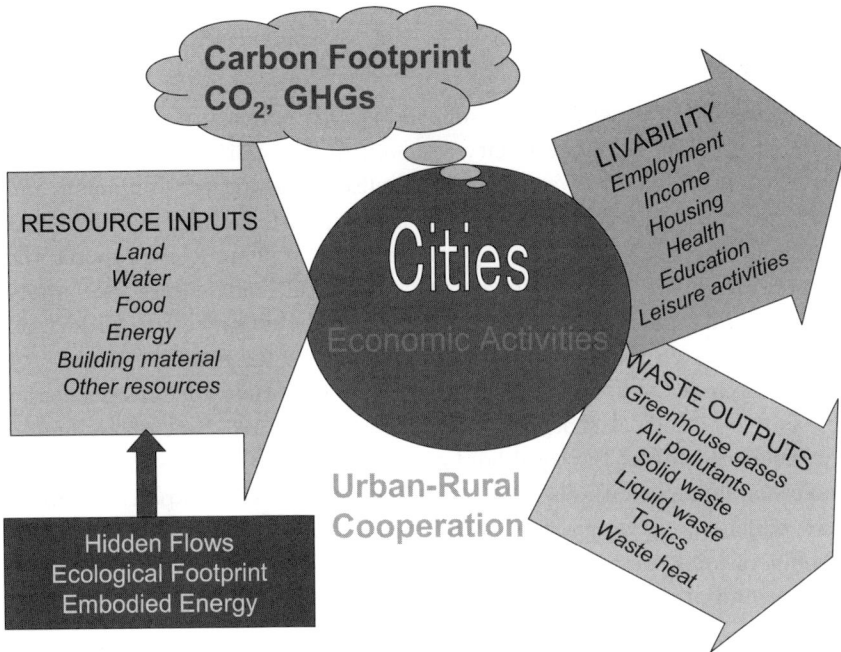

Source: Prepared by the author based on Peter Newman and Jeffrey Kenworthy.

Fig. 7   The City as an Eco-System from the Perspective of Material Circulation.

of waste generated through those activities. In this sense, cities are like eco-systems as Fig. 7 illustrates.

A variety of materials are consumed each day to support the survival and activities of the average person in Japan today: 1.4 kilogrammes of food, 320 litres of water, and the equivalent of 2.4 kilogrammes of energy (crude oil equivalent; total includes household energy and automobile use; figures as of 2000). As a result, a variety of waste and pollutants are generated each day: 1.1 kilogrammes of garbage (municipal waste), 320 litres of wastewater, and carbon dioxide amounting to the equivalent of 8.8 kilogrammes of dry ice.

These figures represent the resources and energy associated with direct consumption by individuals, but besides these amounts, energy is also consumed by industrial and commercial activities. Ultimately, these activities are all for individuals, so they could be interpreted as indirect consumption by individuals. If all those numbers were included, the result would be quite a large figure per person: each person emits nearly 28 kilogrammes of carbon dioxide every day in Japan.

The External Dependency of Cities

Ecological Footprint

To sustain activities within, cities depend heavily on resources from outside. Much of the food ingested by city residents is transported from elsewhere. An enormous amount of soil, water, fertilisers, chemicals, equipment and machines, and fuel are consumed in order to support the affluent food habits of urban citizens. Canadian ecological economist William Rees proposed the term "ecological footprint" to represent the total land required to supply the food and timber products used in a city, in addition to the forest land needed to absorb the carbon dioxide generated by the city.[8]

The area of London is 1,580 square kilometres. Herbert Girardet found that city's ecological footprint to be an amazing 125 times that figure, equivalent to 80% of the total land area of England.[9] The result for Tokyo and other Japanese cities is roughly similar. Countries like Japan and Singapore, which import almost half of their food from overseas, use an enormous amount of land, water, and other resources overseas to produce the food, lumber, and other materials they need.

Embodied Environmental Load

When a product is manufactured, energy is used as an input into a variety of processes, including raw material extraction, production at the factory, transport, and others. If we change our perspective, we can consider the energy incorporated into a product or service, including not only the energy directly used to produce and provide the product or service to the market, but also the energy incorporated indirectly through raw material inputs. This concept is referred to as "embodied energy" and is sometimes also called "life cycle energy". Economic activity requires the inputs of enormous amounts of natural resources, including metal, timber, oil, stone, gravel, and so on.

In 2004, Japan's nominal GDP was 570 trillion yen, matched by natural resource inputs totaling 1.697 billion tonnes. Resource productivity

---

[8]Rees William and Mathis Wackernagel. (1994). "Ecological Footprint and Appreciated Carrying Capacity: Measuring the Natural Capital Requirements of the Human Economy." In *Investing in Natural Capital: The Ecological Economics Approach to Sustainability*, A-M Jansson, M. Hammer, C. Folke, and R. Costanza, (eds.), Washington D.C.: Island Press.

[9]Girardet Herbert. (1999). "Sustainable Cities: A Contradiction in Terms?" In *Sustainable Cities*, D. Satterthwaite (ed.), pp. 413–425.

(GDP per tonne of natural resource inputs) is therefore 336,000 yen.[10] The Japanese government's Fundamental Plan for Establishing a Sound Material-Cycle Society includes a target of raising this indicator to about 420,000 yen in 2015.[11]

Meanwhile, in terms of energy, Japan's primary energy supply was 562 million tonnes (crude oil equivalent), which means that the country's energy productivity (GDP per tonne of energy input, oil equivalent) was about 1 million yen.

Both resource productivity and energy productivity are improving; compared to 1975, the former has improved by a factor of 2.0, and the latter by a factor of 1.4. The inverse of energy productivity indicates how much energy (tonnes, crude oil equivalent) is embodied per unit of GDP, and in 2000, this figure for Japan was 1 tonne per million yen. As a ballpark figure, a purchase worth 1 million yen involves the energy consumption of about 1 tonne (oil equivalent), or about 2.3 tonnes of carbon dioxide emissions.

If we now consider food, the amount of energy consumed at various stages before the food enters our mouths is several times the amount of our food calories intake. For example, fuel is consumed by cultivation equipment, tractors, and fishing boats, and also consumed during refrigeration and canning processes, transportation, distribution, and even refrigeration and cooking at home.

When we attempt to reduce energy consumption, we have a tendency to focus only on the obvious and direct energy consumption, but all consumption activities — whether related to clothing, food, housing, or whatever — can consume energy indirectly in the form of embodied energy. The same thing goes for air pollutants, water pollutants, ozone-depleting substances, and so on, and these are referred to collectively as the "embodied environmental load".

Hidden Resource Flows

Resources covered by calculations of resource productivity deal only with those items that are priced in the market and traded in the economy. For example, in the case of rocks and gravel, the only amount counted is the portion exchanged in economic transactions as construction material. Besides those amounts, however, enormous amounts of soil, rock, and

---

[10]US$1 is almost equivalent to 100 Japanese yen as of April 2009.
[11]Basic Plan for Building a Sound Material Cycle Society.

gravel are moved about at construction sites and through the extraction of underground resources at mines.

Material flows that are traded in the economy are considered "visible" flows, and resource inputs not recorded in economic statistics are referred to as "hidden flows". Examples include the soil excavated at construction sites, the rubble and tailings at mining sites, soil eroded from cultivated land, and trees cut down but not harvested as timber in logging operations. For every tonne of coal mined, it is necessary to move about 4.9 tonnes of dirt and rock. For one tonne of iron, the figure is 5.2 tonnes. For copper, it is 450 tonnes. To extract 100 grammes of gold, 95 tonnes of dirt and rock must be moved.[12]

Urban Activities: Sustained by Vast Amounts of Resources, Energy, and Environmental Impacts

To understand the above discussion, it is not enough to consider only the amounts of resource and energy consumption associated with cities, or the environmental impacts generated in cities. A vast area of forest in the watershed upstream must be maintained to provide a stable source of water to a city. Various products consumed in cities are produced outside the cities, and many resources are consumed in the process of raw material extraction, production, and transport. We must not forget that environmental impacts are generated in all these processes, and that a large amount of the products consumed in developed countries are actually produced in developing countries.

The Role of Urban Environmental Infrastructure

Physical components of a city include housing and commercial buildings, as well as roads and other forms of infrastructure. Activities in a city include the vast flows of people, goods and materials, energy, and information. Thus, the inside of a city is a network of roads, rails, water and sewer lines, electrical grids, gas grids, communications lines, and so on.

---

[12]The reason that rare metals like gold and platinum are so expensive is that they do not exist in abundance, and also that these hidden flows are reflected in the price. In the case of rare metals, the price reflects both the rarity of supply and the difficulty of extraction. It is fascinating to analyse the relationship between the price of an element and the amount of effort required to extract it from the environment, or to see this as an entropy transformation and analyse the relationship between price and changes in entropy.

These networks, if compared with the human body, are similar to networks of blood vessels and nerves; the equivalent to blood and nerve signals flowing through the system would be materials, energy, and information. The arterial blood flowing from the lungs circulates through the body and picks up waste matter from each part of the body as it becomes venous blood. In the body, the liver, kidneys, and other organs are charged with the role of processing the waste matter. The equivalent in a city would be the environmental infrastructure, including facilities that handle wastewater treatment and purification and the waste treatment plants that handle garbage disposal.

If a city's activities exceed certain limits, then material and energy circulation cease to function properly, constraining the city's further economic growth and causing a variety of environmental problems. This is like the city having poor blood circulation, akin to a blockage of the blood vessels. In a city, the cause is often a lack of adequate environmental infrastructure and facilities, the breakdown of these facilities, or lack of capacity. In order to create real eco-cities, the environmental infrastructure must be put in place, and it must be maintained and operated properly.

Transportation, Environmental Burden, and Compact Cities

Mobility, or freedom of movement, is a basic human demand. As cities spread out and cover more land area, it is necessary to connect areas within cities to each other, and also cities to other cities, via efficient and rapid transport systems. To this end, many cities in Europe developed networks of subways, trams, and buses, starting at the end of the 19th century. With the rise of the automobile during the 20th century, cities were created that depended completely on personal car transport — and they are characterised by having lower population density and being more spread out.[13]

Thus, transport is a critical topic when it comes to efforts to create cities with low environmental impacts. First, innovative automotive technologies must be developed to dramatically improve fuel economy. Second, there should be a shift away from the use of private cars in favour of public transport. Third, cities themselves must be redesigned to boost the efficiency of energy use — including not only transport systems but also land use, city layout, citizen lifestyles, and more.

---

[13]Newman Peter and Jefferey Kenworthy. (1999). *Sustainability and Cities*, pp. 27–67. Washington, D.C.: Island Press.

Partly in response to the shrinking population and the aging of society, local cities in Japan are moving toward compact-city designs that involve less horizontal movement. They are using taller buildings and concentrating into the city centre more of the land uses that previously were allowed to spread into the suburbs without any master planning.

Older cities in Europe and the United States are also trending toward compact designs, bringing back tram systems, and so on. Meanwhile, the urban planning trend in younger cities in developing countries is still to promote car dependency. Some cities are expanding without any clear vision of urban development, and the number of cars on the road is increasing rapidly. Without a change in course, energy consumption and carbon dioxide emissions will simply continue to increase.

Thus, improvements in subways, railways, and other transport systems are extremely important when it comes to urban planning in Asian developing countries.

Promoting Eco-Cities: Concepts and Initiatives in Japan

Evolving Policy Objectives for the Urban Environment

Each city can be distinguished by population size and a variety of other characteristics, so the general concept of an eco-city can actually be expressed in a multitude of ways.

Looking back at Japan's experience, the 1960s and 1970s were a period of severe worsening of environmental pollution associated with rapid economic growth. Thus, pollution countermeasures became an absolute priority for environmental policy at the time.

In the 1980s, some successes had been achieved in suppressing pollution, particularly by reducing factory emissions of pollutants to air and water, so citizens began to demand the restoration of nature and historic cityscapes that had been so quickly lost due to rapid urban development. In the context of these changes in public need, Japan's Environment Agency — the predecessor to the Ministry of the Environment — presented the concept of the "amenity town". At the time, critics suspected that this was simply a strategy to distract public attention from the remaining pollution problems, and there was also opposition from civic departments in charge of urban infrastructure construction. Thirty years later, the term "amenity town" is rarely spoken, although the concept has become an integral part of urban planning policies.

During the 1980s, the German concept of the ecopolis also gained some currency in Japan. The 1989 edition of *The Quality of the Environment in Japan*, the annual white paper published by the Japanese government, discussed this concept as follows:

- Utilise the water and materials that sustain urban activities in circulatory way.
- Introduce systems to utilise energy efficiently.
- Conserve and create nature within the city, and create human systems that are compatible with ecosystems.
- By these approaches, create positive urban environments by restoring ecological circulation and make cities self-sufficient and stable as unified systems.

Measures to Make the Ecopolis (Eco-City) a Reality

The 1989 edition of *The Quality of the Environment in Japan* introduces and describes examples of effective measures being implemented in countries around the world to create ecopolises. Amazingly, many are valid even today (in 2009). A selection of them is provided below.

(1) Transportation Measures

- Control vehicle driving in cities by time of day, zone, and type of vehicle (e.g., regulate the access of large trucks into the city centre).
- Institute programmes to reduce car use, such as unified fare systems to promote all types of public transport.
- Introduce programmes to stop engine idling while vehicles wait at traffic lights.
- Consolidate freight logistics through joint collection and delivery; construct truck terminals along perimeter roads around cities; rationalise freight transport, for example, by shifting from the use of small trucks to commercial trucks.

(2) Systems to Restore Water Circulation

- Introduce rainwater storage facilities, such as water-permeable road surfaces that allow rainwater to percolate into the ground, permeable mass etc., such as rainwater reservoirs and collecting ponds. These measures can help prevent floods, as well as reduce urban temperatures through the effects of moisture evaporation from the ground; recharge groundwater, conserve and restore the flow of spring water, and conserve vegetation; and conserve soil organisms.

- Introduce facilities in buildings to utilise "gray" water and rainwater. Use them to promote effective use of water resources and greater water self-sufficiency. Also, where water quality has deteriorated or original natural sources have disappeared, redirect post-treatment clean water back into small watercourses in cities in order to restore their flows, and restore waterside space for citizens to rest and children to play.

(3) Systems for Efficient Utilisation of Energy
- Introduce district cooling and heating systems in city centres.
- Increase thermal utilisation efficiency by introducing heat pumps for residential use.
- Use cogeneration to supply both electricity and heat.
- Develop fuel cells.
- Introduce hot water supply and room heating/cooling systems using solar thermal energy.
- Generate electricity using photovoltaic equipment.
- Generate electricity by wind power.

(4) Measures for Conservation and Creation of Nature in Cities
- Improve regulations to promote tree cover and grass cover in cities (example in Japan: City Parks Law), green conservation areas (e.g., City Green Zone Conservation Law), suburban green conservation areas (e.g., Law for the Conservation of Green Belts around the National Capital Region), and scenic zones (e.g., City Planning Law).
- Implement projects to create urban habitats for small animals (e.g., "Woods for Observation of Nature" and "Urban Ecology Parks").
- Create habitats for wild birds and spaces for people to observe them (e.g., in Japan, the "Small Bird Chirping Woods" programme launched in 1984).
- Federal Law for Protection of Nature and Conservation of Landshaft (Germany). Example: Conservation and restoration of small ecosystems (biotopes) in Berlin by a programme for species conservation.
- Creation of ecological parks in the United Kingdom.

Turning Industrial Towns into Eco-Cities: Initiatives to Create Circulatory Industrial Systems

The amenity town and eco-town concepts can be applied relatively easily to cities that run on commerce. Service industries play a dominant role in cities that prosper from commerce, but this prosperity would not be possible without the existence of industrial cities built around manufacturing industries.

In Japan, industrial cities like Kawasaki and Kitakyushu supported the nation's rapid economic growth after the Second World War, and it was also these cities that experienced the worst impacts of pollution in that period.

In the 1990s, a major effort was made to revolutionise industrial systems and create resource-recycling systems, inspired by the concepts of sound material circulation in the economy, zero emissions, and so on. To deal with an ever-increasing volume of waste, Japan's then-Ministry of International Trade and Industry made "zero emissions" — which until then had been advocated mainly as a concept — a cornerstone of new approaches to regional socioeconomic development based on harmony with the environment. With this approach as a core concept for regional economic revitalisation, the ministry launched the Eco-Town Project in 1997 for innovative urban development that sought to be compatible with the environment. Cities such as Kitakyushu and Kawasaki, which eventually earned status as Eco-Towns, launched urban development initiatives by fostering industries that would be responsible for resource recycling. This approach attracted attention as a way for some cities to reinvent themselves as eco-cities without having to abandon their identity as industrial towns.

The Eco-Town initiatives, with their emphasis on circulatory industrial systems, had a major influenced on Chinese industrial cities where manufacturing industries were growing rapidly. As a result, Chinese cities like Tianjin and Qingdao also promoted urban development projects centering on resource-recycling industries.

Eco-Cities and Low-Carbon Cities

Reflecting upon Japan's experience, we can see the evolution of "eco-city" concepts. The "amenity town" concept aimed for comfortable urban environments (late 1980s), the "ecopolis" concept aimed to create sound material and energy circulation within cities, and to restore natural ecosystems (early 1990s), and the "eco-town" concept promoted urban planning compatible with the environment with the focus on zero-emissions in industrial systems (late 1990s). Then, in 2008, based on the consensus of the G8 Summit, the Japanese government selected "Eco-Model Cities" around the country and offered financial support for their plans.

Eco-Model Cities aim to achieve large reductions in urban energy consumption and carbon dioxide emissions from a long-term perspective up to the years 2050 or 2100. The Japanese government's call for Eco-Model City applicants brought together a cumulative body of knowledge about measures relating to transport, energy, waste, and forests, and so on. Based on the achievements of these sector-by-sector approaches, participating cities are expected to promote the following kinds of measures.

- In a given field (region), incorporate the accumulated knowledge into socioeconomic systems, and seek larger reduction effects.
- To achieve this, instead of the conventional field-by-field or sector-by-sector approach, move toward initiatives based on multi-sectoral, integrated approaches that cities can implement on their own, taking advantage of the special characteristics of each city or region.
- Deliver a broad range of benefits, such as urban and regional revitalisation and quality of life improvements for citizens.

The Japanese government is selecting innovative model cities that implement these kinds of integrated approaches, and intends to further promote these approaches in Japan and overseas. The following are some of the achievements expected of these model cities:

- Dramatic reductions in greenhouse gas emissions, ideally along these lines:
  - Long-term reductions exceeding 50% by 2050.
  - Peak emission levels in the city may slightly increase for a while, but should be followed by substantial declines as soon as possible.
  - Energy efficiency improvements of 30% or more by 2020.
- Innovativeness and potential to serve as a good model
  - Innovative efforts without precedent in terms of integrated approaches.
  - Exemplary or good references for other cities in Japan and overseas.
- Regionally adapted
  - Making the most of conditions and characteristics unique to the city or region.
  - Promotion of self-sufficiency.
- Expected to function smoothly and be fully implemented; achievable and feasible
  - Reasonable initiatives in terms of the targets to be achieved.
  - Backed by the participation of a broad range of stakeholders, including local communities, local businesses, universities, non-profit organisations, etc.

- Likely to be sustainable, by releasing new potential in the city.

  ○ By demonstrating new concepts of urban development, expected to release new potential for the city in the long-term.
  ○ Incorporation of environmental education of the younger generation, which will be responsible for future urban development.

Eco-Cities in Asia

Integration of Concepts: The Low-Carbon Eco-City

Examples from Japan show that the concept of the eco-city is not exactly simple, its objectives are numerous, and its policy priorities change constantly with the challenges of the day.

Eco-cities involve a dimension of environmental objectives that are self-interested at the local level (i.e., it is sufficient to improve the urban environment for local citizens), and those that are not self-interested (i.e., improving the local urban environment also improves the national and global environment).

Cities are increasingly expected to cooperate and tackle initiatives to achieve the latter type of objectives. Most representative of these are initiatives to create "low-carbon eco-cities".

The creation of low-carbon eco-cities demands greater efficiency of energy consumption as well as reductions of carbon dioxide emissions. The pursuit of those goals, however, presents many issues in urban transport and the commercial and residential sectors. Indeed, many of the measures in these areas overlap with measures to coexist with nature, protect bio-diversity, and create societies with sound material cycles. The menu of policies and measures is essentially not much different from those that were proposed as part of the concept of the ecopolis back in the 1980s. Compared to that period, however, there has been remarkable progress in technology. International conventions have also entered into force, such as the Framework Convention on Climate Change, the Kyoto Protocol based on it, and the Convention on Bio-diversity. And perhaps even more important, public interest in and support for eco-cities has become much stronger.

One pillar for the realisation of a low-carbon society must be the integration of a variety of measures — those that seek harmony with the environment, the conservation of bio-diversity, the creation of societies with sound material cycles, and so on as shown in Fig. 8.

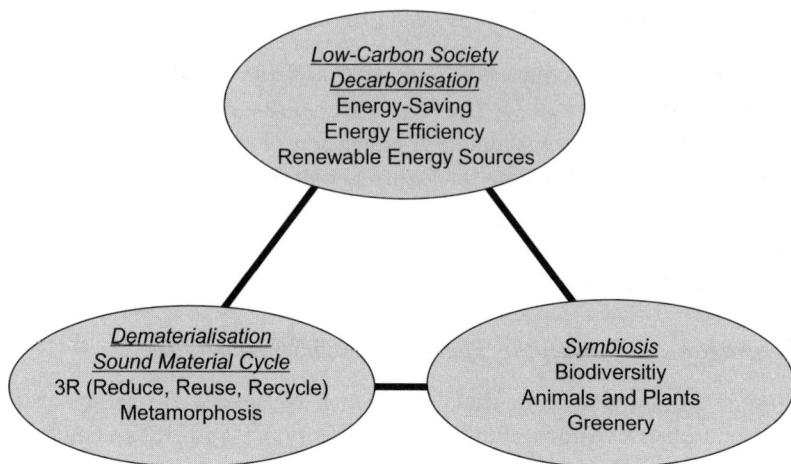

Fig. 8   Multiple Goals of Eco-Cities.

Diverse Initiatives Based on Each City's Uniqueness

Every city has a variety of unique characteristics, so the possible objectives and measures for each eco-city will differ depending on those characteristics.

- Scale (population size, area, etc.): Large, medium, small cities.
- Geographical, climatological, and other natural conditions: Latitude, vegetation zones, etc.
- Socio-economic conditions: Historical context, economics (per capita production and income of citizens, major industries, etc.).
- Divisions of function: Government towns, industrial towns, commercial towns, economic centres, residential communities, etc.
- Governance structures: Relationship between government and citizens, the influence of citizens, etc.

It is necessary to establish policy objectives that respond to the unique characteristics of each city, and to establish a slew of measures in response to those characteristics as illustrated in Fig. 9.

Governance Structures, Citizen Participation

The initiatives to construct ecopolises in Germany were premised upon the economic development; another factor was the autonomous action of a mature civil society. In Japan, the initiatives of environmental

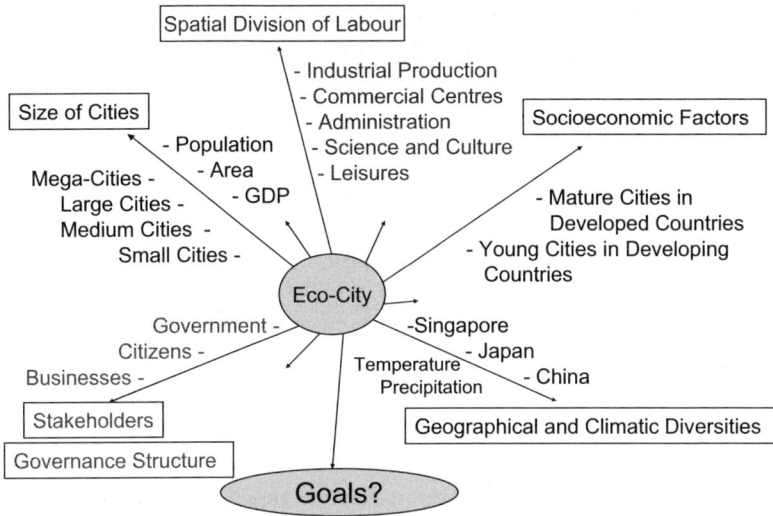

Fig. 9   Different Goals for Different Cities.

non-governmental organisations and other entities in civil society are not as strong, but during the past 20 years, there has been a tremendous transformation in the receptiveness of citizens and corporations to environmental policy.

Planning to create eco-model cities in many of the cities, however, has been done in many cases under the direction of city administrative departments. To generate more impact, it is important to shift towards a movement with more citizen leadership.

Furthermore, few policies can be properly implemented by one city working completely alone within its own jurisdiction. Cities must collaborate with others in the regions around them. One good example in Japan is the trend of urban dwellers participating in the work of maintaining and caring for the forests of mountain villages struggling with shrinking populations. People in cities and in rural communities need to support each other.

Integration with Economic Policy

One of the keys to creating Eco-Model Cities is found in the design of measures to enable win–win situations for both the economy and the environment as demonstrated by the positive feedback cycle in Fig. 3.

Technology has made phenomenal progress since the concept of the ecopolis first appeared in the early 1990s. Meanwhile, the world today (spring of 2009) is confronting a serious global economic crisis, and through what has been called the "Green New Deal", U.S. President Barack Obama has announced policies to commit more effort to developing environmental technologies such as bio-fuels, photovoltaics, and wind power.

This suggests that many environmental technologies have reached the point that they are economically viable, and that the conventional perception that environmental measures are not economically viable has given way to a perception of economic and environmental policies as producing win–win outcomes.

Thus, dramatic advances have been achieved with the economic viability of systems and technological developments. To propel them further, however, more innovation is needed in terms of legislative and tax systems, such as systems that promote the purchase of renewable energy.

Conclusion: International Cooperation

For the creation of eco-cities, it was considered sufficient for cities in the past to simply declare their own local objectives and undertake local initiatives, but today it is essential for a large numbers of cities worldwide to adopt a global perspective, exchange views and know-how, and cooperate on joint initiatives.

Cities in Asian countries need to establish and implement their own policy objectives in response to their own local conditions, of course, but in this endeavour, it is essential that they become aware of the extent to which their own prosperity depends on external factors.

At the same time, however, the most important actors in the creation of eco-cities must ultimately be local: the citizens, corporations, local government, and so on. For them to take action to address environmental problems on a global scale, it is important to create international networks that can facilitate collaboration and cooperation among local actors.

References

Environmental Agency of Japan. (1989). "Kankyo Hakusho" (Annual Report on the State of Environmental in Japan).

Girardet, Herbert. (1999). "Sustainable Cities: A Contradiction in Terms?" In *Sustainable Cities*, D. Satterthwaite (ed.), pp. 413–425. London: Earthscan Publications Ltd.

Imura, Hidefumi and Miranda Schreurs. (2005). *Environmental Policies in Japan*, pp. 15–48. Gloucester: Edward Elgar Publishing Ltd.

Junkan-gata Shakai Keisei Kihon Keikaku.

Ministry of Economy, Trade and Industry of Japan. (2008). "Tsusho Hakusho" (Annual Report on Trade in Japan).

Newman, Peter and Jefferey Kenworthy. (1999). *Sustainability and Cities*, pp. 1–26.

Rees, William. (1999). "Achieving Sustainability: Reform or Transformation?" In *Sustainable Cities*, D. Satterthwaite (ed.), pp. 22–54.

Rees, William and Mathis Wackernagel. (1994). "Ecological Footprint and Appreciated Carrying Capacity: Measuring the Natural Capital Requirements of the Human Economy." In *Investing in Natural Capital: The Ecological Economics Approach to Sustainability*, A-M. Jansson, M. Hammer, C. Folke and R. Costanza (eds.). Washington D.C.: Island Press.

Roelofs, Joan. (1999). "Building and Designing with Nature: Urban Design." In *Sustainable Cities*, D. Satterthwaite (ed.), p. 235.

Satterwaite, David. (1999). "The Key Issues and the Works Included." In *Sustainable Cities*, D. Satterthwaite (ed.), pp. 3–21.

CHAPTER 2

Let's Get Real: Critical Visions and Sustainable Eco-Urbanism

William S. W. LIM*

Since the beginning of this millennium, the turbulent crisis is clearly beyond just economics and climatic. The crisis is systemic in nature. We are witnessing profound transformations of the global economy and power balance with new players from the emerging economies. A New World Order is emerging with different priorities. The world as we know it will not be the same again. Today, the challenge of sustainability requires a new urgency in the context of income disparity between and within countries. The ethical question of sustainability for whose benefit must be seriously addressed in our numerous broad-based actions beyond the criteria of maximising efficiency and profit.

Introduction

Eco-cities is now a fashionable brand to be proudly displayed and identified with. This feedback workshop from the various cities in the region will certainly be useful to compare the experiences and effectiveness of actions taken. On the theoretical level, I wish to share here the challenges in the broader context towards achieving a liveable and sustainable environment in East Asian cities. The analysis will go beyond the applications of present known knowledge and will be based on the *feedforward*[1] approach into the unfamiliar territory of cutting-edge thinking and fundamental changes in the spirit of the post-modern which I have characterised as pluralism, rebelliousness, tolerance of differences, and the firm commitment towards

---

*William S.W. Lim is an independent theorist on Asian cities.
[1] Feedforward control can be likened to learned responses to known cues. Feedback control is reactive; feedforward control is proactive.

vigorously investigating the present untested solutions of new knowledge broadly defined and embraced within the context of radical cultural studies.

This article will be in two parts. First, I will discuss three critical interdependent overviews. They are: 1) escalating climatic crisis and sustainability; 2) unprecedented global financial turmoil and new development model; and 3) Asian urbanism and chaotic order.[2] Second, selected issues of particular relevance to eco-urbanism are identified. They are: 1) sustainable and affordable transportation; 2) energy efficient green buildings; 3) retrofitting; 4) urban agriculture; and 5) recycling.

Critical Overview

(1) Climatic crisis and sustainability — After two decades of largely ineffective international declarations and numerous individual efforts to address the escalating global climatic crisis, conditions are still deteriorating and many serious warning signs are already here. We have reached a moment of truth. Our world is now nearing the dangerous tipping points of environmental calamity which would last for a long period of time and are difficult to arrest and reverse. However, there is a note of optimism that the world is now in the dynamic stage of cutting-edge technological and energy revolution. Furthermore, it has recognised the abundance of available renewable energy resources and their possible effective applications (see Fig. 1).[3] A low-sustainable carbon energy global economy is possible, though the road ahead will be challenging and at least in the beginning, expensive. Major mindset policy changes are essential to overcome the current obsessions in maximising profit and efficiency of the already known, and to encourage creative, innovative ideas in untested territories. We need clear visions and strong collective commitments in achieving a creative and vibrant living environment in the context of a harmonious equitable world for everyone.

To achieve a truly sustainable world is no longer just a utopian dream. Essential initiatives include a large-scale shift to carbon-free

---

[2]William S.W. Lim (1998). "Asian New Urbanism." In *Asian New Urbanism*, pp. 14–32. Singapore: Select Publishing.

[3]Data put together by Worldwatch Institute from various sources. See Flavin, Christopher (2008). *Worldwatch Report 178, Low-Carbon Energy: A Roadmap*, 21. Washington, D.C.: Worldwatch Institute.

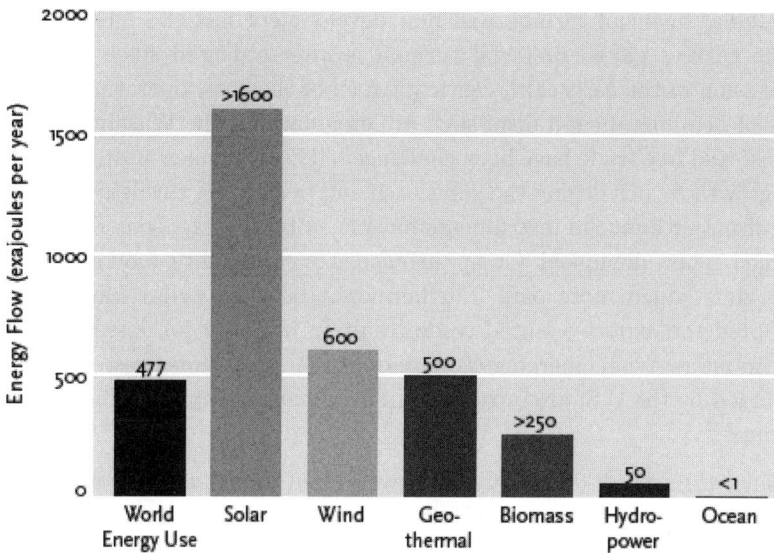

Source: UNDP, Johansson *et al.*, IEA.

Fig. 1 World Energy Use in 2005 and Annual Renewable Energy Potential with Current Technologies.

sources of energy,[4] applications of major advances in energy efficiency,[5] global population stabilisation,[6] protecting and restoring forests, efficient eco-urbanism and dramatic re-orientation in values and lifestyles from the philosophy of greed as well as excessive and wasteful consumerism. Comprehensive sustainable development requires a long-term approach and public commitment well beyond the private business practices with their other priorities and shorter-term considerations. However, we must recognise that many developing countries still require decades of rapid economic growth, and at the same time, the need to minimise pollution and wasteful consumption as well as to achieve an ecologically sustainable economy.

---

[4]Ibid.

[5]See Brown, Lester R. (2008). *Plan B 3.0 Mobilizing to Save Civilization*. New York and London: W.W Norton & Company. Chapter 11: Raising Energy Efficiency, pp. 213–236.

[6]Sachs, Jeffrey D. (2008). *Common Wealth: Economics for a Crowded Planet*. New York: Penguin Press. Chapter 7: Global Population Dynamics, pp. 159–182 and Chapter 8: Completing the Demographic Transition, pp. 183–202. "Crucially, in the medium variant the population stabilises by around 2070 at 9.2 billion; in the low variant, the population stabilises by around 2035 at roughly 7.8 billion," p. 167.

(2) Global financial turmoil and new development model — The severity
of the current global financial turmoil is unprecedented since the Great
Depression in the early 20th century. Much of the basic operating assumptions of neo-liberal capitalism such as deregulations, the Washington Consensus[7] and free trade have been challenged. The illusionary utopian culture
and growth by privileging the super-rich and permitting ruthless manipula-
tion of major financial instruments have been totally exposed. The culture
of greed is now debunked. Great turbulence in commodity, food and energy
prices has added more pain. Furthermore, the crisis today has seriously
disrupted the export-oriented trade resulting in major job losses, particularly in many Asian emerging economies. At the meantime, western governments led by the U.S. are introducing huge financial supports and stimulus
packages.

Since the late 1990s, major new players from the emerging economies are
increasingly claiming their rightful voices in formulating the global agenda.
Though somewhat reluctantly, the inevitable power-sharing and cross cultural recognition are now accepted by the West. It is in this context that
China's response to the current financial crisis should be examined. The
word crisis in Chinese (危机) comprises two characters meaning both dan-
ger (危险) and opportunity (机会). It is therefore psychologically ingrained
in the Chinese psyche to simultaneously tackle the multiple dangers and
explore and uncover new opportunities. This largely explains the quick
response of the Chinese government to attempt a new development model
by critically reviewing, analysing and re-defining their development strategies, environmental, social and economic priorities and income disparity
with a firm political commitment to an unprecedented huge financial pack-
age. Numerous policy actions taken by China should soon result in narrow-
ing rural/urban income disparity, re-introducing universal healthcare and
affordable education for all her citizens. A new development model for the
developing countries is now clearly emerging given priorities to renewable
energy, locally based job creation, eco-urbanism and environmental sustainability, as well as to decrease income disparity between rural and urban and
within cities, and to introduce fair trade instead of the present exploitative
and western-biased free trade.[8] South Korea and Taiwan since mid-1990s

---

[7]Jomo, K.S and Ben Fine, ed. (2006). *The New Development Economics — After the
Washington Consensus.* New York: Zed Books.
[8]Sachs Wolfgang and Tilman Santarius (2007). *Fair Future: Resource Conflicts, Security
and Global Justice.* London & New York: Zed Books: Section "Fair trade instead of

have effectively introduced universal *welfare* as a parallel and inclusive component to previous single-minded economic developmental model. Three essential policies for everyone are now in place. They are: 1) unemployment insurance, 2) healthcare and 3) minimum living standard guarantee.[9]

(3) Asian urbanism and chaotic order — Traditionally, Asian urbanism is differently structured and has over time developed organically. Streets in these cities are dynamic and bubbling with energy and vibrancy. Cityscape is often characterised as a zone of fuzziness where the public and private intermingle, and where the edges of buildings are fluid and constantly changing. "In the tradition of most East Asian civilisations, a 'public' understood in the sense of 'domain' in opposition to the 'private' does not exist."[10] In Asia, chaos, uncertainty, pluralistic richness and evolving complexity are acquired as essential elements of its urban dynamism. The introduction of modernist planning and spatial and usage separations are constantly contested and defied by the dynamic human interactions everywhere.

In recent decades, economic exigencies in many Asian cities have demanded the explosive expansion of urban centres. Following the U.S. capitalist model,[11] traditional downtowns and much of the adjoining areas are demolished to accommodate the modernist infrastructure and financial facilities. When time and where space are compressed immensely, many Asian cities experience the environmental shock of pre-modern, modern and post-modern conditions simultaneously, and in a compact hybrid of contradictions. However, most Asian cities today still maintain their vibrancy because of the chaotic order, pluralistic richness and unintentional complexity. Besides the façade of western modernity along main streets resides a restless, indigenous Asian peculiarity that needs to be better understood.

---

free trade" in Chapter 6: Agreements for Fairness and Ecology, pp. 196–215. Let me quote from this book, "Between 1980 and 2000, the world market prices of 18 important agricultural goods fell by an average of 25% — and by as much as 47% for cotton, 64% for coffee, 60.8% for rice, 71.1% for cocoa and 76.6% for sugar": p. 95 and "US tariffs on sugar were set at 244% of the import price and on groundnuts at 174%, while EU tariffs on beef and wheat were fixed at 213 and 168% respectively": p. 203.

[9]Kwon, Huck-Ju (2008). "Transforming the Developmental Welfare States in East Asia." In *Towards Full and Decent Employment*, J. A. Ocampo and K. S. Jomo (eds.), pp. 330–355. United Nations.

[10]Kuo, Wen-liang (2008). "Optically Irrelevant: A Hypothetical Account of an East Asian Model of Perception." In *Dark Discourse: Reflections of Taiwan City Culture*, Chaolee Kuo (ed.), pp. 49–69. National Taiwan Museum of Fine Arts.

[11]It is important to realise that notwithstanding the vast destruction of Second World War, no traditional central city area in any major European city has been deliberately destroyed for commercial-oriented development.

It is in this context that I have strongly argued in the section *Multiple Modernities and Contemporariness* in my recent book entitled *Asian Alterity*[12] that many universalistic assumptions of Eurocentric modernity are no longer viable paradigms for the non-West to understand contemporary society. In the dynamic global changes of contemporariness, the discourse and applications of the modernity in each country and its cities must evolve within its own traditions and culture.[13] To quote Charles Taylor: "Some of these changes may be parallel, but they will not converge, because new differences will emerge from the old."[14]

Eco-Urbanism

The present single-minded focus by the advanced economies on the pursuit of a high-technological global future and excessive consumerism has left in its wake an unsustainable exploitation of the earth's global resources at the expense particularly of the poor and under-privileged. In the next few decades, unprecedented explosion of the urban population in many emerging economies will continue. However, given the limited resources available in these economies, the present elitist urban practices based on the model of western capitalist modernism are clearly not viable. Sadly, evictions of farmers to build golf courses and high-income low density residential developments are still continuing unabated. In response to challenges of global sustainability and the present global financial crisis, there is now an increasing awareness in the essentiality of public ethical responsibility beyond obsessive priority for monetary gain and the illusionary unrealisable urban imagery.

A truly sustainable world and a liveable environment for everyone is now a necessity and a challenging task. It is no longer just a utopian dream. Renewable technologies, energy efficiency and fundamental policy re-orientation will

---

[12]See William S.W. Lim (2008). *Asian Alterity*. Singapore: World Scientific Publishing Co.: Section 1 "Multiple Modernities and Contemporariness" in Chapter 2: Modernities, pp. 56–62.

[13]Refer to a recent article by Chua Beng Huat, "Disrupting Hegemonic Liberalism: Singapore in Question" delivered at a public lecture at Asia Research Institute, National University of Singapore (Unpublished paper, 2008) and to quote from the article, "There is therefore discursive space for a conceptualisation of a democratic polity that is not liberal but one that privileges the social and to insert this conceptualisation into the theorisation of politics at the comparative and global scale."

[14]Taylor, Charles (2001). "Two Theories of Modernity." In *Alternative Modernities*, D.P. Gaonkar (ed.), p. 172. Durham: Duke University Press.

allow developing countries to increase their reliance on indigenous resources. However, to write critically about sustainability and affordability, as well as liveable and vibrant urban environment, we must ask some hard questions. Sustainability for whom — who benefits and who loses?

(1) Transportation — Notwithstanding the rapid shift to other more efficient energy options, extensive car usage is still the main culprit of urban environmental crisis, and the destruction of the vibrancy in street-life. Public transport ranging from subways, buses and taxis to jeepneys and bicycle rickshaws is an essential source of mobility for the majority and occupies a critical role in urban workability. Cycling and walking should certainly be encouraged with city-wide networks of bicycle lanes and walkways.[15] For cities in the emerging economies, millions will benefit by returning and providing cyclists their rightful status and facilities.

(2) Green buildings — The greatest potential for energy savings in cities lies in the most basic element of energy consumption, i.e., in buildings. Effective actions include the enforcement for new constructions using integration of design with multiple energy efficiency measures in response to local climatic conditions and technical capabilities, the use of compact fluorescent light bulbs (CFLs) as well as mounting solar electric generators on rooftops. Furthermore, Asian cities need to discard the illusionary symbolism of modernity with very tall buildings as these buildings are expensive to construct and maintain.[16] The recent phenomenon in search of the iconic by commissioning international star architects to produce fashionable theme-park trendy images must be contested and debunked.[17]

---

[15]Cycling is now a major mode of urban transport in many major European cities such as Amsterdam and Paris. See Brown, *Plan B 3.0 Mobilizing to Save Civilization*, "The surge to 500 million bicycle owners in China since 1978 provided the greatest increase in human mobility in history... it is bicycles that provide personal mobility for hundreds of millions of Chinese," p. 200.

[16]Buchanan, Peter (2007). "The Tower: An Anachronism Awaiting Rebirth?" *Harvard Design Magazine*, Issue 26, pp. 5–29. To quote from this article, "Sustainability requires not only that we lessen our ecological impacts, but also that we create the urban and cultural frameworks in which we can attain full humanity, in contact with self, others, and nature. This might be the real reason that the tower seems an anachronism," p. 14.

[17]William S.W. Lim (2008). "Debunking the Icon-Myth." Lecture delivered at AAAsia Taiwan Workshop Published in *SA Singapore Architect*, Issue 247, pp. 48–51; in *Architecture + Design (India)*, Special Issue 2009, pp. 60–63 and in *Architecture Malaysia* 21(1): 60–63.

(3) Retrofitting — The sheer number of old buildings that can benefit from retrofitting is staggering. According to an international report, the largest potential within the building sector for reducing greenhouse gases by 2030 is in retrofitting and upgrading equipment.[18] Retrofitting maximises the use of existing architectural resources. This applies particularly to numerous high-rise buildings constructed during recent decades in many major cities of developing economies.[19] To quote Cui Kai, "Renovation promises sustainability — appeals to an appreciation for history and culture — a city, a block, a building can never be what it is but for decades and centuries of construction and renewal."[20]

(4) Urban agriculture — I was once asked after my lecture in Ho Chi Minh City in 2008 whether rich farmland should be preserved within the metropolitan area.[21] My answer was a strong affirmative, as these farms are very productive and are also invaluable in many other ways. They include production of fresh food and vegetables, reduction on transportation load and enrichment of environmental quality. In larger farms, renewable energy such as wind power can be introduced and extensive tree planting and public recreation facilities can be incorporated.

(5) Recycling — Waste recycling makes an important contribution to reducing energy usage and pollution as well as minimising land filling and incinerating waste. In the developed economies, recycling now generates large revenue and new employment opportunities. However, collecting waste for recycling in many poor countries sometimes entail dirty, undesirable and even dangerous work, and workers are often poorly paid. With rapidly improving technology and lowering cost, recycling waste water even for drinking purpose will soon be a viable option for many densely populated Asian cities. In Singapore, recycled water

---

[18]Intergovernmental Panel on Climate Change (IPCC) (2007). *Climate Change 2007: Mitigation of Climate Change*, Contribution of Working Group III to the Fourth Assessment Report of the IPCC. United Kingdom and New York: Cambridge University Press.
[19]It is important to realise that many high-rise buildings are demolished not because they have outlived the economic usage, but because of the increase in permissible development density by the authority resulting in greatly inflated value of the land.
[20]See Foreword by Cui Kai in Yu, Bing (ed.) (2008). *Domus + New Renovation Projects*. China: China Architecture and Building Press.
[21]William S.W. Lim (2008). "Understanding Asian Ethical Urbanism." Lecture to University of Architecture, Ho Chi Minh City, Vietnam (Unpublished paper).

is now supplied at a competitive cost and will be able to constitute 30% of the state's total consumption needs by 2010.[22]

Conclusion

We urgently need more research to better understand the strong linkages and complex interdependency of sustainable development, quality of urban life and spatial justice particularly in emerging economies. To provide the basic needs and amenities for the whole community particularly the poor is not enough. We have to expand the concept of human rights and social justice to include many ethical urban actions such as accessibility and affordability of public transport, healthcare and education as well as to enjoy the facilities of public parks and cultural facilities such as museums, art galleries and libraries. However, this will only be achievable with deliberate public policies towards generous selective subsidisation and broad-based community supports.

The analysis in this article is by no means exhaustive. To achieve a truly liveable and environmentally sustainable eco-city is a difficult task. Each city should set its own implementable targets within a specific time-frame, for example, every three to five years to reduce the carbon foot-print and contribute towards the quality of urban life and global sustainabilities. Two universally applicable actions should be urgently introduced. They are: 1) to reduce or even ban the sale of incandescent bulbs by replacing them with compact fluorescent light bulbs (CFLs) and later with even more efficient light-emitting diodes (LEDs)[23] and 2) to encourage by taxation and legislation the usage of highly efficient hybrid cars, as this will have great environmental impact on air quality particularly in major cities in developing economies.

The urgent challenge today is for Asian societies to pursue an alternative viable development strategy in order to transcend and redefine the dominant logic of materialism and commodification. This can be possible with a strong broad vision of global responsibility, a firm commitment to social justice and an active grass-root participation of the community.

---

[22]PUB Pure Annual Report (2007/2008). Singapore: MediaCorp Pte Ltd.

[23]McKeown, Alice and Nathan Swire (2008). "Strong Growth in Compact Fluorescent Bulbs Reduces Electricity Demand." In *World Watch, Antarctica and Climate Change* (January/February 2009), Vol. 22, No. 1. p. 29. Washington D.C: Worldwatch Institute.

References

Brown, Lester R. (2008). *Plan B 3.0 Mobilizing to Save Civilization*. New York and London: W.W Norton & Company.

Buchanan, Peter (2007). "The Tower: An Anachronism Awaiting Rebirth?" *Harvard Design Magazine*, Issue 26, pp. 5–29.

Chua, Beng Huat (2008). "Disrupting Hegemonic Liberalism: Singapore in Question." Unpublished paper delivered at a public lecture at Asia Research Institute, National University of Singapore.

Cui, Kai. Foreword to Yu, Bing (ed.) (2008). *Domus + New Renovation Projects*. China: China Architecture and Building Press.

Flavin, Christopher (2008). *Worldwatch Report 178, Low-Carbon Energy: A Roadmap*. Washington D.C: Worldwatch Institute.

Intergovernmental Panel on Climate Change (IPCC) (2007). *Climate Change 2007: Mitigation of Climate Change*. United Kingdom and New York: Cambridge University Press.

Jomo, K.S. and Ben Fine (ed.) (2006). *The New Development Economics — After the Washington Consensus*. New York: Zed Books.

Kuo, Wen-liang (2008). "Optically Irrelevant: A Hypothetical Account of an East Asian Model of Perception." In *Dark Discourse: Reflections of Taiwan City Culture*, Chaolee Kuo (ed.). Taiwan: National Taiwan Museum of Fine Arts.

Kwon, Huck-Ju (2008). "Transforming the Developmental Welfare States in East Asia." In *Towards Full and Decent Employment*, J.A. Ocampo and K.S. Jomo (eds.). United Nations.

McKeown, Alice and Nathan Swire (2008). "Strong Growth in Compact Fluorescent Bulbs Reduces Electricity Demand." *World Watch, Antarctica and Climate Change* (January/February 2009), Vol. 22, No. 1. Washington D.C: Worldwatch Institute.

PUB Pure Annual Report (2007/2008). Singapore: MediaCorp Pte Ltd.

Sachs, Jeffrey D. (2008). *Common Wealth: Economics for a Crowded Planet*. New York: Penguin Press.

Sachs, Wolfgang and Tilman Santarius (2007). *Fair Future: Resource Conflicts, Security and Global Justice*. London & New York: Zed Books.

Taylor, Charles (2001). "Two Theories of Modernity." In *Alternative Modernities*, D.P. Gaonkar (ed.). Durham: Duke University Press.

William S.W. Lim (1998). *Asian New Urbanism*. Singapore: Select Publishing.

William S.W. Lim (2008). *Asian Alterity*. Singapore: World Scientific Publishing Co.

William S.W. Lim (2008). "Debunking the Icon-Myth." *SA Singapore Architect*, Issue 24, pp. 48–51; *Architecture + Design (India)*, Special Issue 2009, pp. 60–63, and *Architecture Malaysia*, Issue 21, No. 1, pp. 60–63.

William S.W. Lim (2008). "Understanding Asian Ethical Urbanism." Unpublished paper delivered to University of Architecture, Ho Chi Minh City, Vietnam.

CHAPTER 3

Some Thoughts on the Development of Eco-Cities in Asia

LYE Liang Fook and CHEN Gang*

There is urgency in developing eco-cities or embarking on eco-friendly projects as a means of achieving sustainable development. This paper provides an overview of the rationale, key principles and features of eco-cities. Going beyond concepts and theories, it examines three interesting case studies of eco-cities, namely, the on-going Masdar Eco-city or Masdar Initiative in Abu Dhabi, the failed Huangbaiyu Eco-village in Liaoning in China and the on-going Sino-Singapore Tianjin Eco-city in China. The purpose of showcasing these three examples is to show three different models of building eco-cities or eco-friendly projects with their attendant advantages and challenges. Adopting a policy-oriented approach, the paper further suggests possible actions that can be taken to put the building of eco-cities or eco-friendly projects high on the agenda of Asian governments.

Introduction

A variety of environmental problems including climate change, acid rain, water shortage and pollution, hazardous waste, smog, ozone depletion, loss of bio-diversity and desertification are now affecting our entire world. As the globalisation process deepens and the planet's natural processes transform local problems into transnational and transcontinental issues that demand collective actions, few societies are being left untouched by major environmental problems.

---

*Lye Liang Fook and Chen Gang are Research Fellows in the East Asian Institute of the National University of Singapore. The authors would like to thank Professor John Wong for his valuable comments and contributions to this paper.

Environmental considerations are assuming greater importance in the urban planning processes of an increasing number of governments around the world. One aspect of this increasing mainstreaming of environmental needs is the development of "eco-cities" that seeks to reduce the amount of resource inputs and keep waste outputs to a minimum. In Asia as well as other parts of the world, cities are now absorbing half of the total population. As hubs of prosperity, cities have been blamed for causing environmental degradation due to the high-carbon lifestyle and huge amount of waste generated. It is therefore extremely important to understand that one of the most effective solutions to current environmental problems on a global scale lies on the way in which we plan and build our cities.

There are presently many experiments and developments related to eco-cities in Asia. The Sino-Singapore Tianjin Eco-city, mooted by Senior Minister Goh Chok Tong when he met Premier Wen Jiabao in Beijing in April 2007, is one such example. The Masdar Eco-city in Abu Dhabi is also worth mentioning as it purports to be the world's first carbon-neutral, car-free city to rely entirely on renewable energy. Some scenic and well-planned cities in the region, without the title of "eco-city," in fact have also incorporated many environmentally-friendly ideas and notions from the ecocity-style urban layout and planning in efforts to build themselves into garden cities. This paper will not only analyse eco-cities' important role in the sustainable development of human society, but also highlight the basic ideas and principles concerning such urban planning and construction. By focusing on some of the current practices in Asia, the paper will try to reveal both the achievements and problems in building eco-cities. It will also provide policy recommendations to address urban environmental problems faced by the region. Eco-city planning and construction, including innovative ways of mapping out urban transportation and city layout, and advocating the use of new technology and renewable energy, should become an important area of cooperation in the region to address the increasingly urgent environmental challenges.

Why We Need Eco-cities

People's living standards have improved greatly due to the rapid industrialisation and urbanisation throughout the world in the past 50 years, but these processes have also adversely affected the ecology of our planet. Climate change, water and air pollution, ozone depletion, loss of bio-diversity, desertification and other environmental degradation are now so severe that they not only threaten the sustainable development of the economy, people's health and ordinary life, but also pose an acute political challenge to global governance.

Climate change, mostly caused by greenhouse gas (GHG) emissions from increases in human activities, is one of the most serious environmental problems confronting the international community today. Scientists believe that a continuous temperature rise will lead to frequent meteorological disasters including drought, flood and tropical storms, rising sea levels that may submerge coastal cities and island states, and even change the whole ecological system and cause epidemic outbreaks. The topic had become quite heated in 2007, the Tenth anniversary of the Kyoto Protocol that set mandatory targets for industrialised nations to cut emissions, as new reports released by the Intergovernmental Panel on Climate Change (IPCC) in the same year described the connection between climate change and human activities with a high degree of certainty.

Although global warming affects the ecological system of the whole world and poses a threat to all countries, some regions and countries in Asia are especially vulnerable to this phenomenon due to their special geographic features and weak adaptation capacities. Many Southeast Asian countries are located in tropical areas and some of them are littoral, archipelagic or island states with long coastlines. One of the projected impacts of climate change is sea-level rise, which will bring about saltwater intrusion into surface and groundwater of the coastal areas, reduce output of the fishery industry, and destroy mangrove swamps and the habitats of various benthic organisms due to changes in salinity. Global warming also increases the frequency and intensity of tropical storms, and induces more cardiovascular and respiratory diseases. Some parts of Southeast Asia are already experiencing increasing cases of tropical diseases such as dengue fever and malaria because warmer temperature nurtures the growth of mosquitoes and facilitates vector-borne diseases.

Take the Philippines and Indonesia as examples. These two archipelagic states are believed to be extremely vulnerable to climate change. Indonesia, consisting of about 17,000 islands, may witness 2,000 of them submerged by 2030 due to sea-level rise if the current trend of global warming continues unchecked. The Philippines, with approximately 7,100 islands and rocks, is suffering from more tropical cyclones and flooding that damage the country's agriculture and infrastructure. With frequent precipitations caused by climate change, agricultural outputs could be significantly reduced. Among major continental countries in Asia, China will probably suffer most from the devastating impact of climate change. China admitted in the first National Climate Change Programme that its "annual average air temperature has increased by 0.5 to 0.8°C during the past 100 years, which was slightly larger than the average global temperature rise."[1] The frequency and intensity of extreme climate/weather events throughout China have experienced obvious changes during the last 50 years, with drought in northern and northeastern China, and floods in the middle and lower reaches of the Yangtse River and southeastern China becoming more severe.[2] The rate of sea-level rise along China's coasts during the past 50 years was 2.5 mm/a, slightly higher than the global average,[3] which poses a threat to China's coastal cities, the nation's economic powerhouse. Mountain glaciers in China have retreated at an accelerating rate,[4] reducing water supply to the Yangtse and Yellow Rivers, China's two longest rivers. The prolonged droughts will lead to agricultural output reduction and threaten the food security of the 1.3-billion-people nation.

Climate change and other environmental problems require governments and individuals to take a fresh perspective at how economic and social activities in urban centres can best be organised. Considering the increasing importance of today's cities and urban construction in determining the carbon intensity and pollutant amount of our modern life, how to make our cities more environmentally-friendly and sustainable has become a possible solution to tough environmental problems faced by the international community.

The city exists, like everything else, in an evolving universe, but it appears to have a special role in evolution that may have a great deal to do with how we build and use it.[5] A successful city must balance economic, social and ecological needs from all sides. The notion of an "eco-city" or ecopolis is a big step forward in the long-time evolution of human urban construction. Such a city minimises the required consumption of energy, water and raw materials and its waste discharge of air, solid and water pollutants.

Cities, providing economies of scale and more choices and opportunities, are attracting a rising tide of people hoping for a better life. The year

---

[1] China's National Development and Reform Commission. (2007). "China's National Climate Change Programme." http://www.ccchina.gov.cn/WebSite/CCChina/UpFile/File188.pdf, p. 4.

[2] *Ibid.*, 5.

[3] *Ibid.*

[4] *Ibid.*

[5] Register, Richard (2002). *Ecocities: Building Cities in Balance with Nature*, Berkeley: Berkeley Hills Books, p. 38.

2007 marked a watershed in human history, when for the first time, half of the world's population was living in cities.[6] Yet, cities have simultaneously been blamed for causing environmental degradation due to the high-carbon lifestyle and waste generated. Hence, one of the most effective solutions to current environmental problems on a global scale lies in the way we plan and build our cities.

The notion of "eco-city" proposes a fresh yet practical approach to designing, building and operating cities in a way that the destructive impact of human urban activity upon nature will be significantly reduced. As cities have been expanding into their surrounding areas quickly over the past 50 years, policy makers in many parts of the world have realised that an environmentally-conscious urban planning and development in accordance with local features will have tremendous positive impact upon the natural environment around us.

Ideas and Norms of Eco-City Planning

No single recipe for urban sustainability can be applied to all cities, but the various "eco-city" schemes should strive to conserve, recycle and preserve bio-diversity. More importantly, designers of these cities should always bear in mind that the economic, social and environmental considerations are always interconnected (as highlighted in the introductory chapter), and that current urban development should not compromise the ability of future generations to meet their own needs.

It is important for "eco-city" planners to manage environmental resources as strategic assets that are essential to the long-term interest of urban residents. Environmental resources such as clean air, fresh water, forests and open spaces are often taken for granted by city planners who do not pay enough attention to the efficient and sustainable utilisation of them. In an "eco-city," clean air and drinking water sources that are crucial to the human health should not be polluted in exchange for economic development. Bio-diversity inside and nearby the city should be protected for the balance of nature and the resilience of ecosystems to environmental change. Forests should be preserved not only because they are necessary watersheds and habitats, but also because they absorb huge amount of GHGs and thus slow down global warming. More trees should be planted in the city area or

---

[6]Cities Alliance. (2007). "Liveable Cities: The Benefits of Urban Environmental Planning." Washington D.C. http://www.citiesalliance.org/doc/resources/cds/liveable/cover.pdf, p. 1.

the suburbs to purify the atmosphere and prevent the formation of urban heat island. Other important environmental resources such as wetlands, coral reefs and mangrove swamps should also be preserved in the process of urban expansion.

A typical eco-city should be a low-carbon city with improved public transport and an increase in pedestrianisation and cycling to reduce carbon emissions. To minimise the use of automobiles, the city should be compact and different from the general urban pattern today i.e., skyscrapers in the middle with tens of thousands of acres of ground-scrapers sprawling all around. Instead, the blueprint should be a multi-centre one and in each centre or subcentre, catering, education, medical care and shopping services are available to most residents. Dense subcentres and compact neighbourhood centres are situated fairly close to the major city hub. High-rise buildings are still encouraged in centre areas to save land and reduce long-distance commuting. Some of the outlying communities will be agricultural villages providing their own farm produces for the city hub and subcentres.

High population density, therefore, is a necessity for a sustainable city because it not only reduces the per capita demand for occupied land, but also cuts per capita cost of supplying piped water, sewer systems, garbage collection, postal delivery and other public services. An eco-city must provide easy access to the daily necessities and entertainment by walking, cycling and public transportation. A new transportation hierarchy should be established with preference on pedestrians, cyclists, subways, buses and finally private automobiles. Roads may be narrow to make walking easy and driving difficult.

New energy-saving building materials should be widely used in the construction of an eco-city. To achieve low emissions, architects may need to fit the buildings with solar panels to produce electricity, which will be used for lighting, office equipment and air-conditioning. Better ventilation strategies need to be worked out for reducing dependence on air-conditioning. Blinds, the opacity of windows and airflow need to be regulated throughout the building to conserve energy for heating and for balanced natural lighting.

The eco-city should conserve water resources and interfere minimally with the intrinsic patterns of the water cycle in the ecological system. A compact city layout is necessary to reduce the footprint on the permeable soil, and efficient water recycle systems making full use of creeks and reservoirs should be established to regulate run-offs in the raining and dry seasons, and convert rain water into useful and drinkable fresh water resources. Urban aquifers should be strictly protected from overuse or pollution, while the soil's permeability should be guaranteed to ensure the absorption of groundwater from time to time.

An eco-city should be a "garden city" surrounded by green-belts and woodlands, with the preservation of local species and harmonious co-existence between humans and other creatures. Bio-diversity increases the resilience of eco-systems to environmental changes. Rivers, lakes, wetlands and forest resources can be used as protected areas to add to urban bio-diversity as the city is built. If urban wastes are carefully limited and recycled, and local people take responsibility to ensure their daily activities do not threaten the existence of other species, the city itself can become a botanic garden where urbanism can co-exist peacefully with other animals and plants.

An eco-city also includes the arcologies that take less land, less energy to operate and less connecting materials such as pipes and wires. In an arcological city, major social, economic and civic activities are available within short distances, and farm production is located just outside the city gates. Individual buildings, communities and the city as a whole can then be maintained with great efficiency and little waste.

Translate Eco-City Concepts Into Practice

In order to achieve urban development projects with integrated sustainable solutions across all sectors, eco-city guidelines and objectives have to be woven together with local requirements.[7] Due to the complexity of constructing an eco-city, urban planners need to promote cooperation in a multi-disciplinary planning team as well as among all stakeholders. An eco-city should be understood as a single integrated system (holistic approach) and not as a combination or result of many sectoral developments planned in isolation.[8] The idea of integrated planning is the basis for sustainable urbanism, requiring repeated and ongoing processes of analysis and a multidisciplinary approach to sustainability. In eco-city planning, those sectors related to the metabolic and environmental functions of the city (transport, energy and material flows and socio-economic aspects), which conventional planning considers as subsidiary to urban structure,

---

[7] Gaffron, Philine, Ge Huismans and Franz Skala (2008). *Ecocity Book II: How to Make it Happen*, p. 37. Vienna: Facultas Verlags- und Buchhandels AG.
[8] *Ibid.*, p. 18.

are accorded the same level of importance.[9] Extensive participation is an important part of the knowledge-based eco-city planning because the more the stakeholders are involved in decision-making, the more knowledge they will contribute to the bottom-up planning process. As grass-roots democracy has been regarded as an indispensable element for good environmental governance, public participation should be an interactive process throughout the planning process.

With active participation of different sectors and relevant stakeholders, the whole process of eco-city planning and construction is usually focused on such key areas as urban structure, transportation, energy and other resource efficiency as well as the socio-economic aspects. The main principles for sustainable urban development, i.e., minimising use of land, energy and materials and minimising the impairment of natural environment, should always be followed throughout the construction process.

(1) Urban Structure

The efficient use of land resource is a basic requirement for eco-city planning. Eco-city planners need to pay sufficient attention to the spatial level of quarters and neighbourhoods. It is necessary to optimise the density of settlements with regard to the potentially contradictory requirements of transportation (higher density of origins and destinations), solar architecture (depending on the climate: either avoiding shading between buildings or using it for passive cooling) and quality of life issues (e.g., open spaces for climatic and social functions and personal comfort).[10] Instead of detached, single-family houses with large gardens, compact building structures, such as multi-storey residential, commercial or mixed-use buildings, should be considered. Habitats for plants and animals must be created or conserved in urban contexts, with enough open space and green areas maintained in the forms of gardens, parks, street-trees, green roofs, green facades and natural water features.

(2) Transportation

Eco-city designers should give preference first to the arrangement that reduces the need for transport, then to those measures that encourages travel at low speed, thirdly to public transport and mass-transit, and finally to limited use of car transport. The compact and multi-centric layout of an

---

[9]Gaffron, Philine, Ge Huismans and Franz Skala (2005). *Ecocity Book I: A Better Place to Live*, pp. 37–38. Vienna: Facultas Verlags- und Buchhandels AG.
[10]Gaffron, Philine, Ge Huismans and Franz Skala (2008). *Ecocity Book II: How to Make It Happen*, p. 25.

eco-city should allow most travel to take place on foot, by bike and by public transport. Only a small proportion of population should drive private cars, with special incentives in place to encourage them to buy hybrid vehicles that use energy more efficiently. Yet urban planners should bear in mind that alternatives must be of maximum quality to reduce private car usage. Otherwise, the transport inconvenience will incur public dissatisfaction or even sharp criticism.

(3) Energy and Resource Efficiency

Using energy and other resources efficiently and sustainably is a key part of an eco-city project. Measures should be taken to minimise the energy demand of the built urban structure and minimise energy losses of buildings. The use of fossil fuels for air-conditioning and other electricity supply should be limited while a variety of renewable energy are to be used widely. Urban architectures should design more solar architecture in the city to better tap clean energy from the sun, giving preferences to environmentally friendly and sustainable produced materials. Advanced devices should be adopted to treat wastewater so that it can be recirculated into the water cycle without negative impacts, and the collection and purification of rainwater will help city dwellers use natural resources more efficiently. Solid waste should be recycled or reused, with special devices introduced to use landfill gases as a kind of new energy and thus reduce GHG emissions.

(4) Social Infrastructure and Economic Viability

Besides environmental protection, the eco-city as an attractive and prosperous place has to provide a satisfying social and economic infrastructure for a high-quality life. One important element is easy access to day-to-day facilities. Kindergartens and elementary schools should be located within walking distance, while other schools, clinics and hospitals should be within walking/cycling distance or maximum 30 minutes by public transport. Leisure and recreation facilities such as cinemas, theatres and fitness centres should also be within walking distance or easily reached by public transport.

Economic viability is another important aspect to consider in building an eco-city. To achieve economic sustainability, it is generally helpful to involve a plurality of investors including owner-inhabitants, real-estate companies and professional developers right from the start. A public-private partnership is one of the tools available for implementing eco-cities, with different partners from the public and the private sectors working together.[11] Co-operation of all sectors on eco-city projects makes it possible to divide the risks among partners, to attain the public, social and societal goals with reduced funding from public sources, and to raise the return on investment on related private investments.[12] Short-term investments and returns should not be the only indices for measuring the profitability of an eco-city project, whose long-term success relies on whether it helps to create a unique city context with significant reduction of pollution, minimised use of fossil fuels and other resources, improvement in people's health, high quality of life, less car accidents and more convenience for social activities.

(5) Monitoring and Evaluation

When the physical construction has completed, it is time to evaluate the real performances of the eco-city and test whether the planning hypotheses are validated. Certain monitoring and evaluation mechanisms and procedures must be in place to ensure that the urban development process serves the goals of conserving resources, reducing pollution, increasing green spaces and improving people's residential life. Such evaluation is also important for getting valuable empirical knowledge that can be used as reference information for future improvement and other eco-cities' design. One indispensable feature of the eco-city is public participation, so a good monitoring system not only depends on technical data-collection such as on energy saving, emission reduction and water consumption, but also depends on well-designed social feedback mechanisms that assimilate public opinions and assessments. Continuous evaluation with the participation of all relevant stakeholders is essential for maintaining the vitality of the eco-city, which needs to rely on qualitative and quantitative tools to assess whether the proposed environmental, economic and social objectives have been met. Appropriate adaptations and adjustments must be made from time to time in response to the latest evaluation result.

Highlights of Selected Eco-Cities

To operationalise the ideas and principles of eco-cities listed above, this section will look at selected eco-cities that are being built or have been built. The eco-cities cited here have the touted qualities of encompassing

---

[11] *Ibid.*, p. 36.
[12] *Ibid.*

the three harmonies, i.e., that of contributing to the economy, protecting the environment and meeting social considerations. Three eco-cities will be examined. They are Masdar Eco-city in Abu Dhabi; the Huangbaiyu Eco-village in Liaoning province; and, the Sino-Singapore Tianjin Eco-city in Tianjin municipality.[13]

These three eco-cities are chosen because they are well-known and are generally regarded as cutting-edge projects. The Masdar Eco-city is an ambitious project to create an environmentally friendly living space under harsh desert conditions. The Huangbaiyu Eco-village was presented as a model of how communities could be better organised in a rural setting. The Sino-Singapore Tianjin Eco-city, with the high-level support of the governments of Singapore and China, aims to convert otherwise non-arable land (salt farms and vacant land) into productive use.

These three examples are not meant to be exhaustive but rather to provide a flavour of the different varieties of eco-cities already out there. Several aspects of each eco-city will be highlighted here including the nature of the project, the land area, the amounted invested, the investors and the nature of the government's involvement. More focus will be placed on the Sino-Singapore Tianjin Eco-city since a major aim of this paper is to share the Singapore perspective on this project. (See Annex A for a comparison of the Masdar Initiative, the Huangbaiyu Eco-village, and the Sino-Singapore Tianjin Eco-city).

Masdar Eco-City

The Masdar Eco-city or Masdar Initiative in Abu Dhabi, the capital of the United Arab Emirates (UAE), has been touted as the world's first zero-carbon, zero-waste, car-free city that will be 100% powered by renewable energy.[14] This is a bold initiative as the UAE is reportedly the world's second highest per capita emitter of carbon dioxide and other GHGs.[15] To explore a more viable development model in the long-term,

---

[13]There is also the well-known Dongtan Eco-city on Chongming Island that got off on a promising start in 2005, but has since run into difficulties. This project is looked at in detail by other experts in this volume.

[14]Masdar Initiative (2008). "Masdar Conveys Abu Dhabi's Vision on Future Energy to US Congress." Press Release, 19 June. http://www.masdaruae.com/text/news-d.aspx?_id=62.

[15]*Gulf News Online* (2008). "Experts Urge UAE to Cut Carbon Emissions Sharply." 14 May. http://archive.gulfnews.com/indepth/cityscape08/more_stories/10212996.html.

the eco-city will allow Abu Dhabi a means to diversity its economy (heavily dependent on oil and gas industries) and develop knowledge-based industries related to the environment.

The eco-city will be a six square kilometres walled community built next to the international airport in Abu Dhabi. Phase I is underway and expected to be completed in December 2009. By 2016, when the entire city is ready, there will be an estimated 40,000 people and 1,000 businesses in the city. The city aims to have a car-free environment that will boast walkways and a light rail line complemented with a personalised rapid transit (PRT) or podcars powered by renewable energy. The lack of cars will allow for narrow, shaded streets that will also help to funnel breeze from one side of the city to the other. All waste will be composted and recycled. Power will come from photovoltaic panels fitted on rooftops and a solar power plant. Water needs will be met by recycling and a desalination plant that runs on solar power.

Economically, the eco-city will complement Abu Dhabi's economy by spearheading the growth of the clean energy sector. In collaboration with the Massachusetts Institute of Technology, the Masdar Institute of Science and Technology (MIST) has been established to focus on graduate research related to core energy and sustainability technology. MIST is expected to be home to 100 students and faculty by fall 2009.[16] The Innovation and Investment Unit of the Masdar Initiative has invested in advanced energy and sustainability technology by foreign and local companies. The Carbon Management Unit of the Masdar Initiative seeks to broker investments to reduce GHG emissions under the UN Clean Development Mechanism.[17] These growth areas are aimed at generating employment and benefitting the residents of the eco-city.

The Masdar initiative is headed by the Abu Dhabi Future Energy Company (ADFEC), a wholly-owned subsidiary of the Mubadala Development Company. The latter is an investment and development arm of the government of Abu Dhabi. The ADFEC reportedly has access to a budget

---

[16]Beginning in September 2009, the MIST will offer five, 24-month Master of Science programme in the areas of information technology, water and environment, engineering systems and management, material science and engineering, and mechanical engineering. The Masters programme will be expanded over the years. A Ph.D. programme will commence in 2011 upon the graduation of the first batch of Masters degree students. See official site of the Masdar Initiative at http://www.masdaruae.com/index.aspx.
[17]*Ibid.*

of US$22 billion for the Masdar Initiative.[18] The master plan of the eco-city was drawn up by world renowned architect Norman Foster while the World Wildlife Fund is providing the sustainable concepts based on the ten guiding principles of its One Planet Living Programme.[19]

The Masdar initiative has the strong commitment and support of the Abu Dhabi government, in terms of the political leadership and financial resources being brought to bear on the project. It also appears to have access to the relevant expertise, experience and technology. Since 2006, it has been off to a strong start. However, it remains to be seen to what extent the project, when it is finished, would adhere as closely to the high standards of a carbon-free and waste-free environment as envisaged by its developers. Also, practical considerations such as the high noise level due to its location near the airport and the degree of social acceptance of a car-free environment have yet to be proven.

Huangbaiyu (黄柏峪) *Eco-Village*[20]

Huangbaiyu Eco-village in Liaoning province was meant to be a model of how technology and knowledge could improve villages' lives in a rural setting. The houses would be built based on renowned American architect William McDonough's "cradle to cradle design," where the materials for construction would be sourced locally and reused with little or no wastage.[21]

---

[18] *Time* (2007). "Renewable Energy: Desert Dreams." http://www.time.com/time/specials/2007/article/ 0,28804,1712863_1712864_1712857-1,00.html.

[19] The ten guiding principles are zero-carbon, zero-waste, sustainable transport, local and sustainable materials, local and sustainable food, sustainable water, natural habitats and wildlife, culture and heritage, equity and fair trade, and, health and happiness. For further details, please see http://www.oneplanetliving.org/.

[20] The Huangbaiyu Eco-village is technically not an eco-city as it located in the rural areas. However, it is included here because it is an environmentally-friendly project that aims to achieve environment protection, economic growth and social objectives. In particular, the project has a strong social orientation of providing a model of low-cost living for villagers in a rural setting. The project is also located in Liaoning, close to the Sino-Singapore Tianjin Eco-city, both in Northeast China. It offers an interesting contrast to what Singapore is offering in neighbouring Tianjin.

[21] In the "cradle to cradle" design, everything is reused by either returning to the soil as non-toxic "biological nutrients" that will bio-degrade safely, or returned to industry as "technical nutrients" that can be infinitely recycled. This design method is the brainchild of the famous American architect William McDonough. For more details, see http://www.mcdonough.com/. See also *Newsweek*. (2005). "Designing the Future; In a New Interview Series, Newsweek Talks to a Leading Ecological Architect Whose Goal is Nothing Less Than Eliminating Waste and Pollution." 16 May.

Each house would be built using local materials, all of which would be either bio-degradable or easily recyclable. The walls of each house would be made of pressed-earth blocks (as opposed to kiln-fired bricks) a half-metre thick to provide proper insulation. Between the blocks would be straw, a by-product of the local rice industry. Solar panels on the rooftops would provide electricity and heated water.[22] All the houses were supposed to face south in line with a traditional Chinese preference as well as to maximise their exposure to sunlight. There would also be a bio-mass gasification factory to burn the animal, human and agricultural waste to produce energy.

Construction of the eco-village started in 2005. The target was to build a total of 400 houses to support a population of 1,400. To contribute to the economic well-being of the farmers, the houses would be centralised in a town centre so that the hitherto smaller plots of farmland could be consolidated to increase the land available for farming and other development. There were apparently also plans for the farmers to be employed in local industries to earn additional income. In this way, the farmers would have the financial means to buy the new houses that would be built.

The project was under the auspices of the non-profit China-U.S. Centre for Sustainable Development with representatives from the business, government and non-governmental organisations on its board. The Co-chairs of the board are Madam Deng Nan, daughter of the late Chinese leader Deng Xiaoping (on the Chinese side) and William McDonough (on the U.S. side).[23] The master plan for the eco-village was jointly designed by a U.S.-China team. The centre provided technical assistance and some materials to build the eco-village while the funding for the project came from a local entrepreneur (Dai Xiaolong) and the local government.

The project, however, did not proceed as planned. The 400 houses due in 2008 were not constructed. The 42 houses erected so far were not built according to specifications, meaning they could not achieve the energy savings they were meant to deliver. Each house was supposed to cost no more than US$3,500, but cost overruns have doubled that figure.[24] They were too

---

[22] *Newsweek International* (2005). "Building in Green; Can China Move 400 Million People to its Cities without Wrecking Environmental Havoc? Eco-Urban Designer William McDonough Says Yes — And Beijing is Listening." 26 September.

[23] The China-U.S. Centre for Sustainable Development was conceived in April 1999 when Chinese Premier Zhu Rongji visited Washington for meetings on "Cooperation on Environment and Development" with U.S. Vice President Al Gore. A Memorandum of Understanding forming the China-U.S. Centre was signed by China and the U.S. See official website at http://www.chinauscentre.org/purpose/history.asp.

[24] *Newsweek* (2007). "Trouble for China's Model Green City." 10 May.

expensive for the villagers. The farmers were also reluctant to move in because the houses were packed together with little space around them. Their poultry could not fit into such a setting. Also, the houses do not face south.[25]

The construction of the Huangbaiyu Eco-village ran into a number of problems. Foremost among them appeared to be the different expectations on both sides on what the project was and the benefits it would bring to the villagers. The American team at the China-U.S. Centre for Sustainable Development reportedly made it clear from the start that they would supply the vision but not the investment. However, the local perception, especially among the villagers, was that the project would bring them money and jobs. Indeed, visits by several U.S. delegations to Huangbaiyu did raise expectations that the U.S. would eventually invest in a factory in the village. The villagers also did not grasp the normative and abstract concept of living in harmony with the environment.

Another problem seemed to be a lack of proper supervision and management of the project on both the Chinese and U.S. sides. The U.S. side did not ensure that what was in the master plan was implemented. On the Chinese side, Dai Xiaolong, the main financier who is also Chairman of the Huangbaiyu Village Committee, had a huge say in developing and building the project. He made adjustments to the original designs without anyone stopping him. The government of Benxi City (本溪市) where the eco-village was located, also largely left it to Dai Xiaolong to run the show. In addition, it was questionable to what extent the design of the eco-village took into account the views and preferences of the farmers given the extremely low take-up rate after the first 42 houses were completed.[26]

Sino-Singapore Tianjin Eco-City

Overview

Unlike the Masdar Eco-city which is a key project led by the UAE government and the Huangbaiyu Eco-village which was driven by the non-profit China-U.S. Centre for Sustainable Development, the Sino-Singapore

---

[25] *BBC News* (2006). "Making Cities Work: China." 21 June. http://news.bbc.co.uk/go/pr/fr/-/2/hi/asia-pacific/5084852.stm.

[26] Apparently, only two families have moved to occupy two of the 42 houses. See "China Green Dreams: A Not So Model Village." Video Clip by Public Broadcasting Service at http://www.pbs.org/frontlineworld/fellows/green_dreams/. See also *Sydney Morning Herald.* (2006). "China's First Eco-Village Proves a Hard Sell," *The Age* (Australia), 26 August 2006 and "Green Dream Vanishes in Puff of Reality." 26 August.

Tianjin Eco-city is a flagship project that has the support and attention of the governments of Singapore and China at the highest levels and across the whole of government.[27] Besides its strong environmental features and emphasis on commercial viability, the project seeks to fulfill a number of other objectives.

The Sino-Singapore Tianjin Eco-city was mooted by Senior Minister Goh Chok Tong and agreed to in-principle by Premier Wen Jiabao when they met in Beijing in April 2007.[28] The project was regarded as mutually beneficial since Singapore and China could jointly share their experience and expertise and achieve a demonstration effect that went beyond the confines of the project itself. Both sides have moved briskly to implement the idea. The major milestones in the development of the Sino-Singapore Tianjin Eco-city are at Annex B.

There are several purposes behind the Sino-Singapore Tianjin Eco-city project. At the strategic level, it marks Singapore's continued strive to stay relevant to China's rise by identifying a niche area for collaboration with China. In doing so, Singapore can leverage on China's growth. On China's part, the project will enable the country to devise a model that balances the goals of economic growth, environment protection and social harmony, one that is based on Singapore's own developmental experience which may be more realistic and attractive to China compared to other models. This is in line with the top leadership's call for a scientific concept of development enshrined in the constitution of the Chinese Communist Party. The project will also facilitate the implementation of China's regional development strategies.[29]

At the political level, the project will provide a platform for existing and aspiring political leaders and officials as well as businessmen from both sides to jointly work together. In doing so, they will get to know each other better which will in turn facilitate their work in China. More importantly, both sides will attain a comfort level that would lay the groundwork for stronger political and economic ties in the future. Although this point is

---

[27]Singapore's Ministry of National Development. (2008). "Speech by Minister Mah Bow Tan at the Ground-breaking Ceremony of the Sino-Singapore Tianjin Eco-city in Tianjin," Press Release 28 September.

[28]*Straits Times*. (2007). "Singapore, China to Jointly Develop an 'Eco-City'." 26 April.

[29]Singapore's Ministry of National Development. (2008). "First Meeting of the Sino-Singapore Tianjin Eco-City Joint Working Committee in Tianjin." Press Release, 31 January.

not often stated publicly, it is an important consideration at least from the Singapore side. Singapore wants to build a long-term relationship with China that can withstand hiccups that may occur from time to time.

From the operational perspective, the project, if successful, will demonstrate how an attempt to balance economic growth, environment protection and social harmony can be viable. The demonstration effect would be significant as there will be potential for replication elsewhere in China and possibly even other parts of the world.[30] The impact would go beyond the economic realm to cover the broader perspective of how societies could be organised while enhancing the environment and contributing to economic growth.

Distinctive Features of the Sino-Singapore Tianjin Eco-City

The distinctive features of the Sino-Singapore Tianjin Eco-city can be viewed from two levels. The first, at the broad strategic level, will examine the framework of cooperation that oversees the implementation of this project. This framework is lacking in most other eco-city projects. The second, at the operational level, will highlight the features directly related to the project. These features may be common to other eco-city projects although the extent of these features and the targets set may differ. The focus on the key features is not meant to suggest that this project is either bound to succeed or will not succeed. Such a question is beyond the scope of this paper. Rather, the focus on the key features is intended to highlight some of the major differences between this project and other projects elsewhere.

(1) Framework of Cooperation

The Sino-Singapore Tianjin Eco-city project is not an ordinary commercial undertaking. In most other eco-city projects, the government's involvement is either minimal or even non-existent. The usual practice is to let the private sector take the lead on the project with the government playing the role of creating the right conditions for the project to succeed. In contrast, on the Sino-Singapore Tianjin Eco-city project, the Singapore and Chinese governments have not only attempted to create the right conditions for

---

[30] *21st Century Business Herald.* (2008). "Zhongxin shengtaicheng shi zhongguo xinxing chengshihua de yige shiyanchang." (Sino-Singapore Eco-city is an Experiment in China's New Model of Urbanisation), 5 July.

the project to take off, but also brought it under an official supervisory mechanism.

In fact, the project has been set within the framework of bilateral cooperation between the two countries. In this sense, both governments regard the project's development as indicative of the substantive relations between the two countries. If the project progresses well, this would strengthen bilateral ties. If it does not, this would likely have some negative impact on bilateral relations. It is reasonable to assert that neither the Chinese nor Singapore governments would want to draw such a linkage if it was not confident that the project would have a fair chance to succeed.

The two sides have already set up a mechanism to oversee the development of the project. The mechanism can be divided into two main levels (see Fig. 1). The highest and first level is the Joint Steering Committee (JSC) comprising heads of the relevant ministries and government agencies from both countries and the Tianjin municipal government. Co-chaired by Deputy Prime Minister (DPM) Wong Kan Seng and Vice Premier Wang

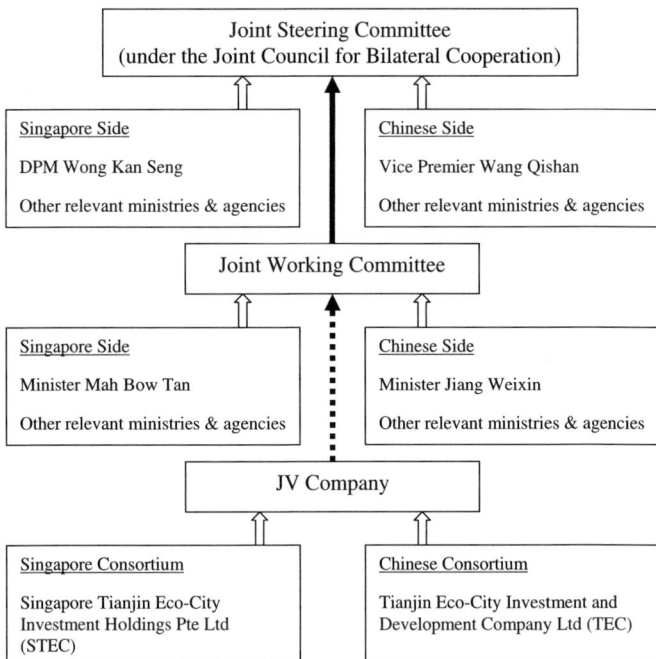

Source: Authors' own compilation.

Fig. 1   Overview of Supervisory Mechanism.

Qishan, the JSC examines all major or policy issues related to the development of the eco-city.[31] The JSC itself reports to the Joint Council for Bilateral Cooperation (JCBC) that oversees all aspects of cooperation between Singapore and China.[32]

Under the JSC, the relevant ministries and agencies on the Singapore side include the Ministry of National Development, Ministry of Environment and Water Resources, Ministry of Foreign Affairs, Ministry of Trade and Industry, Building and Construction Authority, International Enterprise Singapore, Jurong Town Corporation, National Parks Board, Public Utilities Board, Urban Redevelopment Authority, Housing and Development Board, and National Environment Agency. On the Chinese side, the relevant ministries and agencies include the Ministry of Housing and Urban-Rural Development, Ministry of Environmental Protection, Ministry of Land and Resources, Ministry of Foreign Affairs and other relevant agencies.

The JSC held its inaugural meeting in Tianjin in September 2008. At that meeting, DPM Wong and Vice Premier Wang noted that the development of the eco-city had made "rapid and good progress" since the idea was mooted about one-and-a-half years ago. Most significantly, the meeting agreed that the key areas of work ahead would not only include the physical and infrastructural development of the eco-city, but also cover the formulation of policies which was in line with the vision of the eco-city and the principle of the three harmonies (i.e., harmony between man and man, between man and the environment, and between man and economic activities) to complement and support the project's development.[33]

The second level of the supervisory mechanism is the Joint Working Committee (JWC). The upward pointing bold arrow line indicates that the JWC reports its key deliberations directly to the JSC. Co-chaired by Minister for National Development Mah Bow Tan and Minister for Housing and Rural-Urban Development Jiang Weixin, the JWC addresses operational issues related to the development of the eco-city.[34] So far, three JWC meetings have been held since the signing of the Framework Agreement on the Development of the Eco-city in November 2007.

---

[31] Wang Qishan's predecessor on the JSC was Madam Wu Yi who stepped down as Vice Premier in March 2008.

[32] The JCBC was established in 2003.

[33] Singapore's Ministry of National Development. (2008). "Inaugural Sino-Singapore Tianjin Eco-city Joint Steering Council Meeting." Press Release, 3 September.

[34] Jiang Weixin's predecessor on the JWC was Wang Guangtao who stepped down in March 2008.

The JWC has addressed issues such as the KPIs to guide the planning and construction of the eco-city, the Master Plan for the entire 30 square kilometres, the detailed plan for the 4 square kilometres start-up area; the work schedules and key milestones of the project; and, the roles, powers and responsibilities of the Eco-City Administrative Committee (ECAC) that will administer the eco-city. The JWC also draws upon the resources and expertise of the relevant ministries and government agencies on both sides to carry out its tasks.

The above supervisory mechanism was formalised with the signing of the "Framework Agreement on the Development of an Eco-City in the PRC" in November 2007.[35] The agreement was signed by Prime Minister Lee Hsien Loong and Premier Wen Jiabao at the Istana, the official residence of the President, during the visit of Premier Wen to Singapore in November 2007. In addition to the Framework Agreement, a Supplementary Agreement was also signed at the same time between Minister Mah Bow Tan and Minister Wang Guangtao (former Minister of Housing and Urban-Rural Development) to facilitate and support the joint development of the eco-city in accordance with the Framework Agreement. These agreements underscore the active role that the governments on both sides have played and intend to play to ensure the success of the project.

Besides the official supervisory mechanism, there is the commercial component that comprises the JV company. The rationale of having a JV company is to ensure that the eco-city will be guided by sound commercial principles in its development. This will ensure its financial sustainability. Operationally, the JV company exists as an independent entity. Nevertheless, the JV company indirectly reports the progress or issues that cannot be resolved at their level to the JWC which in turn reviews or addresses them. In this way, the JWC can give the project an added push when needed. This indirect relationship between the JV company and the JWC is denoted in the figure by the upward pointing bold dotted line.

Known as the Sino-Singapore Tianjin Eco-City Investment and Development Company, the JV company has an initial registered capital of RMB 4 billion (US$583 million) with equal contribution from the Singapore consortium and the Chinese consortium.[36] The Singapore consortium,

---

[35] Singapore's Ministry of National Development. (2007). "Agreements to Develop Eco-city in China Signed." Press Release, 18 November.

[36] Under the JV Agreement signed on 1st July 2008, the Chinese consortium will transfer land for the development of the eco-city to the JV company as its contribution in kind

the Singapore Tianjin Eco-City Investment Holdings (STEC), is currently wholly owned by Keppel Corporation. Keppel, however, is seeking international institutional investors to coinvest in STEC. Already, the Qatar Investment Authority has entered into a Memorandum of Understanding (MOU) with Keppel to accept Keppel's invitation to participate as an equity investor in the project by taking up a 10% stake in STEC.[37]

The Chinese consortium, the Tianjin Eco-City Investment and Development Company (TEC), is led by the Tianjin TEDA Investment Holding Company. The Tianjin TEDA Investment Holding Company is wholly-owned by the Tianjin municipal government. The company has spearheaded the development of the Tianjin Economic and Technological Development Zone (TEDA) since 1984. The company is also involved in various sectors such as property, finance, transport and energy in the Tianjin Binhai New Area (TBNA, with a total land area of 2,270 square kilometres) where both TEDA and the Sino-Singapore Tianjin Eco-city are located.[38] The Tianjin TEDA Investment Holding Company therefore brings to the JV company not only valuable experience and expertise, but also a strong network for conducting business.

Most recently, the JV company signed on its first business partner when a MOU was signed in January 2009 with Sembawang Engineers and Construction Pte Ltd to work on the feasibility study for the developments of a US$1 billion solar polysilicon production plant in the Sino-Singapore Tianjin Eco-city. Sembawang will be the project sponsor and developer of the plant and will lead a consortium of private investors to fund the development.[39]

(2) Other Key Features of the Eco-City

The Sino-Singapore Tianjin Eco-city aims to be environmentally-friendly, socially harmonious and economically sustainable. It is located in the Coastal Leisure and Tourism Zone of the TBND. In terms of the time-line, the target is to complete the 4 square kilometres start-up area by 2013. The

---

to the registered capital of the JV company. The Singapore consortium's contribution to the registered capital will be in the form of cash.

[37]Keppel Corporation. (2008). "Joint Venture to Jointly Develop Eco-city in Tianjin, The People's Republic of China," Press Release, 1 July.

[38]See website of Tianjin TEDA Investment Holding Company at http://www.teda.com.cn/shouye/index.asp.

[39]Keppel Corporation. (2009). "Sino-Singapore Tianjin Eco-city Signs MOU with First Business Partner for US$1 Billion Project," Press Release, 22 January.

entire development is expected to be completed in 10 to 15 years' time, with a projected population of 350,000 residents.[40]

A major feature of the eco-city lies in its conversion of otherwise unproductive land to good use, where ecological rehabilitation is balanced with urban development (see Fig. 2). The eco-city will be built on a 30 square kilometres site consisting largely of non-arable land, including salt farms and vacant land. There will be a central core (known as the eco-core) of conserved ecological wetlands and rehabilitated water bodies including a wastewater pond currently being used as an effluent discharge ground. The areas surrounding the eco-core will be divided into four main districts, each

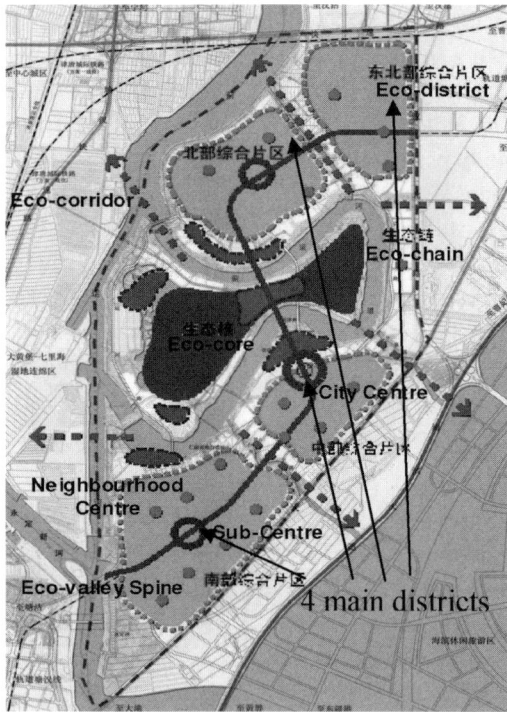

Fig. 2   Basic Layout of Eco-City.

[40]Singapore's Ministry of National Development. (2008). "Sino-Singapore Tianjin Eco-city Draft Master Plan Unveiled," Press Release, 17 April. (http://www.eco-city.gov.cn/eco/shouye/zongtiguihua/index.html_1094844436.html).

to be served by an urban subcentre. Each district will have a mixture of residential, commercial, industrial, cultural and recreational land.

The second key feature of the eco-city is the focus on maximising convenience for residents by locating the necessary services and facilities nearby. The basic building block of the eco-city is the eco-cell that integrates different land uses within a modular 400 metre by 400 metre grid. Education institutions, commercial areas, workplaces, and recreational areas are distributed within these eco-cells which are in turn sited within walking or cycling distance of residential areas. Together, the eco-cells form neighbourhoods, districts and eventually urban centres.

The main mode of transport will be a light rail line running through the eco-city. This will be complemented by cycling paths and green connectors. There will also be a secondary network of buses or trams. The goal is to make commuting via public transport and non-motorised means so convenient that residents will gradually rely less on or even relinquish the use of private vehicles. Certain incentives may also be introduced to achieve this goal.[41] This approach takes into account current realities of individual preferences of owning private cars as a status symbol.

The third distinguishing feature of the eco-city is its strong message of social harmony or more specifically, efforts to meet the needs of ordinary people. The eco-city has positioned itself as a model of harmonious living where people from all walks of life, regardless of their income or social status, can come together. This is akin to Singapore's concept of neighbourhood communities where different ethnic groups, professions and religions can co-exist as a vibrant and cohesive entity. In particular, at least 20% of the residential areas in the eco-city will be set aside for public, subsidised housing.[42] To meet this goal, Singapore and China aims to leverage on their experience of providing public housing and devise the most feasible way forward.[43] It remains to be seen how this will be operationalised.

---

[41] *Lianhe Zaobao.* (2008). "Zhongxin hezi gongsi chengli, Tianjin shengtaicheng cong guihua jinru shizhan" (Sino-Singapore Joint Venture Company Established, Tianjin Eco-City Moves from Master Planning into Real Combat), 2 July.

[42] *First Financial Daily (Shanghai).* (2008). "Zhongxin Tianjin shengtaicheng zongti fangan chulu, 2020 nian jiangda 35 wanren" (Sino-Singapore Tianjin Eco-city Master Plan is Released, in Year 2020 the Population will Reach 350,000), 7 May.

[43] *Lianhe Zaobao.* (2008). "Tianjin shengtaicheng jiangjian gongwu ge jieceng renmin neng hexie gongchu" (Tianjin Eco-city will Build Public Housing, Various Social Groups can Live Harmoniously), 17 April. See also *Straits Times.* (2008). "HDB-style Living in Tianjin Eco-city," 17 April.

Related to the goal of social harmony is the resettlement of a group of about 2,000 villagers that would be affected by the development of the eco-city. Elsewhere in China, there have been umpteen instances of resettlement cases gone awry, leading to affected residents protesting against the developers and local authorities. Given the sensitivity of resettlement cases, the Singapore and Chinese sides have paid particular attention to address the concerns and needs of the would-be affected residents. It has been reported that the 2,000 villagers who need to relocate will be guaranteed jobs and housing in the eco-city.[44] Meticulous handling of this issue will generate good publicity for the eco-city and strengthen its positioning as a place for people from all walks of life.

A final attractive feature of the eco-city is the emphasis on implementing the best practices from both the Singapore and Chinese sides. Both sides appear willing to share and learn from the other. The collaboration can be described as a partnership rather than a one-way street of one side telling the other side how things should be done. By jointly contributing, the parties involved would have greater vested interest to see the ideas to their fruition. For instance, the green area per person in the eco-city is set at 12 square metres by 2013 (a Chinese standard as opposed to the 8 square metres per person in Singapore). In terms of water quality, the target is to make all water in the eco-city portable (a Singapore standard). All buildings in the eco-city will conform to green building standards that will marry Singapore's green mark with China's green standards.[45]

Some Challenges and Problems of Building Eco-Cities

The notion of a sustainable low-carbon city offering an alternative to the current model of high energy consumption and high wastage presents an extremely attractive proposition. Terms such as "low carbon city," "compact city," "renewable city" and "environmentally-friendly living or transport" have suddenly become mainstream language. Yet, the goal of

---

[44] *Straits Times.* (2008). "$9.7 billion Price Tag for Landmark Tianjin Eco-city," 7 May.
[45] On transportation, the target is to achieve at least 90% of residents walking, using public transport or cycling when commuting within the eco-city by 2020. Another target is to have 100% barrier free access for residents in the eco-city. In terms of economic contribution, the target is to have at least 50 R&D scientists and engineers per 10,000 workforce in the eco-city by 2020. Also, at least 50% of the employable residents in the eco-city should be employed in the eco-city by 2013. A total of 26 KPIs (22 quantitative and 4 qualitative ones) have been agreed to by both sides. They can be found at http://www.tianjinecocity.gov.sg/KPI.htm#21.

achieving a low-carbon footprint is wrought with challenges and difficulties. In some instances, the euphoria surrounding the building of an eco-city begins on a high-note but the momentum then peters out when difficulties are encountered on the ground. In other instances, the eco-city that is being built fails to live up to its much touted environmentally-friendly or energy saving qualities. This section will highlight some of the challenges and difficulties of building eco-cities.

Green agenda not commonly shared. The green agenda has so far not received the level of attention that it deserves from various governments and even among the different levels of governments within the same country. There are many reasons behind this apparent inertia. One reason is the continued preoccupation of present governments on growth and development with scant regard for protecting the environment. To them, environmental protection is secondary to the primary goal of generating employment and creating wealth. Another reason may be the strong vested interests of those related or linked to fossil-powered industries that hamper the switch to non-fossil-powered means. Other reasons may be the lack of a proper regulatory framework or incentives to encourage the growth and implementation of green concepts and technologies; the concern that environmental protection will incur additional costs; and, the perception that developed countries should lead and shoulder greater responsibilities in fighting climate change and global warming.

Insufficient awareness of the normative value of eco-cities. Very often, when eco-cities are mentioned, the centre of attention is usually on the physical structure, design appeal and environmentally-friendly features of eco-cities. What is often neglected is the more important need to generate greater awareness of the rationale and benefits that an eco-city will bring to the people who would directly benefit from such a project. As a result, there is very little local understanding of how an eco-city can improve the quality of life of the people. There is thus a lack of local buy-in and support critical to the success of any eco-city project.

Lack of effective supervision and enforcement mechanisms. At times, impressive-looking plans and nice-sounding concepts fail to be implemented due to the lack of effective supervision and enforcement mechanisms. Also, different agencies that have oversight on environment-related issues may also fail to coordinate with each other, leading to delays or weak implementation. The result is an eco-city that ends up not being built or even if it is built, it does not live up to what it is expected to deliver in terms of its environmentally-friendly features.

Insufficient detailed local plan making and performance indicators. At times, there may also be insufficient detailed local plan making and key performance indicators to translate abstract environmental concepts into manageable and measurable stages or phases for implementation. This not only makes it difficult to translate existing broad plans into action but also causes difficulty in tracking the progress of the development of the eco-city.

Failure to identify with local circumstances and needs. For an eco-city to be successful, it must not only be in line with the overall national development plans but also must be relevant to local circumstances and needs. There have been instances where the development of an eco-city fails to take into account the way of life and material standards of the local population they are meant to benefit. Hence, what is built is not practical or is expensive, or even goes against local preferences or practices. The local community ends up by not supporting the project or even worse, rejecting the project.

Lack of political support and sufficient funding. There have also been instances where the development of an eco-city has been hobbled by a change in political leadership especially at the local level. The previous leadership may have been supportive of the project but the subsequent leadership may not accord the project the same level of support due to various reasons. Without or due to a lack of political support, it is usually difficult for an eco-city project to take off. In other instances, the developer may lack sufficient financial resources to build the eco-city. There may also be unexpected cost-overruns due to unforeseen circumstances, thereby leaving the developer with the difficulty of mustering additional financial resources to complete the project.

Some Suggestions for Regional Cooperation

Regional governments are realising the urgent need for collective action to reduce GHG emissions. As mentioned in the introductory chapter, at the 13th ASEAN Summit and the Third East Asian Summit (EAS) in Singapore in November 2007, the *ASEAN Declaration on Environmental Sustainability* and the *Singapore Declaration on Climate Change, Energy and the Environment* were respectively adopted.[46] In addition, the East Asia

---

[46]For details of the *ASEAN Declaration on Environmental Sustainability*, please refer to ASEAN Secretariat website at http://www.aseansec.org/21060.htm. For details of the

Summit (EAS) Energy Ministers (that met in Singapore in August 2007) and the inaugural EAS Environment Ministers (that met in Hanoi in October 2008) have separately met to look at what they can further do within their respective areas of specialisation. In particular, the EAS Environment Ministers had focused on the main theme of "Achieving Environmentally Sustainable Cities in East Asia".

Below are some key recommendations to foster regional cooperation related to the development of eco-cities:

- **Elevate** the development of eco-cities as an important item on the national and even regional agenda. Each government must demonstrate the necessary political will to tackle climate change and global warming in a concerted manner.
- **Take** practical and incremental measures to incorporate eco-friendly features into urban design and planning over time. The development of eco-cities need not involve a big-bang approach. Instead, it should proceed in a manner and pace that each country is comfortable with. Such an approach will take into account the diverse socio-economic and political conditions as well as the different capabilities of each country. In this way, every country can play a role in reducing its carbon footprint.
- **Develop** individual country action plans related to the development of eco-cities or the incorporation of eco-friendly features into urban design and planning. In this way, each country can lay out in a transparent and predictable manner the actions that it intends to take over a period of time. Where possible, such action plans can be reviewed by other countries so that further suggestions or improvements can be made to these plans.
- **Generate** greater awareness of the rational and long-term benefits of developing eco-cities among the *people* as well as the *private* and *public* sectors (or what is commonly known as the 3 Ps). This can be achieved through various measures such as conducting regular campaigns, providing incentives and systematic education. The will result in stronger and broader ground-level support for any environment-related initiatives.
- **Develop** human resource capabilities related to environmental protection and eco-cities so that there is a ready pool of talent able to implement the green agenda.

Singapore Declaration on Climate Change, Energy and the Environment, please refer to ASEAN Secretariat website at http://www.aseansec.org/21116.htm.

- **Facilitate** the sharing of experience, expertise and technology related to eco-cities such as green building, transportation, water management, bio-diversity conservation, urban greenery, sanitation and waste management, the 3Rs (Reduce, Reuse and Recycle), and air, noise, water and land pollution control. This may be done through existing regional or international platforms or new platforms that may be deemed necessary.
- **Target** capacity building (related to the building of eco-cities) as a priority area under the ASEAN plus Three Cooperation Fund launched in 2008. By raising the capacity of the countries concerned, they would then be in a better position to carry out environmentally-friendly initiatives including the building of eco-cities.
- **Attract** and strengthen collaboration with the private sector to develop eco-cities by providing various financial incentives and tax relief measures. An eco-city has to be commercially viable to be sustainable and the involvement of the private sector is usually the best way to achieve this objective. The various governments may also consider providing some seed money to kick-start the building of eco-cities given the huge outlay that the private sector may otherwise have to incur.
- **Expand** the existing ASEAN Initiative on Environmentally Sustainable Cities to include other non-ASEAN countries in the region. This will readily provide access to a bigger pool of experience, expertise, technology and even best practices from both the public and private sectors.

Annex A: Comparison of Some Eco Projects.

No.	Name of Eco-City Project	Nature of Project	Location & Land Area	Investment Amount	Investors	Nature of Government Involvement	Launched Date	Plans and Status
1	Masdar Initiative	Touted as world's first carbon-neutral, car-free city which will also be 100% powered by renewable energy	Abu Dhabi 6 sq km	US$22 billion	Abu Dhabi Future Energy Company (ADFEC)	ADFEC is a wholly owned subsidiary of the Abu Dhabi government through the Mubadala Development Company	Announced in March 2006 Ground broke in February 2007	Construction began in early 2008 Phase 1 to be completed in December 2009 To support 50,000 people and 1,000 businesses when fully completed in 2016.
2	Huangbaiyu (黄柏峪) Eco-Village	A model of low energy housing in a rural setting (where about 1,400 farmers lived in an agricultural area covering 135 hectares or 1.35 sq km)	Liaoning —	RMB 30,000,000 (US$4.5 million)	A local entrepreneur (Dai Xiaolong) & local government	Dai Xiaolong, also Chairman of Huangbaiyu village committee, played a major role in developing and building the project	Site chosen in 2003 First demonstration house built in April 2005	Construction began in August 2005. First 42 houses constructed by 2006 but not up to specifications The plan for 400 houses by 2008 was not met

(Continued)

Annex A (Continued).

No.	Name of Eco-City Project	Nature of Project	Location & Land Area	Investment Amount	Investors	Nature of Government Involvement	Launched Date	Plans and Status
3	Sino-Singapore Tianjin Eco-city (天津滨海新区生态城)	An economically thriving, environmentally friendly, socially harmonious and resource-efficient city	Tianjin Binhai New District 30 sq km	RMB 50,000,000,000 (US$7.3 billion)	Keppel Corp to lead Singapore consortium. Tianjin TEDA Investment Holdings to lead Chinese consortium	Joint Steering Committee Joint Working Committee	Announced in April 2007 Ground breaking in September 2008	Start-up area (4 sq km) to be ready by 2013 Entire area to be ready by 2020
4*[49]	Dongtan Eco-city (东滩生态城)	Touted as China's first sustainable eco-city	Chongming island, Shanghai 86 sq km	N.A.	Shanghai Industrial Investment Corporation (SIIC) & Arup	SIIC is a large investment group company owned by the Shanghai municipal government	In August 2005, Arup signed contract with SIIC to undertake the integrated master planning for Dongtan	Construction to start in 2009 (delayed since late 2006). Phase I of 1 sq km with about 10,000 people to be completed in 2010 (This has been scaled back) To accommodate 500,000 people by 2050

[49]Dongtan Eco-City is not elaborated in this paper as other paper presenters will be examining this project separately. Some details of this project are included here merely for comparison purposes.

Annex B: Key Project Milestones (most recent first).

Date	Event	Remarks
Year 2008		
28 Sep	Ground-breaking ceremony for Phase I of the 4 sq km start-up area took place, witnessed by Singapore's Senior Minister Goh Chok Tong and Chinese Premier Wen Jiabao.	Ground-breaking was earlier scheduled for July 2008. Singapore agreed to push back the ceremony as the Chinese authorities have their hands full after the May 12 Sichuan earthquake and the Beijing Olympics in August 2008.
	The eco-city service centre was also unveiled.	
3 Sep	Inaugural Joint Steering Council (JSC) Meeting of the Sino-Singapore Tianjin Eco-city.	The meeting agreed that the key areas of work ahead will include not only the physical and infrastructural development of the eco-city but also the formulation of policies which are in line with the vision of the eco-city and the principle of the "three harmonies," to complement and support its physical development.
1 Jul	3rd JWC (in Tianjin) discussed proposed changes to the Master Plan for the eco-city and preliminary detailed plans for the 4 sq km start-up area.	Co-chaired by Ms Grace Fu (Senior Minister of State, MND) and Mr Qiu Baoxing (Vice Minister, Housing and Rural-Urban Development Ministry).
	Second Supplementary Agreement signed to formalise the roles, powers and responsibilities of the Eco-City Administrative Committee (ECAC) to oversee the planning and development of the project.	
	Two other commercial agreements signed. The first was an agreement between the Singapore Consortium and the Chinese Consortium on the formation of a joint venture (JV) company to develop the project. The second was an agreement between the ECAC and the JV company to formalise the commercial terms of the project.	

(Continued)

Annex B: (Continued).

Date	Event	Remarks
6 May	Tianjin municipal government released the Master Plan for public consultation. It received over 200 views from the public.	Further refinements will be made before the Master Plan is submitted for approval by the Chinese authorities.
17 Apr	Master Plan of the eco-city released by Singapore's Ministry of National Development.	
8 Apr	2nd JWC (in Singapore) endorsed the draft Master Plan. The JWC noted that work has commenced on the 4 sq km start-up area.	Co-chaired by Mr Mah Bow Tan (Minister, MND) and Mr Qiu Baoxing (Vice Minister, Housing and Rural-Urban Development Ministry).
31 Jan	1st JWC (in Tianjin) gave in-principle endorsement of the KPIs to guide the planning and construction of the eco-city. The KPIs highlight concepts like the preservation and restoration of the natural ecology, recycling and efficient use of resources, social cohesion, green consumption and low carbon emission.	Co-chaired by Mr Mah Bow Tan (Minister, MND) and Mr Wang Guangtao (Minister, Housing and Rural-Urban Development Ministry).
Year 2007		
18 Nov	Two agreements were signed. Prime Minister Lee Hsien Loong and Premier Wen Jiabao signed the "Framework Agreement on the Development of an Eco-City in the PRC." The agreement spelled out supervision mechanism for the project.	The agreements were signed during Premier Wen Jaibao's visit to Singapore.
	Minister Mah Bow Tan and Minister Wang Guangtao signed a Supplementary Agreement to facilitate and support the joint development of the eco-city in accordance with the Framework Agreement.	

(Continued)

Annex B: (Continued).

Date	Event	Remarks
	It was also announced that the eco-city would be developed by a Joint Venture (JV) company. The Singapore consortium would be led by Keppel Corporation while the Chinese consortium would include companies like the Tianjin Binhai New Area Urban Infrastructure Construction Investment Company, Tianjin TEDA Investment Holdings Company and the China Development Bank.	
7 Nov	Minister Mah Bow Tan led a delegation to Tianjin to attend a Joint Working Committee meeting in Tianjin. The meeting discussed proposed sites for the eco-city, key project milestones as well as matters related to Premier Wen Jiabao's forthcoming visit to Singapore in the same month.	His Chinese counterpart was Wang Guangtao (Minister, Housing and Urban-Rural Development Ministry).
4–8 Sep	Minister Mah Bow Tan led a delegation on a working visit to China. The team visited some of the candidate cities (Tianjin and Tangshan) to have a better understanding of the conditions of the sites that have been proposed for the eco-city. A team from Keppel Corporation led by Executive Chairman Lim Chee Onn joined Minister Mah on the visit.	Keppel Corporation was appointed to lead the Singapore consortium.
25 Apr	Senior Minister Goh Chok Tong raised the idea of developing an eco-city when he met Premier Wen Jiabao for discussions in Beijing. Both leaders agreed to pursue this idea.	

CHAPTER 4

Building Ecotopia: Critical Reflections on Eco-City Development in China

POW Choon-Piew and Harvey NEO*

Although the idea of constructing an "eco-city" has been bandied around since the 1980s, the concept remains somewhat elusive and controversial for a number of reasons. First, while its physical form and design appeal have often been widely touted by urban planners, architects and government officials, the deeper normative tenets of building an eco-city are surprisingly ignored. Second, the lack of an "actually existing" or successfully implemented eco-city project particularly in the Asian context suggests considerable amount of resistance and difficulties (in terms of planning, politics, economic costs, etc.) that the concept faces in practical terms. In this paper, we aim to address some of these fundamental debates in the eco-city concept with an empirical focus on China. Apart from critically reviewing the literature on eco-city (and related notions of urban sustainability and ecological modernisation), we will use the (failed) example of Shanghai's Dongtan Eco-city project (jointly developed by the British and Chinese governments) to discuss the relevance and challenges of translating the eco-city planning concept and ideal on the ground.

Introduction

In her book *Towards Green Civilization* (*Zhouxiang lushe wenming*), the author Guo Yanhua (2004) argues that the eco-city (*shengtai chengshi*) as an urban form and planning ideology presents a viable solution to many of urban China's environmental problems. The eco-city, according to Guo, promises economic progress, social harmony and ecological protection

---

*Pow Choon-Piew is an Assistant Professor in the Department of Geography at the National University of Singapore. Harvey Neo is an Assistant Professor in the Department of Geography at the National University of Singapore.

and represents the apotheosis of China's pursuit of green civilisation. Our purpose in this paper is not to take umbrage with such optimism. Rather, we take a critical stance to examine how ideas about constructing the ecotopia is being mobilised and "imagineered" by the state and developers in the context of urban China, and more specifically Shanghai.

To be sure, the concept of sustainable urban development is by now a widely used phrase. First popularised through 1989 United Nations Brundtland Report, sustainable development has immense influence on many fields of research across the humanities and sciences. We now speak of sustainability in many facets of human life, in effect breaking the word "development" in sustainable development into more manageable analytical bits. Hence, urban sustainability, social sustainability and economic sustainability have all become key focus across academia and policy making. Given that the world now has more people living in urban areas than rural ones, the question of urban sustainability is particularly pertinent.

The problems in defining, ascertaining and operationalising "sustainability" have long been recognised (see Haughton, 1999; Klauer, 1999; Satterthwaite, 1997). Fowke and Prasad (1996) have identified a staggering 80 conceptions of sustainable development. It thus flows that defining urban sustainability is similarly fraught with difficult and contention. Banister (1998: 65) has noted that:

> the main objective [of urban sustainability] is to improve the quality of life by providing affordable housing, employment opportunities... It also aims to provide quality of life through open space and green space, and it could include cultural, leisure and recreational resources.

Conspicuously absent from his definition of urban sustainability are explicit references to the environment. This is curious given the unambiguous environmentalist underpinnings of "sustainability". Nonetheless, it does illustrate that urban sustainability is "an inherently multi-dimensional concept" and indeed, it could very well be that the many "disparate environmental, social and economic factors involved are mutually incommensurable" (Stirling, 1999: 119). Given this, it is clear that urban sustainability has a clear ethical dimension (Rogers, 2000). To elaborate, what is sustainable and what can (and should) be sustained in a given city would always have to be questioned. This in turn implies that "urban sustainability" is a place-dependent concept: what is desirable and sustainable in one city may not be the case in another.

It is from this part conceptual (in the sense that working towards urban sustainability is necessarily contentious and place-dependent), part normative position (in the sense that moral ethical decisions have to be taken in achieving urban sustainability) that we attempt to grapple with the notion of eco-city. Our main goal is to illustrate, through the example of urban China, the difficulties in conceptualising, planning and actually building an eco-city in a rapidly developing growing region.

The paper is divided into four sections. Following this introduction, we will briefly discuss the notion of environmental sustainability and its relations to urban development. We will also trace the genesis and conceptual underpinnings of the eco-city idea. This discussion will lead us into our case study of eco-city planning in Shanghai, China. Here, we will discuss the urban development trajectory of Shanghai as well as the potential contradictions inherent in some of the normative ideals of eco-city and the socio-political context of China. We will conclude by speculating on the future of eco-city in general and particularly in China.

Environmental Sustainability, Urban Development and Eco-City

Cities are net emitters of carbon dioxide. As cities are densely populated, they are unable to produce enough resources (food and energy, etc.) to sustain themselves. To put it crudely, cities are fundamentally environmentally unsustainable and are kept viable only by drawing essential materials from their hinterlands or further afield. It is thus not surprising that some have criticised the term "sustainable city" as being an oxymoron. The emergence of the eco-city concept is an extension of both sustainable city and urban sustainability. More generally, it can be viewed as part of the relentless search for the ideal city. We find it useful to background the debates on urban sustainability with the concept of ecological modernisation. Broadly, the *theory* of ecological modernisation speaks of "win–win situations, manageable futures and prosperous development *with* rather *against* nature"; it argues that "sustainable futures can be attained under conditions of a continuously growing capitalist economy by making use of negotiated, problem-specific settlements among different and divergent policy actors" (Keil and Desfor, 2003: 30).

Indeed, cities are typically the economic drivers of their respective countries and are continually growing. The United Nations Department of Economic and Social Affairs (Population Division) has projected that in 2050, the percentage of urban residents in the world will be 69.6%, up from 50% in 2008. "Ecologically modernising" the city essentially means making city-living a possibility when future urban population increases dramatically. It is predicated upon the use of good technology to achieve this ambitious goal. Ecological modernisation literature distinguishes between "weak" and "strong" categories. Weak ecological modernisation is described as economic, technological (narrowly defined), instrumental, technocratic, neo-corporatist, closed and national while strong ecological modernisation is ecological, institutional, systemic, communicative, deliberative, democratic, diverse, open and international (Christoff, 1996).

Whether one draws on the weak or the strong version of ecological modernisation, it is clear that institutions (including state and non-state ones) and technology are critical. In particular, urban environmental governance, under a strong ecological modernisation regime, "reveals a complex interaction between the state, civil society and nature; constructed through discursive processes of environmental politics and policy making" (Keil and Desfor, 2003: 28). Harnessing the positive power of technology and enlightened governance, many urban places have initiated both modest (e.g., tracking carbon footprints of cities, see Wackernagel, *et al.*, 2006) and more ambitious schemes (e.g., low-carbon economies, see Local Government Association, 2009) to be sustainable.

While ecological modernisation and eco-city draw from different disciplines and literatures, they share some cognate ideas. To elaborate, we find "strong" ecological modernisation illuminating the key points of the eco-city concept; specifically its emphasis on open, international orientated policies aimed at systemic change in the ecological performances of places. Moreover, both ideas, at their most anthropocentric forms, can be seen as a theory of "capitalist survival" (Keil and Desfor, 2003: 32). Their promise of radically transforming social/urban spaces is eloquently spoken but not yet materialised. Indeed, scholars of ecological modernisation have typically speak of two different sets of concern viz. the *theory* of ecological modernisation as opposed to the *practice* of ecological modernisation.

As will be seen, constructing the eco-city similarly has two distinct sets of focus. We argue that the theory (or the conceptual underpinnings) of eco-city comprises many ideals that have yet to be actualised in practice. Indeed, we wish to argue that parts of the theory of eco-city are impracticable in particular spatial contexts. What then are the main tenets of the eco-city?

As with ideas of urban sustainability, sustainable cities and ecological modernisation, there is no one fixed definition of the eco-city. Guy and Marvin (2001) argue that we need to move from a singular model of what sustainable city is to one that speaks of multiple models of sustainable city. In view of the alignment of sustainable and eco-cities, it is not surprising that eco-city is similarly multi-faceted. While we will not deliberately distinguish between the two concepts, where appropriate, we will draw attention to the distinctiveness of the eco-city concept.

The idea of an eco-city can be traced to the mid-1970s when Richard Register and his colleagues in Berkeley founded "Urban Ecology" to "rebuild cities in balance with nature". Specifically through the following ten principles, they wish to create ecological cities (Roseland, 1997: 197–198):

(1) Revise land-use priorities to create compact, diverse, green, safe, pleasant and vital mixed-use communities near transit nodes and other transportation facilities.

(2) Revise transportation priorities to favor foot, bicycle, cart and transit over autos, and to emphasise "access by proximity".

(3) Restore damaged urban environments, especially creeks, shorelines, ridgelines and wetlands.

(4) Create decent, affordable, safe, convenient and racially and economically mixed housing.

(5) Nurture social justice and create improved opportunities for women, people of colour and the disabled.

(6) Support local agriculture, urban greening projects and community gardening.

(7) Promote recycling, innovative appropriate technology, and resource conservation while reducing pollution and hazardous wastes.

(8) Work with businesses to support ecologically sound economic activity while discouraging pollution, waste and the use and production of hazardous wastes.

(9) Promote voluntary simplicity and discourage excessive consumption of material goods.

(10) Increase awareness of local environment and bio-region through activist and educational projects that increase public awareness of ecological sustainability issues.

As a whole, these principles towards the creation of eco-city drew from pre-existing ideas in their time (e.g., social ecology, bio-regionalism,

the Green Movement) and were also harbinger of future urban-
environment theories (ecological modernisation, sustainable development,
and local/community economic development). It is perhaps understandable
that this manifesto cannot specifically foresee nor take into account contemporary environmental challenges like the rise of greenhouse gas emissions.
Some might even argue that the largely local and at best regional orientation of eco-city, as it was first conceptualised, precludes the consideration
of such transboundary and global problem as greenhouse gas emissions.
Nonetheless, many have attempted to actualise one or more of these ten
principles. Yet not all ten of the principles are equally easy to achieve.
Clearly, they encompass multiple-scale initiatives and consist of both fairly
intuitive, non-contentious exhortations (e.g., "restore damaged urban environments") as well as more controversial ones (e.g., "nurture social justice")
which could fundamentally change the social, economic and political environment of a given place. More importantly, these principles also illustrate
that eco-city building is not just about the "reordering of the physical fabric of the city" (Guy and Marvin, 2001: 133); it also aims to improve its
social and environmental well-being.

Thus, for state authorities and other relevant actors, constructing an
eco-city is in part a complex normative project. This in itself should not
be surprising because as indicated earlier, different urban residents might
demand different kinds of amenities and urban structures, apropos to their
social, cultural context. Further to that, different political and social systems will mean different ways and processes of building an eco-city. This
suggests that there may not be a prescribed type of eco-city (despite the
clearly laid out principles) nor a standard way of working towards it. The
following case of Dongtan in Shanghai will illustrate both these two con-
tingencies. What and who defines the visions and contours of the Dongtan
Eco-city? How are the processes in executing the plans for such an eco-city
tied to the political and ideological processes in China? Before proceeding
further, it is timely to briefly review China's recent environmental policies.

Greening China

Since economic reform, environmental degradation in China has increasingly dominated domestic and international news headlines. While few
industrial nations in the world can lay claim to having developed economically without leaving behind a trail of ecological damages, environmental

degradation in China has now become so severe that it not only threatens public health but also poses an acute political challenge to the ruling Communist Party.

To be sure, China's political leaders are cognisant of the need to tackle the country's mounting environmental problems by overhauling the legacy of Deng's "growth-first" philosophy. It is perhaps significant to note that in his annual address to the country in 2007, Prime Minister Wen Jiabao made 48 references to the "environment", "pollution" or "environmental protection" (Kahn and Yardley, 2007). It is also significant that between 1996 and 2004, China's investment into environmental pollution control went up to over 900 billion yuan, amounting to 1% of that period's GDP. In 2006, expenditure on environmental protection was also formally itemised in the State's financial budget.

According to a recently released White Paper on Environmental Protection (1996–2005), China aims to reduce energy consumption per unit of GDP by 20% before 2010. In addition, the total amount of major pollutants discharged will be reduced by 10% while forest coverage will be raised from 18.2% to 20%. In order to achieve this goal, the Chinese government has come up a broad strategy to actively speed up "Three Changes". First is the change from emphasising economic growth at all costs to emphasising both environmental protection and economic growth; second is to synchronise environmental protection and economic growth rather than allowing environmental protection to lag behind economic development; and third is the change from mainly employing administrative measures in environmental protection to comprehensive use of legal, economic, technical and necessary administrative measures to solve environmental problems. In a nutshell, the new white paper emphasises a harmonious and holistic system encompassing economic, social and cultural resources while establishing stable economic growth with minimal cost to environmental resources as well as a high awareness of the environment.

At the national and local levels, China has also established a system of environmental protection standards. National-level environmental protection standards include environmental quality standards, pollutant discharge (control) standards, and standards for environmental samples. Local environmental protection standards include environmental quality and pollutant discharge standards. By the end of 2005, over 800 national environmental protection standards were enacted by the State. At the local level, the municipalities of Beijing and Shanghai as well as provinces such as Shandong and Henan had promulgated over 30 local environmental protection standards. In recent years, the Chinese government has focused its pollution-control efforts on what are known as the "key regions", with marked achievements to its credit. The "key regions" refer to the three rivers (Huaihe, Liaohe and Haihe), the three lakes (Taihu, Dianchi and Chaohu), the major state projects (the Three Gorges Project and the South-North Water Diversion Project), the "two control's area" (sulfur dioxide control area and acid rain control area), Beijing and the Bohai Sea <http://www.china.org.cn/english/MATERIAL/170402.htm> [20 May 2009].

During the Tenth Five-Year Plan period, the state also set aside 111.9 billion yuan from the central budget for environmental protection. Specifically, 108.3 billion yuan from the treasury bonds was used to control the duststorm sources threatening the Beijing-Tianjin area, to protect natural forests, to turn cultivated farmland back into forests or pastures, to control pollution around the Yangtze River's Three Gorges Dam area and its upstream, as well as pollution on the Huaihe, Liaohe and Haihe rivers, Taihu, Dianchi and Chaohu lakes, to industrialise the reuse and recycling of sewage and garbage, and to reclaim wastewater.

Despite these environmental policies and rhetoric, enforcement of these regulations appears to be weak. In the face of mounting critique against China's dismal environmental track record, flagship projects such as the high-profile Dongtan Eco-city project have emerged as important hallmark projects that will not only showcase China's green efforts but also transform the country's profile and image. It is in this context that we now turn to examine the Dongtan Eco-city project.

Dongtan and its Ecological Imaginary

> "Shanghai will grow. The question is how will it grow. We can programme into its DNA a sustainable growth pattern. We have to make cities, as much as we can, future proof". (Alejandro Gutierrez, Arup's master planner behind Shanghai's Dongtan project)

As part of the state's efforts to promote "green civilisation" in China, the Dongtan Eco-city project was conceived as a prestige urban project to be emulated by the rest of China and even the world. Located in the eastern part of the Chongming island, the Dongtan Eco-city project represents China's first attempt at building a sustainable urban model from scratch. Owned by the Shanghai Industrial Investment Corporation (SIIC), the Dongtan project was contracted to the British engineering firm Arup[1] following an international master plan competition which features some high-profile firms such as the late icon of American architecture Philip Johnson/Alan Ritchie (USA). Reportedly, designers from Johnson's company flew back and forth to the site several times, making plans for a leafy low-density suburb built around a huge manmade lake. Unknown to Johnson's staff, SIIC had also commissioned a series of ecological master plan with the Atkins group (London-based with China offices) and Architecture-Studio (Paris-based with one permanent agency in Shanghai).

As the firms each touted their proposals to the SIIC, none of the proposals went anywhere because SICC was not even sure what it wanted (McGray, 2007). But as the record will show later, it was Arup with its concept of "integrated urbanism" that eventually seized the day. Reportedly, the Arup team had pulled together experts from its offices around the world to work on this grand project that the firm had been looking for. Right from its inception, the project enjoyed political patronage from both sides. As Moore (2007) observes:

> "So impressive were the groundbreaking plans, drawn up in conjunction with the British Engineering firm Arup, that former British Prime Minister Tony Blair himself helped launch the project in 2005 with Hu Jintao, the Chinese President — and earlier this year Gordon Brown, the British Prime Minister pledged that it would be the model for similar towns in Britain. 'Britain and China will lead the world in the creation of eco-cities', the Prime Minister boasted".

Collectively, these transnational architectural firms, are part of what Olds (2001) terms as the dream team of "global intelligence corps"; adept in the production of gleaming new urban spaces and highly stylised and seductive images of urban modernity. One of the key factors behind Arup's success is the formation of "long-term relationships" with architects (Olds, 2001:217). An interesting question to consider here is how are these highly mobile images (liquid image) of ecological modernity produced and circulated? Furthermore, what are the economic, social and intellectual underpinnings of the production of these images and global expertise? More importantly, how are these images and plans translated on the ground? The next section will briefly sketch out Arup's plans for the Dongtan development.

---

[1] Arup was founded by Ove Arup in the 1940s and is based in London with 86 offices in more than 30 countries and a staff of almost 9,000, including 1,500 in China.

Arup's "Intergrated Urbanism"

"It is what we call integrated urbanism: we look not just at the environment, but also at social and economic aspects: employment opportunities, the way people work, the way people play, the way they move around the city." (Roger Wood, project manager at Arup)

According to Arup's planning report, the Dongtan Eco-city will be built in three successive phases with the first phase projected to be completed by 2010, just in time for the Shanghai World Expo. The planned community at Dongtan is targeted to reach 500,000 residents by 2050 while retaining much of the natural wetlands. Using CAD software, the planners for Dongtan "started dropping blocks of buildings on the site and counting heads" (McGray, 2007) and realised (quite miraculously) that the island could sustain up to half a million population at an optimum density of 50 people per acre. Arup's programmers also wrote software that stitched together databases detailing the inputs and outputs of urban facility, process, product and human activity on the island. In sum, Arup's vision is at once technological, instrumental, technocratic and neo-corporatist.

The plan also envisioned a self-sustaining city with an ecological footprint of two or less (two hectares of land to accommodate consumption and waste generated by each person). In addition, the city will be planned according to a compact urban design and with a standard fare of ecologically friendly features such as solar powered water taxis, buses powered by hydrogen fuel cells (no petrol or diesel vehicles allowed in the city); organic farming; recycling of waste; and relying on renewable energy (generated by wind turbines and bio fuels from agricultural waste). For urban built environment, high-tech green building technologies will also be adopted. All in all, Dongtan's development is said to combine traditional Chinese design with latest green technologies.

According to Arup, the key principles underpinning Dongtan's sustainability framework are:

(1) To preserve the wetland habitat.
(2) To create an integrated, vibrant and evolving community.
(3) To improve quality of life and create desirable lifestyles.
(4) To create an accessible city.
(5) To ingrain contemporary Chinese culture into the city fabric.
(6) Managing the use of resources in an integrated manner.
(7) Working towards carbon neutrality.

(8) Utilising governance to achieve long-term economic, social and environmental sustainability.

Interestingly, the framework does not mention public participation. That such a "people's dimension" is conspicuously absent from the Arup's key principles is not unexpected. As mentioned earlier, the eco-city ideal involves more than just a physical and environmental transformation of a city but aims for a socio-political change as well. At the end of the day, the relationship between Arup and the Shanghai authorities, despite its co-evolving and cooperative nature, is still one of patron and client. Bearing this in mind, we offer some preliminary reflections of this relationship.

Reflections

Notwithstanding the high-level political support and commitment by the municipal and Central governments in China, many critical questions remain. Will Dongtan devolve into what critics term as a "Potemkin eco-village" or worse still an eco-themepark catering to the wealthy urbanites for a "feel-good" weekend getaway? Already, detractors have criticised the Dongtan project as "the ultimate greenwashing tool" and "a show-case eco-city [that] can do little on its own to save China from itself". While the jury is still out on whether Dongtan can live up to its "bright green reputation", we can already detect some disjunctures between Dongtan's development and the ideals and tenets of eco-city. First, the Dongtan project has remained "nothing but a pipe dream". As Moore (2008) notes:

> "The greenfield site, a lush area three-quarters of the size of Manhattan, remains untouched — and planning permission won by the Shanghai Industrial Investment Corporation (SIIC), the property developer that commissioned Arup to design and build the city, has lapsed".

Even if the Dongtan project is eventually built, environmentalists have argued that any building work could have a serious impact on the rare birds that visit the area. More seriously, Arup's envisaged plan to house 40,000 people in the island by 2010 and 400,000 by 2020 has also raised questions about the potential eviction of hundreds of farmers who are currently living there. In fact, few of the villagers in Chongming island have even heard about the Dongtan project, much less Arup's grand plans to transform the island into China's first eco-city. In this respect, a major objection may be levelled at the Dongtan Eco-City project's lack of grassroots participation and involvement, a central tenet of the eco-city. Indeed, many other eco-city developments eschew the *tabla rasa* approach of Dongtan (where the city is literally built from scratch) in favour of a more *in situ* approach (e.g., Curitiba in Brazil and Cleveland in USA).

Ultimately, the preceding paragraphs appear to be moot with the arrest (and depose) of the former Shanghai Mayor Chen Liangyu in 2006 on charges of corruption and property related fraud. Reportedly, the ruling Communist Party, suspicious of Shanghai's political clout, had purged the city's leadership. Dongtan, being a pet project closely related to the deposed mayor has now become a casualty of China's internal politicking and "a symbol of political overreach" (Montlake, 2008). In our most recent visit to Shanghai in February 2009, we were made aware that the Dongtan project is on a permanent hiatus, with no indication of when it would be built. When we asked a member of the Dongtan project team in Arup about the status of the Dongtan project and when work might resume; she answers, somewhat obliquely, that "this (i.e., the Dongtan project) has become a political thing, so it's rather sensitive now". The leadership change in the Shanghai local government certainly has much to do with the termination of the project (although it must be emphasised that no official announcement to this effect has been made). Still, much can be learned from this alleged failure, particularly when eco-city building has aroused increasing interest in many other Chinese cities (e.g., Tianjin).

The Dongtan project, as it is envisioned, hopes to assemble much of its design appeal and symbolic power through an appeal to technology wizardry and putting in place the right urban form. This in itself is a necessary component in constructing an eco-city. Yet as David Harvey (1997) notes, a key challenge in any urban development project is to understand urbanisation as a group of fluid processes in a dialectical relation to the spatial forms to which they give rise and in which they contain. The task then is to enlist in the struggle to advance a more socially just, politically emancipatory and ecologically sane mix of spatio-temporal production process. In Harvey's term, what needs to be done is to move away from a fixation over "utopianism of spatial form" and begin to engage with "utopianism of processes". What Dongtan has failed to take into account of, perhaps future eco-city plans can endeavor to pay attention to.

Much like what the Dongtan project would probably have become, we suggest that many actually existing eco-city practices (and processes) are decoupled from its ideological roots. This is not to point fingers at the "global intelligence corp" for touting a "flawed" product because, as mentioned earlier, their product can only be as complete as what the client demands. It must be reiterated that we are certainly not opposed to the idea of eco-city nor are we discounting the importance of technology, planning and architectural designs. The experience of the Dongtan project does, however, compels us to question if the eco-city concept can be meaningfully divorced from its quite explicit socio-political ideology. Can it stand purely on its environmentalist and technological roots? While we acknowledge there cannot be just one model of eco-city, we question if the road towards urban sustainability (of which the eco-city is a major key strategy) can proceed without actively developing socio-political sustainability.

Moreover, the lack of grassroots participation, the general consensus that this is a project driven in part by a strategy of place marketing, and its close association with the local government meant that with a change in the leadership of the local government (not uncommon in the context of China), backing for the project could be suddenly withdrawn. This is likely the case for the Dongtan project in Shanghai.

The construction of eco-city thus not only involves active physical construction but also more subtle re-construction and de-construction of what it means to be an eco-city. Beyond this, as we have learnt from the Dongtan experience, it also takes tremendous social-political resolve and stability to materialise any vision of the eco-city. The latter might be the key reason that will ensure the success of the Sino-Singapore joint Tianjin Eco-city project. Such government-to-government co-operation is less likely to be derailed by complex local politics, as was probably the case in Shanghai.

On the positive side, Dongtan's plan and concepts have in fact raised the bar in the theoretical discourse about eco-city planning. Its experience has influenced plans for other new eco-developments that are currently being built. Just by existing in its idealistic paper form, Dongtan has a lot to teach the world about the art and science of planning green cities. For Arup, while Dongtan's fate could very well serve as a strictly conceptual model, there is evidence that it is thinking beyond Shanghai. Plans are in progress to build more eco-cities in China, notably the Changxing Eco-city (in Beijing) and Wanzhuang Eco-city (located between Tianjin and Beijing) <http://www.arup.com/china/project.cfm?pageid=11316> [1 May 2009]. Arup also has three other eco-friendly projects in the works to re-develop existing Chinese cities of Langfang, Jinan and Suzhou, using the same concepts as Dongtan (Heim, 2007). Clearly, eco-city building in China has not always been a smooth-sailing process but there are, to be certain, some positive signs emerging as many local governments now place environmental health at the forefront of their urban policies. Some notable examples here include Yangzhou's Eco-city Plan (a Sino-German cooperative programme) which emphasises the importance of local public participation and conserving the old city fabric, instead of the usual practice of razing old neighbourhoods and building new ones. For its effort in improving urban residential environment and promoting ecological development, the Yangzhou prefecture was awarded the UN-Habitat Scroll of Honour in 2006 <http://www.unhabitat.org/content.asp?typeid=19.&.catid=490.&.cid= 2843> [20 June 2009]. Over in rural areas, the environmental agenda has also taken shape in the form of "eco-villages", the most famous example here being the Huangbaiyu project in Liaoning Province. Spearheaded by the China-U.S. Center for Sustainable Development, the eco-village which was supported by local public-private partnership was jointly designed by William McDonough and Tongji University. Even though the project was beset by several intractable problems and disappointments (see, for example, May 2008), like the Dongtan project, they both yield important lessons for local governments and foreign firms hoping to build future eco-developments in China. Returning to the theme of optimism expressed by Guo (2004) in her study of China's *march towards green civilisation*, the overall trajectory towards urban sustainability will hopefully be an encouraging one, even as issues of social polarisation and the social sustainability in urban China may become more apparent in time to come.

References

Banister, David. (1998). "Barriers to the Implementation of Urban Sustainability." *International Journal of Environment and Pollution*, 10: 65–83.

Guo, Yanhua (2004). *Towards Green Civilization (Zhouxiang lushe wenming)*. Beijing: China Social Sciences Press.

Christoff, Peter. (1996). "Ecological Modernization, Ecological Modernities." *Environmental Politics*, 5: 476–500.

Fowke, Raymond and D.K. Prasad. (1996). "Sustainable Development, Cities and Local Government." *Australian Planner*, 33: 61–66.

Guy, Simon and Simon Marvin. (2001). "Constructing Sustainable Urban Futures: From Models to Competing Pathways." *Journal of the International Association for Impact Assessment*, 19: 131–139.

Harvey, David. (1997). "The New Urbanism and the Communitarian Trap." *Harvard Design Magazine*, Winter/Spring (1).

Haughton, Graham. (1998). "Environmental Justice and the Sustainable City." *Journal of Planning Education and Research*, 18: 233–243.

Heim, Kristi. (2007). "Can a Bold New 'Eco-City' Clear the Air in China?" http://seattletimes.nwsource.com/html/businesstechnology/2004033679_ chinagreen.html [1 May 2009].

Keil, Roger and Gene Desfor. (2003). "Ecological Modernization in Los Angeles and Toronto." *Local Environment*, 8: 27–44.

Klauer, Bernd. (1999). "Defining and Achieving Sustainable Development." *International Journal of Sustainable Development and World Ecology*, 6: 114–121.

Local Government Association. (2009). "Creating Green Jobs: Developing Low-Carbon Economies." http://www.lga.gov.uk/lga/aio/1509491 [1 June 2009].

May, Shannon. (2008). "Ecological Citizenship and the Plan for Sustainable Development." *City* 12: 237–244.

McGray, Douglas. (2007). "Pop-Up Cities: China Builds a Bright Green Metropolis." *Wired Magazine*, 15:5.

Moore, Michael. (2008). "Chinese Eco-City Stuck on Drawing Board UK-China Venture; Exercise in Urban Rural Symbiosis Stalled." *Reuters News*. http:// www.ottawacitizen.com/travel/Chinese+city+dream+stuck+drawing+board/ 992012/story.html [8 February 2009].

Olds, Kris. (2001). *Globalization and Urban Change: Capital, Culture, and Pacific Rim Mega-Projects*. New York: Oxford University Press.

Rogers, Raymond. (2000). "The Usury Debate, the Sustainability Debate and the Call for a Moral Economy." *Ecological Economics*, 35: 157–171.

Roseland, Mark. (1997). "Dimensions of the Eco-City." *Cities*, 14: 197–202.

Satterthwaite, David. (1997). "Sustainable Cities or Cities that Contribute to Sustainable Development?" *Urban Studies*, 34: 1667–1691.

Stirling, Andrew. (1999). "The Appraisal of Sustainability: Some Problems and Possible Responses." *Local Environment*, 4: 111–135.

Wackernagel, Mathis, Justin Kitzes, Dan Moran, Steven Goldfinger and Mary Thomas. (2006). "The Ecological Footprint of Cities and Regions: Comparing Resource Availability and Resource Demand." *Environment and Urbanization*, 18: 103–112.

CHAPTER 5

Moving Toward Eco-Friendly City: Perspective on Thailand

Rujiroj ANAMBUTR*

This paper explores policies and projects related to the concept of eco-city in Thailand and reports on their levels of achievement and challenges. It is found that the concept is recognised and well received by the state, private sector, and academics, though still somewhat limited in its application. There are several relevant projects initiated by the government at the local levels. The estimated achievements of these projects are positive while several of them are in the early stages of operation. Major obstacles to these projects are the lack of implementation mechanisms and unintegrated plans. "Sufficiency philosophy" is a major policy implemented with efforts from various sectors, though its application is still limited to rural areas and small communities rather than in cities and urban areas. Lessons are drawn from the successes and challenges of these projects. Major considerations for future actions and initiatives include the need for political stability, true leadership, integrated plans, applicable implementation as well as building knowledge and experiences through research and co-operation.

Introduction

Thailand, in these past few years has been in a difficult period of political uncertainty. A lack of true leadership during this period has left initiatives in the area of environmental concerns moving along at a gradual pace. Political parties are more concerned with popular policies designed to win over the hearts of the majority of the population. As the economic crisis struck,

*Rujiroj Anambutr is a Senior Lecturer and Chairman of the Masters Programme in Landscape Architecture in the Department of Urban Design and Planning, Faculty of Architecture, Silpakorn University, Thailand.

the government has allocated resources in areas that will best support the economic livelihood of the people. New initiatives in environmental areas are not on the top of the priority list at this time. However, the existing projects that have been already initiated are not obstructed. They are progressing steadily, being pushed by the state agencies with help from private organisations and interest groups.

For this reason, several urgent environmental concerns that have been on the public focus in the past few years such as global warming and climate change are not getting as much attention at this time. However, there are a number of significant projects either directly or indirectly related to eco-cities which are still operating steadily with good prospects. Some examples of significant policies and projects are highlighted below.

Projects and Policies Related to Eco-Cities in Thailand

Thailand National Environmental Performance Assessment

A brief overview of the "Thailand National Environmental Performance Assessment (EPA) Report" prepared by the Department of Environmental Quality Promotion, Ministry of Natural Resource and Environment, Thailand, and Project Secretariat of the United Nation Environment Programme (UNEP) Regional Resource Center for Asia and the Pacific is necessary here. The project is led by the Asian Development Bank and the UNEP in co-operation with the Institute for Global Environmental Strategies (IGES) and the National Institute for Environmental Studies of Japan (NIES). Participating countries are those in the Greater Mekong Subregion (GMS): Cambodia, Lao People's Democratic Republic, Myanmar, Thailand, Vietnam, as well as Yunnan Province and Guangxi Autonomous Region of the People's Republic of China.

The goal of the project is to promote sustainable development in the region by assisting government agencies in assessing the progress of environmental management which will to some degree reflect the achievement Thailand has made in this area. The assessment focuses on seven main environmental concerns, namely, forest resources, water resources, land degradation, inland water pollution, solid waste management, hazardous substance management and climate change. Although the coverage of the assessments are not focused specifically on the situation of the city and urban areas, certain environmental concerns such as water pollution, solid waste management and hazardous substance management either originate from or directly affect the environment of cities and municipalities in the areas under study. The project assessed the performance over time and gave indicators, ratings, and future directions of the situation to each of the environmental concerns and also provided recommendations for environmental management. The report is particularly useful as it not only assesses how a country has performed but also provides warning indicators that can guide future actions. The lessons of success and challenges faced by countries can provide a useful basis to foster dialogue and cooperation among countries that share similar ecological systems.

EIA and Special Protection Zones Designated by ONEP

The Office of Natural Resources and Environmental Policy and Planning (ONEP) has designated several areas with exceptional natural and cultural resources as Special Protection Zone. These areas are basically popular tourists' destination, namely, Hua Hin, Phuket, Krabi, Phang-Nga, Samui, etc. Rapid tourism development in these areas has led to uncontrollable growth and physical development, destroying natural and cultural resources which attract tourists in the first place. The agency realises that such a vicious cycle will eventually cause irreparable damage to those areas. Numerous hotels, accommodations of various types and price ranges are springing up everywhere. The physical environment has been changing so rapidly without any proper controls and plans. ONEP's control of physical development is through Environmental Impact Assessment (EIA) reports which is mandatory for large-size and special types of buildings and projects. For smaller projects in these special protection zones, owners need to file the Initial Environmental Examination (IEE) Reports for approval by the local boards appointed by the central government before the project can proceed. However, a study of the IEE and EIA processes has revealed that, on average, a local IEE report takes a much shorter time than the EIA report which is approved by the central EIA board. It is still inconclusive that the local approval process is more efficient and that the delegation of environmental responsibility to the local authority helps to better preserve these protected areas. Upon unverified visual survey of these areas in question, there seems to be rampant violations of physical development control which are potentially damaging to the environment. Perhaps the problem lies in the enforcement or in the approval process, which remains to be closely and systematically scrutinised.

Sufficiency Philosophy

Since 1972, Thailand's revered King Rama IX enunciated the idea of "sufficient consumption" to the Thai people. Since then His Majesty has advocated the concept continuously. It was not until around the 1990s that the royal idea caught on and was heeded by the masses, starting with government agencies. During the 1997 economic crisis, the idea started to be materialised though not very clearly. State agencies and private organisations have since been trying to decipher the rather elusive concept in order to implement it. It was only within this decade that the royal advice has come to fruition, with several state agencies brainstorming and coming up with a clearer definition and guidelines for application. The meaning of the concept "sufficiency" as interpreted and agreed upon by state agencies are as follows:

Sufficiency is a philosophy and a directive for all modes of conduct, for a way of life and living for the public at all levels, from family to community to the state. The philosophy should govern the administration and development of the country to the optimum (or moderation), especially in economic development in the age of globalisation.

Three Qualities of Sufficiency:

(1) Being sufficient, taking the "middle path", in moderation.
(2) Being reasonable.
(3) Immune to outside and inside changes and challenges.

(Ministry of Interior, 2004)

A prior condition to the philosophy is that its conduct must be based on the foundation of knowledge and integrity. The goal of sufficiency is to reach a balance in the way of life, be ready for changes and fluctuation, and be ready to face globalisation (and not to be engulfed or overwhelmed by it).

As an example of the nation-wide implementation by the government, the Ministry of Interior has drawn up a framework for action. Certain principles and tactics must be kept in mind, which are: development plan must "work with" not "work for" the people, practice must be "learning by doing", and with a technique of "provoking thought, creating consciousness, and asking the right questions", not "spoon-feeding" which often results in inaction.

According to the Ministry, sufficiency must become the foundation for the way of life of the people in villages. The vision states that within 2011, people will be satisfied with their lives through practicing sufficiency. The steps to be taken are:

2008 — to raise consciousness and understanding of the value of sufficiency.
2009 — to create community's force to drive toward sufficiency.
2010–2012 — to create sustainability for the sufficiency way of life.

To assess the success of the implementation, a 6×2 matrix of indices were formulated to guide the action for the communities that practice sufficiency. The indices are (Ministry of Interior, 2008):

(1) Lower expenses

　1.1 Grow home kitchen gardens
　1.2 Stop gambling and booze

(2) Increase revenue

　2.1 Household second career
　2.2 Use appropriate technology

(3) Frugality

　3.1 Household has savings
　3.2 Community has savings group

(4) Learning

　4.1 Community transfers knowledge or folk wisdom
　4.2 Household has learnt and practiced sufficiency in daily life

(5) Environmental conservation and sustainable uses of natural resources

　5.1 Community uses raw material in a sustainable way in making a living
　5.2 Community grows shady trees to make the village more liveable

(6) Reciprocity

　6.1 Community takes care of those less fortunate
　6.2 Community has unity.

For each index, the participating communities are scored for carrying out related activities. A score of 1–3 is given for each index according to the number of activities performed. For example, if 50% or 50–75% or more than 75% of all the households in a community have kitchen gardens, then a score of 1, 2, or 3 is awarded respectively to the community. The scoring will be reported to the state agency overseeing the project which will draft the performance report.

According to 2008 report, there were 43,261 targeted villages, and 86.2% of those have already practiced sufficiency, and 18% of them (or 6,802 villages) have reached a certain degree of success and can become learning centres for others. Every province has at least a few demonstration projects to substantiate the policy.

Sufficiency is obviously related to sustainability. It is also inherently related to the eco-friendly concept. Sufficiency is a philosophy and a state of mind. To know when is "enough" or "sufficient" in all aspects of life is quite abstract and difficult to pin-point. It is specific and different to each and every person. It may well start with an accounting of the expenses and revenue of the household. Good accounting gives a clear picture of how much is enough to survive comfortably, as well as what is not necessary. Changing the way of life and agricultural practice to suit the nature and environment will help to reduce what is not needed, such as planting a good combination of fruits, vegetables, and herbs to be used as bio-insecticide, and raising animals as a source of food and labour in the farms or paddy fields, with manure to be used as organic fertiliser or to generate electricity. The right "balance" will fulfill the basic needs of a household, even those with small plots of land. Once the needs are fulfilled, the rest is surplus that can be traded for profit. The sufficiency philosophy is not at all against profit; rather, it is a clear, moderate path to wealth as long as those who practice it know their level of "sufficiency" and cut down on things that are not necessities. One way to reduce the unnecessary is by living in better harmony with nature and understanding the ecology of the area. That is a path toward an eco-friendly way of life and profession. There are numerous examples of this "New Theory" communities where agriculture and animal raising that is combined with the practice of financial frugality have yielded positive results and brought about wealth and well being to the communities.

Although it is stated that the sufficiency philosophy can be practised in any manner at all levels, the projects and concrete procedures as set by the state have been mostly for the communities in the rural areas. How can sufficiency be applied to the other entities, especially the big cities where the environment is most adversely affected? Academics in the related fields have been trying hard to grasp the concept and finding a way to implement the philosophy with more concrete procedures.

Eco-City Concept in Large Cities in Thailand

Bangkok and the Global Warming Problem

Bangkok is the largest and the capital city of Thailand. It is struggling to become a world-class city as envisioned by many despite its many shortcomings: urban sprawl, underutilised super-blocks, traffic congestion, inefficient transportation, over-crowdedness, etc. All these have led to several environmental concerns.

Bangkok is the centre of everything for Thailand, with its population of approximately 10 million people. It struggles to function as a city for its residents. Bangkok Metropolitan Administration (BMA) is a local autonomous government responsible for almost all aspects of the city. With such heavy responsibilities, BMA has taken the environmental challenges, especially global warming quite seriously. It is one of the large world cities that releases a great number of Greenhouse Gases into the atmosphere. BMA participated in the C40 Climate Summit in 2007 in New York City and has since drawn up its own action plan to alleviate the global warming problem, in cooperation with academics, the private sectors and its citizens.

In brief, the existing conditions in Bangkok with regard to the global warming problem is not so healthy. Travelling on the roads is the main mode of transport in the city. Over 50% of travelers use private cars and around 47% use public transport in the form of buses and taxis. The limited-range railed Mass Transit serves less than 1 million people a day. This results in 60,000 tonnes of carbon dioxide per day released from vehicles alone.

The city generates 8,500 tonnes/day of solid waste. Disposal is mainly by sanitary landfill which generate 500 tonnes of methane/day or equivalent to 11,000 tonnes of carbon dioxide/day. Bangkok discharges approximately 2.4 million cubic metres/day of wastewater and only half is treated properly. Its estimated BOD pollution is at 500,000 kg/day which will cause another 1,000 tonnes/day of carbon dioxide. Moreover the largest source of CO_2 is from electricity generation which is estimated at 40,000 tonnes/day. see Table 1.

It is quite surprising to see that the amount of CO_2 Bangkok has released per year is among the highest compared to other big cities of the world. Its annual CO_2 release is lower than Tokyo and New York, but higher than London and Toronto. When the amount of CO_2 released per person per year is calculated, Bangkokians are among the highest. On average, a Bangkokian releases 7.3 tonnes of CO_2 annually, compared to a New Yorker (7.1 tonnes), a Londoner (5.9 tonnes), and a Tokyo resident (5.7 tonnes).

Table 1

Source	CO$_2$ Tonne/Day	%
Electricity	40,000	33
Fuel Consumption	60,000	50
Solid and Liquid Waste	11,000	9
Other (est.)	9,000	8
Total	120,000	100

Source: BMA (2008).

Perhaps this may be attributed to the inefficient way Bangkokians travel and the intensive energy uses in offices and residences.

By BMA estimation, all the trees in Bangkok can absorb CO$_2$ no more than 500 tonnes/day which accounts for only 0.5% of all CO$_2$ released in Bangkok. By the author's rough estimation, based on Bangkok's population of 10 million, Bangkokian's CO$_2$ footprint as estimated by BMA is 7.3 tonnes/person/annum will total approximately 73 million tonnes/annum. A large tree absorbs 20.3 kilogrammes per year. Therefore, Bangkok needs at least 3,080,168,780 full grown trees to reach a CO$_2$ neutral state. An average full grown tree with 8 metre crown diameter covers an area of around 60 square metres. Therefore, Bangkok will need a planting area of 184,810 square kilometres to be CO$_2$ neutral. It is worth nothing that the total area of the whole country is only around 500,000 square kilometres.

In a drive to alleviate the dire circumstance, BMA has set up task forces to study and draw up action plans to reduce CO$_2$. In an effort to find a solution and at the same time to raise awareness among citizens, a survey was carried out among the public, experts, state agencies, private sector and NGOs. The results have shown that there was some understanding of the problem among those who responded to the survey and there were five main suggestions to reducing CO$_2$ in Bangkok:

(1) Improving mass transit system and solving traffic problem.
(2) Increasing usage of alternative energy to reduce dependence on fossil fuel.
(3) Improving buildings to become more energy efficient.
(4) Improving disposal of garbage and wastewater.

It is admirable that BMA has acknowledged that it is a part of the global problem and is actively trying to find solutions. The action plan proposed by BMA is commendable but the success of implementation is still in question. At this juncture, it seems that we are still in the early stage of raising awareness. The most obvious campaigns are in the area of education and awareness and they seem to work well. BMA has many projects like handing out free cloth bags for grocery shopping to reduce the demand for plastic bags. This is a good beginning to educate people and start altering their behaviour.

Some academics have criticised such common effort of "paper or plastic" as too little. There is much more to be done. For example, to solve the traffic problem, more extensive network of either underground or elevated mass transit is needed. The mass transit extension projects are in process, but the mega-projects need time and heavy investments. Even when the new ongoing extensions are in operation, the network will still not be extensive enough to become the main mode of mass transportation in the near future. More urgent solutions and actions are needed.

What is needed to solve the traffic problem?

It is proven that altering behaviour can be done but not sustainable as long as it is not as convenient or cost effective in the short run. To be able to sustain eco-healthy behaviour, such as abandoning private cars to use mass transit, a concerted effort by all parties is needed rather than just words. A serious problem requires a drastic solution.

Bangkok's traffic has been notoriously acute and chronic for longer than anyone can imagine. Most residents in Bangkok rely on their private cars for daily travels. Hence to reduce car usage cannot be done by mere request. Even the railed mass transit alone will not be sufficient to significantly reduce the number of cars on the streets. Bangkok's anatomy, with endlessly winding, non-gridiron small roads and lanes, is in itself a major hindrance for people to get onto the mass transit line. To get people to leave their cars at home, there must be concerted plans to:

(1) Improve sidewalk network and physical condition.
(2) Relocate hawkers out of the sidewalk and find other places for them to trade.
(3) Provide bicycle paths and parking spaces, and promote their usage.
(4) Provide networks of public transportation to connect residential areas and mass transit stations.
(5) Provide sufficient car parks in mass transit stations in the outskirts.
(6) Build more and better walking networks in business and retail commercial areas.
(7) Provide incentives to business to connect its establishments to the public walking networks. The design of new development must respond and facilitate pedestrians at ground, above-ground or overhead level.
(8) Reduce or eliminate the number of parking spaces required by the building code in the inner city for new developments.

(9) Apply Congestion Charges for the private vehicles entering the inner
city. (Anambutr, 2006)

Though the above ideas are recognised by the BMA, there has been little
follow-up and the actions taken are not well integrated.

Green City Chiang Mai: An International Cooperation Project

This is one creative project demonstrating an effort to move a small step
closer toward an eco-city in Thailand. The project involves international
cooperation between Chiang Mai City, and educational institutions and
research institutes of the Netherlands in 2008. The project is aimed at
improving the quality of Chiang Mai, Thailand's second largest city and
the Northern hub, using the "Green City" concept. It is expected that the
problems of flooding and air-pollution which reach a serious level season-
ally can be reduced with greening of the city. The three phrases of the
project are: (1) Identification of problems in the city, with participation by
local residents administrations and organisations. (2) Outlining the plan
for the greening of Chiang Mai, formulated by landscape architects and
planners. (3) Organising a workshop to devise implementation mechanisms
based on the plan from the 2nd phase. The workshop included experts
from the Netherlands to provide and exchange experiences and advice on
technical knowledge of planting to reduce pollution, promote institutional
development and capacity building.

Chiang Mai is probably one of the most appropriate targets for such
a demonstration project. It is not as big and problem-ridden as Bangkok,
but big enough to have complicated urban and ecological problems. It is
also a living ancient city with valuable cultural and social aspects, and a
famous tourists' destination. The project tackles probably the weak points
in eco-city building in Thailand. They are the lack of technical knowledge
on challenging issues and weaknesses in implementation which has been the
failure of so many initiatives. Should the project be successful, it can serve
as a model for not only other cities in the country but also in Southeast
Asia. However, its success still remains to be seen.

Cabinet Resolution on Action Plan for Sustainable Green Communities

In 2008, the Cabinet passed a resolution on the Action Plan for Sustainable
Green Communities prepared by the ONEP. The Plan aims to alleviate the

global warming problem in the country through creating more green areas. In essence, it called for local administrations, government agencies, private sector, educational institutes, religious organisations, NGOs, and community leaders to cooperate to provide more sustainable green space in their areas of responsibility. There are clear vision, goals, objectives and action plans set for the project. For example, the action plan calls for all central and local state agencies to have or develop at least 30% of green space with tree plantings on existing lands and 50% on newly acquired lands with new construction. These apply to state land, public land, government offices, infrastructure land, monastery estates, schools and public open spaces. Creating network of green spaces and retention reservoirs are encouraged where possible. Recycling and sufficiency principles are suggested for the maintenance and up-keep of these newly created green spaces. The action plan targets a concrete result within four years since the beginning (2011). The responsible agencies are required to file reports on the progress and to provide explanations if any goal is not met. The action plan has been well received by the agencies, but its result still remains to be seen.

The "Liveable City" or "Healthy City"

The Ninth National Economic and Social Development Plan has listed "Liveable City" development as a national agenda. The aim is to improve the quality of life with more balanced development among economic, social, and environmental objectives for all the cities, towns, and communities in the country. Based on the two well-known surveys, the Mercer Quality of Living Survey and *The Economist's* World's Most *Liveable* Cities that ranked cities where international businesses would choose to locate their operations, and the World Health Organisation's (WHO) concept of "Healthy City" 1995, Thailand's own liveable city index was developed.

There are six main criteria for assessment: safety, education, hygiene, recreation, economic stability and public transportation. The Ministry of Interior has further defined ten characteristics for a Thai liveable city. They are: good city plan, infrastructure and public services, open spaces, parks, and recreation spaces, historic and archeological significance and sense of place, natural water bodies, cultural heritage, civic mindedness, good physical and mental health, job opportunities and low-living expenses, and good governance. The ministry has implemented the concept and set up guidelines according to the criteria for all local administrations to take action accordingly. The ministry's implementation is rather process-oriented, giving a direction for local governments to follow as a means to improve the quality of their communities.

In 2008, the Office of National Economic and Social Development in cooperation with Chulalongkorn University devised a set of measurable, quantitative indices for ranking of cities, towns and communities, adapted to suit the country's context and with readily available data and statistics. The introduced indices was later used annually to assess and rank cities, towns and communities and provide a comparable standard for the community to know at which levels they stand compared to others. This is useful for local governing agencies to see not only their achievements but also the areas which they can improve or pay more attention to.

Environmental Awareness and Education

Environmental education has been a part of primary and secondary education in Thailand for over a decade. In terms of informal education, the EPA report (2008) has summarised:

> "There are 55 environmental education centres [called the Provincial Environmental Education Centres (PEEC)], supported by the Department of Environmental Quality Promotion. PEEC's partners are local administrative organisations, national agencies, schools and teachers, women's groups, monks, NGOs and the private sector. PEECs organise and conduct capacity building programmes (e.g., training of teachers and local government staff) and also serve as discussion centres."

The public is also made aware through other informal channels such as various forms of media, the internet and campaigns which seem to be quite effective. It is obvious that environmental awareness has been raised among the public, especially the younger generation who are more receptive to popular media and the internet. However, the general population is still bombarded heavily with consumerism messages. Though the awareness may have been raised, it is doubtful whether positive environmental attitudes, and even more importantly, more environmentally-friendly behaviour, are also being raised at the same time.

Carbon Label on Consumer Products by the Industries, Driven by Global Trend

Businesses and private sector have also started to do their part to be environmentally friendly. With global economic downturn looming, it is foreseeable that fiercer competition and more stringent trade barriers will be in place because countries are trying to protect their own domestic industries. Other than FTA mechanisms, it is predicted that regional organisations such as the EU will place stricter environmental requirements on imported products to their member countries. Carbon labelling is one example under such requirements and may become the global trend within the next year. Thai leading business corporations are in the early stages of studying the carbon labelling process for food and garment products, which include calculating the carbon emitted during the manufacturing of such products, finding ways to reduce emissions, and increasing efficiency of the production process and personnel in order to be able to compete in the world market. There are currently only six manufacturers studying the process. In addition, the tourism and hotel industry is also starting to take a serious interest on this issue.

Challenges Facing the Move Toward Eco-Friendly City

Political Instability

In the past years, Thailand has been in the worst political turmoil, with three prime ministers in one year. It is most obvious that policies and projects at the national level have been suspended at decision-making level. For a while, there is little leadership. State agencies are adopting a "wait and see" attitude. Even when a new government is in place, only a few politicians pay attention to environmental concerns because there are more urgent issues at hand: how to restore not only citizens, but also foreign governments and businesses confidence in the political system. This is much more important and by no means an easy task.

An example can be drawn from the national energy policy and automobile industry policy. There is an urgent need for national decision and directives for the promotion and use of alternative fuels: Gasoline, Gasohol (E85, E20), Bio-diesel, Compressed Natural Gas (CNG) and Liquified Petroleum Gas (LPG). There are always pros and cons attached to each alternative, either in itself (i.e., availability, pricing, taxes, investments, facilities, fuel price fluctuation, etc.) or in connection with other important issues such as competing needs and pricing between food and fuel in agriculture. This also directly affects the eco-car project, the prospective champion product second to the one-tonne truck manufactured in Thailand. With uncertainty clouding the energy policy, eco-car development by foreign companies may be held back resulting in the delay of incoming foreign investments at a time when the government urgently requires a revival of national economy.

It is quite clear that the government's decision on this matter will not hinge on the country's prosperity and environmental concerns alone. Short-term considerations that directly affect the government's reputation and creditability will weigh heavily on its decision. Not surprisingly, new initiatives for environmental projects are not a top priority unless they are somehow tied to the economic interest of the ruling elite.

Global Economic Crisis

The world is facing an economic crisis. The situation in Thailand is not much better than elsewhere. The Manufacturing Product Index is at 6.6% in November 2008, a 10-year low. Export growth is down 17.7% and tourism is down 22.4%. Our GDP increases at 0% and contracted 2.5–3% from the previous quarter (Bank of Thailand Briefs, 2008). The newly appointed Thai government is trying its best to restore political confidence, remedy the hardships and quickly address the problems surfacing more and more with each passing day.

It is obvious that several important environmental concerns will have to take a lower position on the priority list. This is not just happenning to Thailand but occuring elsewhere as well. The vocal voices on the urgent problem of global warming and climate change which were hot topics in the past few years has died down temporarily. The world's focus is now on the revival of the economies. It is also unfortunate that global environmental problems that can cause economic disasters in the long-run, such as climate changes that may affect agricultural production in many countries, are neglected for the time being.

Urban Policy and Planning

The population and economy of Thailand has been growing steadily resulting in increasing demand on land. Rapid sprawl in almost every urbanised areas has been encroaching onto suburban agricultural lands despite numerous attempts to control urban expansion. At the same time, forest land has been exploited for agricultural use due to lack of strict enforcement.

Urban sprawl has become common problems in several towns and cities in Thailand. This results in wasteful infrastructure developments, especially for transportation. The quality of life of the lower income who are forced to live at the outskirts are not necessarily better off. They bear the burden of travelling to their workplaces and face the inconveniences of being far from public services, such as schools and health facilities. In many places, even basic necessities such as water supply and electricity are inaccessible. The problem of urban sprawl has been recognised a while back by state and planning agencies. While the comprehensive plans of several communities issued by the state have tried to draw limited boundaries for urban expansion, in actual implementation local political forces have hindered such attempts. In addition, there is a lack of integrated plans in terms of the construction of roads and highways. Such construction are mostly driven by the political motives of those in power to better respond to their constituents. The city plans are seldom followed to the point where it can be effective in solving the sprawl problem.

However, there is still hope with our outdated urban planning laws. The state is at the moment in the process of amending the 1974 Planning Acts. In essence, the amendment is focused on four main areas:

(1) Introducing the country plan and the regional plan to promote better conformity and transfer of policy from the national to the local levels through a series of plans.
(2) Increasing citizen participation in the process.
(3) Granting an automatic continuity to the previous mandated five year comprehensive plan validity.
(4) Making minor improvement to the Special Area Planning Law.

When the amendment is passed, it should improve the situation to some degree and increase cooperation and integration of plans among state agencies responsible for urban development, especially in terms of roads, highways and infrastructure development and planning. The implementation of more integrated planning would hopefully drive urban growth to more desirable directions, but that remains to be proven. If such basic obstacles are overcome, planners would be able to proceed to tackle the more challenging task such as how to make the city more ecologically-friendly or the known concepts of "smart growth".

Unintegrated Plans for Urban Development

The lack of integration among relevant state agencies has long marred the urban development efforts to the point of failure. An obvious example is the city's comprehensive plan which lays out the directions and areas for future expansion. However, since the city plan is carried out by the local administration while almost all infrastructure agencies are responsible to the central government, more often than not, the budget for infrastructure is not allocated according to the city plan. This is one major reason for the lower success level of comprehensive city planning in Thailand. There are too many instances of such discrepancies to be mentioned here. However, the amendment of the urban planning act calls for a better integration of specific plans by relevant agencies playing vital roles in urban development. It is hoped that the situation will improve.

Lack of Technical Knowledge and Implementation Experiences

Upon reviewing several documentation on environmental plans and performance assessments, it is obvious that two major obstacles to the success of existing projects stem from the lack of knowledge and experiences both in technical areas as well as in the implementation process. For many projects, the sound intentions and policies set by the central government are well communicated to the local authorities. Unfortunately, the lack of applicable guidelines or definite procedures for actions has lead to unsatisfactory results or even inaction. While academic institutions are trying their best to conduct more research and development in environmental and ecological areas, it seems that there is not enough knowledge or experiences in the field to ensure successful outcomes. Several institutes and agencies have sought help from international institutes and organisations. More research, practices, and cooperation are needed to transfer knowledge and experiences within and outside Thailand.

Lessons Learned and Some Thoughts on Future Directions

The reason this paper uses the name "eco-friendly city" instead of "eco-city" is because most of the projects implemented so far have aimed at raising the environmental quality of people in the city and community mostly at the more basic levels: better quality of life, waste disposal, health and sanitation, energy saving, more green space, less pollution and hazardous materials, etc. The idea of a full-fledged eco-city where city and ecology co-exist in harmony, with carbon neutral and balanced biological footprints, near zero-emissions, recycling of water and waste, and new ways of eco-friendly thinking and living, still exists only as an ideal and theory in quite a limited circle among academics.

In the past, the idea of a new eco-town set up near Bangkok to solve its over-populated and over-centralised problems have surfaced from time to time. For instance, when the new Parliament Building was proposed, there was an idea that this was an opportunity for designing a new eco-town in Nakon-nayok or Chacheongsao Provinces which could set an example for the whole country to follow. Such ideas dissipated quickly after initial exploration. There were heated political debates on its feasibility which got nowhere. There were also a lack of transparency and conflict of interests on land ownerships.

It is fortunate that the academics realise the value of the concept and is striving continuously in their studies, research and experiments to preach and disseminate their ideas and knowledge in various areas such as concepts, processes, planning and designs of cities down to green buildings, and even in terms of construction materials. Hopefully, what they know will translate into practical benefits in the near future.

Based on the achievements and obstacles of existing eco-related projects in Thailand, there are a few thoughts that may be worth taking into considerations. They are:

True Leadership is Needed

Though having a central government has its own advantage in driving environmental movements, the lack of true leadership and decisive decision-making can be a cause of delay for several environmental projects.

True leadership may not be limited to the people holding offices. A precious demonstration of leadership can originate from the application of the "Sufficiency Philosophy" of His Majesty the King Rama IX. The state agencies have spent years painstakingly studying, interpreting and finally providing the operational meaning, understanding and policies down to implementation procedures. The experiments and practices took several more years before satisfactory results started to yield. However, those evidence of success are still primarily evident at a small scale or in rural communities with agricultural practice while, in theory, the philosophy can be applied to different forms and sizes of organisations, cities and towns. More study is needed to encourage forward thinking and devise operational procedures for these entities to embrace the philosophy.

Decentralisation Works

According to the EPA report, among the member nations, Thailand's performance is moving in the right direction. One of the contributing factors is the decentralisation policy, the delegation of administrative and environmental responsibility to local governments. Decentralisation policy in Thailand has started for a certain period of time. It was at first believed that local governments, especially small municipalities, did not have either the capability or the integrity to carry the burden of such responsibilities. As time passed, objective assessment has revealed that in certain areas local administrations were quite capable. Especially where local people participate in the process, environmental problems could be better managed due to genuine concerns and a sense of ownership. Where there are still problems involving the lack of specific knowledge and know-how, the central government can then step in to fill this void.

Concrete Benefit is the Motivation: Better Education is Needed

In different circumstances, an eco-friendly practice can be either costly or beneficial compared to the current practice. To make people realise the benefit of sound environmental practice, better education is needed. Either that or environmental solutions must encompass short-term economic benefits also.

For example, due to fossil fuel price rises, a large number of motorists voluntarily turned to bio-diesel and Gasohol adaptation of their car fuel systems because it makes more economic sense. On the other hand, adapting the engines on older cars results in increasing air-pollution in the form of polluted gas and dust particles converted, though this fact is hardly considered by car owners.

The motivation for the switch here is purely the cost not environmental consciousness. It is an easy decision to practice eco-friendly when short-term benefits can be readily realised. However the more complicated solution and higher costs or inconvenience to those who practice waste recycling for instance, will require much longer time, better understanding and greater awareness to accomplish. More environmental education through formal and informal channels are needed. Businesses have started to be concerned and capitalised on environmental themes to enhance their corporate images as the public has become better educated in this area.

Economic Crisis Can Be an Opportunity

Some have seen the economic crisis as an opportunity to advocate "sufficiency" as a way out. This is certainly logical since sufficiency is tied to sustainability. To be sufficient is to optimise, which in this situation would mean a reasonable level of consumption, i.e. consuming only what is necessary and the rest can be surplus. The focus is not only on how the resources are utilised but also the way people adjust their level of feeling "sufficient" to an appropriate degree according to the situation. Moreover, the economic slowdown allows people time to reflect on the value and quality of life. Cities and communities, which are much damaged physically and culturally through rapid, uncontrolled growth and tourism, now have the time to recuperate and rethink. This may be one great opportunity to seriously study the application of sufficiency to cities, towns, and communities. As the saying goes: "Necessity is the Mother of Invention". With the right attitude, there is a chance that initiatives will follow.

While advocating sufficiency as one solution, the government is allocating much of the available budget to stimulate spending in a hope of reviving the domestic economy through consumption. These two seemingly opposite actions are not necessary in conflict. Careful considerations in channeling the budget to promote sufficiency and sustainability should be very beneficial in both the short and long runs.

Better Integration is Urgently Needed

Post-war urban development in Thailand has met with limited success. One factor hindering the implementation of city plan is the lack of integration among responsible agencies. To be able to put an eco-city idea into practice requires the cooperation of all sectors. A lesson can be drawn from the sufficiency projects which has proven that an unprecedented concerted effort from all parties involved is not only possible but also fruitful. However, this calls for true commitment and devotion from all sides. Perhaps, this brings us back to the issue of true leadership that is lacking.

From Policy to Implementation to Enforcement, More Knowledge is Needed

Most of the project reports examined have stated that a key shortcoming lies in the area of transferring policy into implementation and concrete action. This problem has been the weakest link especially in urban development where the implementation mechanisms are not effective or simply not available. Time and effort are needed to study and experiment with project implementation that will suit the country's context. This will require cooperation among academic institutes, state agencies, private sector and citizen groups.

In summary, the concept of an eco-city is still thriving in Thailand. Upon examinations of related projects and activities, it should be safe to assume that the move towards the direction of being eco-friendly is alive and well, though still in its early stages. In terms of balance, it is clear that the tip is still in favour of cconomics especially at this difficult time. Nevertheless, the government has been moving steadily to create a better environment for the country as well as actively acknowledging its part in the environmental problems the world is facing. To be sure, most of the eco-friendly projects have been initiated only within the past ten years. While they have yet to be declared a success, their performance so far has been quite heartening. The author is hopeful that despite this difficult period, the eco-city concept will still remain on the agenda and further progress will be continuously made not only in academic circles but also expand to other stakeholders.

References

Anambutr, Rujiroj. (2006). "Liveable Cities and Energy Conservation." In the Proceedings: Annual Seminar of the Thai Urban Designer Association, Bangkok.

Bangkok Metropolitan Authority (2008). Action Plan for Reducing Global Warming Problem for Bangkok 2008–2013.

Department of Environmental Quality Promotion and Project Secretariat UNEP Regional Resource Center for Asia and the Pacific. (2008). "Thailand National Environmental, Performance Assessment (EPA)." Ministry of Natural Resource and Environment, Bangkok.

Department of Local Administration, Ministry of Interior and the National Economic and Social Development Board (NESDB) (2007). Liveable City Manual, Bangkok.

Delinews (2009). Environment, Global Warming Affect Manufacturing. January 4.

NARCIS Project: Green City ChiangMai (2008). http://www.narcis.info/research/RecordID/OND1331035/Language/en/;jsessionid=vv4z9t06lkod.

Ministry of Interior. (2008). "Report on the Result of Sufficiency Economics Implementation for the past 9 months (December 2007-August 2008)."

Ministry of Interior. (2007). "Guidelines for the Creation of 'Liveable Cities and Communities' for Local Administration." Bangkok.

Muneesawang, Sirirat (2008). The Impact of the Concept of "Liveable City" on Physical and Environmental Development: A Case Study of Phitsanulok." (Unpublished paper).

National Social and Economic Development Board. (2006). "Progress Report on Liveable City and Community." Bangkok.

Office of the Natural Resources and Environment Policy and Planning, Ministry of Natural Resource and Environment. (2007). "State of Environmental Quality Report: 2006." Witoon Karn Pok Printing.

Office of the Natural Resources and Environment Policy and Planning, Ministry of Natural Resource and Environment. (2004). "Measures for Increasing and Management of Sustainable Green Areas in Communities." Ministry of Natural Resources and Environment, Bangkok.

Office of the Natural Resources and Environment Policy and Planning, Ministry of Natural Resource and Environment. (2005). "Manual for Operation on Natural Resources and Environment for Ministry of Interior."

The National Municipal League of Thailand (NMT). (2008). "Reducing Global Warming for Local Administration." http://www.sumc.in.th/images/document/20070528121202rsmwo.pdf.

CHAPTER 6

Challenges to Implementing the Eco-City Concept in Indonesia's Major Cities

Suraya A. AFIFF*

This paper calls for the need to take on board the rights of the individuals particularly their ability to input their views and concerns into the political process while implementing the eco-city concept in Indonesia's major cities. The paper observes a tendency for state actors to collaborate with business interests to the total disregard of public or individual interests in the name of implementing eco-friendly projects. By examining the politics behind the use of open green spaces in Jakarta, Bandung and Malang, the paper shows that city administrations sometimes allow private businesses to gain access to the development of green spaces even though such actions go against planning regulations. There is a need to accommodate the voices of the less influential so that the benefits of eco-friendly projects can be more evenly distributed and not just confined to the rich and powerful.

Introduction

There are various theoretical perspectives and approaches in regard to eco-city concept. Whenever the implementation of the eco-city concept is primarily based on the technocratic solution, the urban environmental discourse might provide legitimacy for the state to continue to justify violent action against some poor city dwellers. In this paper, therefore, I argue it is important to consider the human rights perspective and political process in the application of the eco-city concept in Indonesia's major cities. Based on

*Suraya A. Afiff teaches environmental politics at the anthropology graduate programme at the University of Indonesia besides her involvement with KARSA (the Learning Circle on the Reformation of Village Institution and the Agrarian Reform), Yogyakarta, Indonesia.

Indonesia's experience that I will further discuss in this paper, the organisation of space in urban areas is often strongly biased toward economic growth, in which the government prefers to facilitate the interest of private enterprises. Business groups have relatively good access to government and politicians. With their financial power, some business conglomerates could influence or even modify government policy so that it would benefit their company's agenda. Concerned citizens and the poor communities, on the other hand, often have less power than corporations to oppose or shape government policy.

Using examples in Jakarta, Bandung, and Malang, this article focuses on the politics of open green space (*ruang terbuka hijau* or RTH) areas within the city. The debates about open green space areas are a good example due to several factors. Open green space areas in a city has various ecological functions. Therefore a city must set aside a certain percentage of their total land area for this purpose. However, most city governments in Indonesia prefer to provide these areas for commercial purposes rather than leave them undeveloped. Even though it is stipulated in the spatial planning regulation that these areas should be open green space, some city administrations go against these regulations by facilitating private business interests to gain access to these areas. In regard to the poor citizens, however, local governments often evicted squatters by using environmental protection concerns to legitimise their actions.[1]

Urban poverty is one of the major issues found in many cities in the Third World countries (Brockerhoff and Brennan, 1998). This picture is no different from the situation found in Indonesia. Slums and poor neighbourhoods partly emerged as a result of urbanisation process as many people from the rural areas or small towns migrate to the big cities hoping to get a better job. Urbanisation itself has been seen as an unavoidable consequence of the modernisation process as a society moves or transits from a condition of "undeveloped" to "developed" country. Based on a World Bank study (2003), it was estimated that by 2025 over 60% of people in Indonesia will live in the urban centres. As more people come to the city,

---

[1] I am indebted to Khalisah Khalid and Vinsensius Santoso, both are activists from Wahana Lingkungan Hidup Indonesia (Indonesian Environmental Forum), who have introduced me to this issue. Khalid wrote a paper about the policy of open green space and the eviction of the urban poor in Jakarta while Santoso wrote about the environmental grassroots movement against housing developers in Malang city, East Java. Many of the information and ideas in this paper have been inspired by my discussion with both of them.

the demand for housing increases. As government fail to provide housing for the lower income class, slum areas and "illegal" settlements emerge uncontrolled, and create pockets of poverty complexes within the city. Some of the areas occupied by squatters are often classified in the city spatial planning regulations as green open space (*ruang terbuka hijau* or RTH) that might encompass city parks (*taman kota*), green belt areas, areas along the river banks, or urban forest (*hutan kota*) areas. Based on the regulations, all of these areas mentioned above are supposed to be prohibited from settlements. In the name of environment and public interest, city government forced these poor settlements out of the areas without providing them with fair and appropriate solutions. Since the city government regarded the land as "state land" (*tanah negara*), so those who occupied this land are considered "illegal" squatters. Therefore, no compensation is provided during the eviction process.

Government actions against the squatters, which is known in Indonesia as "*penggusuran*" (eviction), sometimes overlap with private company interest to develop the area. In these cases, it was the private developers who provided financial support to the government to do the eviction. After the areas has been cleared of settlements, the sites are then developed into shopping malls, hotels, housing or apartment complexes mostly for middle and high income citizens. This government's "*penggusuran*" policy has been criticised by rights activists who argue that this is discrimination against the poor citizens. This case supports what many political ecologists have been repeatedly arguing that urban environmental space is a product of the socio-political process (Heynen *et al.*, 2006). This means we must pay attention to questions such as how environmental discourse have been contested by various actors in the city and who has gained control over the political process and who has been excluded from this process.

The rest of the paper will be organised as follows. I will begin the next section with a brief review on how different authors define and apply the eco-city concept. This review indicates that there are various definitions and ways to implement the concept and there should be no universal paradigm imposed since the local social and political conditions are often different from one country to another (Myllylä and Kuvajab, 2005). The difference is not necessarily between countries in the North and South hemispheres. Even among countries in Southeast Asia, for example, social and political conditions in terms of social equity, corruption, democratic process, transparency, and other key elements of good governance are not the same. Then in the next section, I describe the current debates about open green space in Indonesia. I derive the examples for this section from cases in the three cities — Jakarta, Bandung, and Malang. Based on these examples, I point out three key issues that in my view would be the key challenges to implementing the eco-city concept in Indonesia. The first issue is regarding the politics of urban spatial planning. Here I attempt to show how economic forces strongly influenced the way spatial planning regulations have been implemented by the city administration. In some instances, the city government even manipulates their own spatial planning regulations to facilitate private sector economic interests. The second aspect that I will discuss concerns the issue of political participation. I point out the persistent limitation of civil society and the poor to influence the city government policy despite the fact that Indonesian democracy has made tremendous progress after 1998. The third aspect relates to the politics of knowledge production. In this section, I attempt to show that knowledge production is not a neutral process. Some knowledge, such as scientific or Western knowledge often is hegemonic over the local knowledge. What kind of "nature" has been produced in the urban space also hinges on who defines the knowledge that is used as the basis for government policy and action.

A Brief Review on Urban Environmental Discourse

It is not my intention in this section to provide an extensive review concerning the terms and concepts used by various authors in global urban environmental discourse. Based on these literatures, there are three aspects that I would like to point out here. First, authors often used different terms to refer to a rather broad concept that aims to find a balance between ecological, economic growth, and social goals in urban development. Some prefer the term urban sustainability or environmentally sustainable city (e.g., Blassingame, 1998; Bugliarello, 2006; Lundqvist, 2007; Nurhidayah, 2008) inspired by the concept of sustainable development which was first promoted by the Brundtland Commission report in 1987 (Drakakis-Smith, 1995). Others, however, prefer the term eco-city or ecological city (e.g., Haughton and McGranahan, 2006; Roseland,1997; Wang and Ye, 2004), the term that was popularised by Urban Ecology, a Berkeley (California, U.S.) based non-profit organisation formed in 1975. This organisation organised the first international conference on eco-city that was held in Berkeley, California, in 1990. Up to 2006, five conferences on this topic have been organised in several countries namely Australia, Sinegal, Brazil, China, and India (Lundqvist, 2007; Roseland, 1997).

Secondly, there is no single definition, approach, model or theoretical concept that has been widely used to guide the way to achieve ecological city or sustainability in city development (Haughton and Mcgranahan, 2006; Lundqvist, 2007). Urban Ecology, for example, defines the eco-city concept very broadly as a goal "to rebuild cities in balance with nature". They also promoted ten principles for practitioners to create ecological cities (Roseland, 1997). Lundqvist (2007), on the other hand, suggests the UN Habitat II guidelines as the basic definition of the concept and as a starting point to design the implementation strategies and actions. Meanwhile, in the first of his three series articles on urban sustainability, Drakakis-Smith (1995) elaborates on his suggestion about the concept, which he argues must encompass the philosophical approach (a macro-dimension) and programme level activities (a micro-dimension). He argues there are five elements in order to achieve sustainability in an urban context. These five key components are: 1) equity, social justice and human rights; 2) basic human needs; 3) social and ethnic self-determination; 4) environmental awareness and integrity; 5) awareness of inter-linkages across both space and time (p. 664). In term of dimensions in the eco-city concept, according to Roseland (1997), these dimensions include urban planning, transportation, health, housing, energy, economic development, natural habitats, public participation and social justice. This implies that an interdisciplinary approach would be needed to create an eco-city.

Authors have divided views about the lack of coherent concept and models to achieve an ecological city. Those who view this situation as a weakness argue that we need some universal guidelines that we all can refer to. On the contrary, others who view it as a positive situation argue that some flexibility in the way to achieve the eco-city goal is needed since local social, economic, and political conditions vary from one place to another. Some argue that we should avoid imposing one universal approach and model to every case and place. Therefore, some authors such as Myllylä and Kuvajab (2005) believe that what is needed is "locally defined 'sustainable city' models that consider local societal and cultural resources and constraints along with environmental improvements".

The third issue that is worthy of highlight here is the tendency for the application of eco-city concept in the Western countries to be greatly influenced by ecological modernisation thought, which emphasises a technological solution in their approach (Myllylä and Kuvajab, 2005). The problem is that when a technological solution is used as the main strategy to create eco-cities in the South countries, it might create what Myllylä and Kuvajab (2005) describe as "ecological islet" where an enclave of well-designed, clean and "green" neighbourhood is built for middle-upper class income citizens who can afford to live there and be surrounded by poor and polluted settlements. Therefore, they suggest that the sustainable city concept must encompass three aspects: political, urban governance, and socio-economic and cultural aspects.

Based on the above issues, I found the political ecology framework useful in helping me to think critically about the way environmental discourse in urban development have been contested by government officials, activists, communities, and scholars in the Indonesian context. Political ecologists have emphasised multi-level analysis to trace the linkage of local, national, and global forces that shape environmental degradation and change. They also argue that access and control over resources are unequal among actors. The state is an important actor since it often determines who can gain access to what resources and for what purpose. Furthermore, many political ecologists today also turn to discourse as a tool for analysis, which is inspired by Michael Foucault's point of view. Discourse analysis allows them to understand who is being included and excluded from the process. Whose knowledge is being used as a basis for legitimising actions by powerful actors such as the state would be important in the analysis of the discourse about environmental degradation and protection (Peet and Watts, 2004; Robbins, 2004; Watts, 2000).

In my next section, I will discuss how urban environmental discourse in particular the discourse about open green space in the city has been currently contested in Indonesia. I focus on the debates about open green space (*ruang terbuka hijau* or RTH) in the three cities — Jakarta, Bandung, and Malang — since it allows me to highlight some challenges in the creation of eco-city models in Indonesia.

The Current Debates about Open Green Space in Indonesia

The recent debates about the need to protect and expand the open green space in big cities have been partly triggered by huge floods that hit Jakarta since the early 2000s. It was argued that one way to prevent floods is through the creation of substantial percentage of areas within a city as open green space or *ruang terbuka hijau* (Tanaga, 2007; *Trubus*, 2008). According to the current spatial planning regulation (Law No. 26/2007), the open green space area in a city shall be at least 30%, the idea that has been promoted in the 1992 Earth Summit in Rio de Janeiro, Brazil. However, in practice, open green space in many cities in Indonesia has been significantly reduced due to city administrations often viewing it as "unproductive land". They regard it as financially burdensome to maintain the area since they cannot gain any economic benefits from it. Therefore, many city administrations prefer to facilitate private sectors to develop the area in order to generate revenue for the city.

In the Jakarta metropolitan city, for example, the reduction of *ruang terbuka hijau* (open green space) can be observed from the goal as is outlined in the spatial planning regulation. The spatial planning guideline in 1965–1985 mentioned that 27.6% of the total land cover in the city of Jakarta has to be set aside as open green space. This number has been reduced to 26.1% in the spatial planning of Jakarta for 1985 to 2000. And in the spatial planning for 2000–2010, it is reduced again to only 14% (*Kompas*, 2008). Yet, the current figure of the Jakarta open green space is only 9.6% of the total 65,000 hectares of Jakarta Metro City (*Jakarta Post*, 2008). Therefore there is a gap between the target goal, which is 14%, and the reality where only less than 10% of the total area of Jakarta is set aside as open green space.

Despite the fact that most big cities in Indonesia do not meet the requirement of having 30% open green space areas as stipulated in the national spatial planning law, there is no penalty or consequences for those who fail to meet the goal. In fact, the law could not stop the persistence of local government practice to reduce the existing open green space areas for business or commercial purposes. The example here is the current debates about the plan of the Bandung city administration (West Java) to allow PT. Esa Gemilang Indah, a private business entity, to develop Babakan Siliwangi, a 3.8 hectare of urban forest area in Bandung for commercial activities. This government plan was met with strong criticism from the public. A coalition of scholars, artists, activists and concerned individuals emerged to oppose the plan. As a result, the city government delayed the plan, although the project was not shelfed. If Bandung's Mayor continues with his project plan, the current 8.6% of open space area in Bandung will be reduced (*Tempo*, 2008). This shows that even if a city has a significantly low percentage of open green space, this situation does not automatically make them more committed to prevent more open green space from being converted to commercial use.

Privatisation of city parks and forested areas in Malang city, East Java, for commercial purposes is continuing despite the fact that green open space for this city has been reduced to only about 4% of the total land area (*Tempo Interaktif*, 2004). This government policy led to strong opposition by some scholars and environmental activists in East Java (Santoso, 2008). The case here involved a conversion of 28.2 hectares of city parks and forested land areas ex-APP (Agriculture Extension Academy) located in central Malang. A politically well-connected business individual who bought the area turned it into a housing complex for the upper income class. According to Santoso (2008), the government sold this piece of land to a private company in 1992, but it was not until 2007 that the development of the area took place due to various reasons. Santoso argues that part of the reason was that there was strong opposition from the public to the government action. Interestingly, the development of more than 200 housing complex in fact violates the local government regulation (Perda 7/2001) that stipulated the area to be an open green space for Malang city. Although a coalition comprising scholars, activists and some politicians who opposed the plan were successful to halt the construction plan for some years, after 1998, this coalition unravelled and was no longer able to stop the conversion of one of the best remaining forested areas in Malang city (Santoso, 2008).

Based on the above cases, I argue at least that there are three aspects that need to be considered in regard to the debates about eco-city concept and goal, i.e. the politics of urban spatial planning, the issue of political participation, and the politics of knowledge production. I will discuss them further below.

The Politics of Urban Spatial Planning

Khalid (2008) makes an interesting argument about the politics of conversion of open green areas in Jakarta. She claims that about 1,960 hectares of land that were previously designated as open green space in Jakarta has been converted into commercial purposes, as can be observed from Table 1. Only 282 hectares of these open green space, she argues, has been occupied by urban poor settlements. Yet, she argues, instead of blaming the commercial businesses, Jakarta officials would usually blame the poor community and evict them from the land they occupied, such as the case of forced eviction experienced by about 200 households who had been living in the BMW park which she observed.

It was a common practice for the government to revise the zoning restriction in the spatial planning document in order to accommodate private sector interest. One of these examples cited by Santoso (2008) involved a case in Malang where in order to accommodate the developers' interest, the local government attempted to revise the area classification as stipulated in the spatial planning guideline so businesses could begin to develop the area.

Table 1   RTH in Jakarta that has been Converted into Business Purposes.

Area	Size	Original Use	Conversion
Kelapa Gading	1,288 hectares	Water catchment area, rice field	— Shopping Mall Kelapa Gading (in 2005: 6 hectares) — Kelapa Gading Square (in 2003: 17 hectares)
Pantai Kapuk	831 hectares	Protected forest	— Pantai Indah Kapuk Housing Complex — Mutiara Indah — Damai Indah Golf Course
Sunter	1.459 hectares	Water catchment area	— Sunter Agung Housing Complex — Automobile Assembling Complex — PT. Astra Komponen, Astra Daihatsu, PT. DENSO Indonesia, PT. Dunia Express Trasindo
Hutan Kota Senayan	279 hectares	Public facility	— Mulia Hotel — Sultan Hotel — Semanggi Gas Station — Senayan Residence Apartment, Hotel Century Atlet — Simprug Golf Course — Plaza Senayan
Hutan Kota Tomang	70 hectares	City forest	— Mall Taman Anggrek — Mediteranian Garden Residence I dan II

Source: Khalid (2008).

The inconsistency of local government to fulfil the spatial planning guideline document was confirmed by participants who attended the meeting about spatial planning organised by National Planning Agency in March 2004 (Bappenas, 2004). Since corruption has been a common practice in Indonesia and became rampant after the decentralisation era, government enforcement has been mostly weak against those who are financially powerful. Furthermore, there is no single case where government officials are imprisoned due to a violation of spatial planning regulations.

Furthermore, an Environmental Impact Statement (or AMDAL), which is required when changes are being made to an existing project to develop an area previously classified as protected forest or green areas, is also an empty document since it is not strictly adhered to. Again, money talks more in re-directing, modifing, and changing government policy in Indonesia.

Political Participation

Since 1998, Indonesia has become a democracy. However, this does not mean that the access and mechanisms for the poor community and other concerned citizens to voice their concerns have been improved. The Santoso (2008) case on the grassroots movement in Malang against the property developers shows that grassroots coalition against the Malang government plan to allow conversion of the open green space was ironically weakened after the reformation (*Reformasi*) era. The case in Bandung also shows that although grassroots coalition against the local government project to convert the area has halted its progress so far, it has not ended the project since the coalition failed to obtain a written commitment that will guarantee that the Mayor would stop the project. There is still no clear mechanism in place that allows genuine participation.

Whose Knowledge and Whose "Nature" Counts?

The third issue that challenges the achievement of social justice dimension in eco-city goal concerns the process to create the "natural" space in the urban context. Here, I draw from political ecologists' idea about "nature" as a product of cultural construction (Robbins, 2004). In the Jakarta forced eviction case against 200 households who lived in the BMW city park, the urban poor community and their activist allies requested the Jakarta governor to allow a small percentage of the area in the BMW park to be allocated for urban poor settlement. Despite the agreement by the urban poor community to redesign their settlement so that it would not thwart government plan to rebuilt the area as an public open space, Jakarta's governor declined the request for various reasons. Partly, this was due to the fact that the city government had already planned to collaborate with a private sector to develop the area into a sporting facility (Khalid, 2008).

This example shows that the idea about what is considered as "open green space" and how we create such an area depend on who has the power to decide what this area should look like. This would also have implications on whose knowledge is being used or allowed to be incorporated in the production of this (human-made) "nature".

Conclusion

I hope the cases and descriptions in this paper allow us to see some of the key challenges that might be found in the implementation of the eco-city concept in Indonesia. I am fully aware that what I have described in this paper might not provide the whole picture. Nevertheless, I hope the points that are raised about the importance of human rights and the political process related to the eco-city concept are worth considering.

References

Alberti, M. and L. Susskind. (1996). "Managing Urban Sustainability: An Introduction to the Special Issue." *Environ Impact Assessment Review*, 16: 213–221.

Bappenas (2004). "Rilis Berita: Diskusi Reformasi Penataan Ruang."

Blassingame, L. (1998). "Sustainable Cities: Oxymoron, Utopia, or Inevitability?" *The Social Science Journal*, 35(1): 1–13.

Brockerhoff, M. and E. Brennan. (1998). "The Poverty of Cities in Developing Regions." *Population and Development Review*, 24(1): 75–114.

Bugliarello, G. (2006). "Urban Sustainability: Dilemmas, Challenges and Paradigms." *Technology in Society*, 28: 19–26.

Drakakis-Smith, D. (1995). "Third World Cities: Sustainable Urban Development, 1." *Urban Studies*, 32(4&5): 659–677.

Haughton, G. and Gordon Mcgranahan. (2006). "Editorial: Urban Ecologies." *Environment and Urbanization*, 18(3): 3–6.

Heynen, N., M. Kaika, and E. Swyngedow. (2006). "Urban Political Ecology: Politicizing the Production of Urban Natures." In *In the Nature of Cities: Urban Political Ecology and the Politics of Urban Metabolism*, N. Heynen, M. Kaika, and E. Swyngedow (eds.), pp. 1–20. New York: Routledge.

Haughton, G. and G. McGranahan. (2006). "Editorial: Urban Ecologies." *Environment and Urbanization*, 18(3): 3–6.

Jakarta Post. (2008). "Jakarta to Plant 30,000 Trees." 29 November.

Khalid, K. (2008). "Kebijakan Ruang terbuka Hijau dan Penggusuran Miskin Kota di Jakarta Study Kasus Penggusuran Taman Bersih, Manusiawi dan Berwibawa (BMW)." (Unpublished paper).

Kompas. (2008). "Panen Buah-buahan di Kota Jakarta." 12 December.

Lundqvist, M. (2007). "Sustainable Cities in Theory and Practice: A Comparative Study of Curitiba and Portland." Fakulteten för samhälls-och livsvetenskaper, Karlstads unversitet.

Nurhidayah, L. (2008). Toward Environmentally Sustainable City in Indonesia: Case Study on Environment Protection in Surabaya. http://ssrn.com [23 January 2009].

Peet, Richard and Michael Watts (eds.) (2004). *Liberation Ecologies: Environment, Development, Social Movement.* Second Edition. London and New York: Routledge.

Robbins, Paul. (2004). *Political Ecology: A Critical Introduction.* Oxford: Blackwell.

Roseland, M. (1997). "Dimensions of the Eco-City." *Cities,* 14(4): 197–202.

Santoso, V. (2008). "Gerakan Lingkungan Dalam Pusaran Kapital: Telaah Kritis Konversi Lahan APP Menjadi Perumahan Mewah Ijen Nirwana Residence di Malang, Jawa Timur." (Unpublished paper).

Tanaga, S. (2007). "Pertahankan Eksistensi Taman Kota." 18 June. http:// bandungheritage.org

Tempo. (2008). "Berebut Jantung Bandung." 6 October. http://majalah.tempointeraktif.com/id/arsip/2008/10/06/LIN/mbm.20081006.LIN128375.id.html

Tempo Interaktif. (2004). "Ruang Terbuka Hijau Malang Tinggal Empat Percent." 13 August. http://www.blog.tempointeraktif.com/hg/nusa/2004/08/ 13/brk, 20040813-36,id.html.

Trubus. (2008). "Ruang Terbuka Hijau Antara Tuntutan dan Kebutuhan." 3 May. http://www.trubus-online.co.id/mod.php?mod=publisher&op=viewarticle& cid=4&artid=1272.

Myllylä, S. and K. Kuvajab. (2005). "Societal Premises for Sustainable Development in Large Southern Cities." *Global Environmental Change,* 15: 224–237.

Wang, R. and Y. Ye. (2004). "Eco-City Development in China." *Ambio,* 33(3): 341–342.

Watts, M. (2000). "Political Ecology." In *A Companion to Economic Geography,* E. Sheppard (ed.), pp. 257–274. Wiley-Blackwell.

The World Bank. (2003). "Cities in Transition: Urban Sector Review in an Era of Decentralization in Indonesia." East Asia Urban Working Paper Series, Dissemination Paper No. 7.

CHAPTER 7

Eco-City: China's Realities and Challenges in Urban Planning and Design

WANG Tao and SHAO Lei*

There are many challenges in carrying out the eco-city programme in China. Although sustainable development is urgently needed by Chinese cities, there is no consensus on what a sustainable city or eco-city is, especially when it comes to its physical appearances. And if sustainable development is to be achieved through urban planning, some of the intrinsic questions of the profession cannot be avoided. This paper introduces some realities of the sustainable urban development programme in China, and discusses the strategies and objectives of eco-city development in the context of urban planning and urban design.

Background

China has been experiencing a rapid urbanisation process since it started economic reforms in the 1980s. The backlog of urbanisation caused by the urban-rural dualist policy in the planned economy period has been gradually released, resulting in rampant urban growth in terms of the concentration of both population and economic activities. From 1978 to 2005, the number of cities in China has increased from 193 to 661, among which 49 cities have a population exceeding 1 million. In 2006, among the 1.3 billion population of China, 44% are registered as urban residents while the remainder 56% as farmers. The rate of urbanisation is estimated at an annual 1%

*Wang Tao is an executive editor-in-chief of Community Design Journal by Tsinghua University. He is leading the R&D Section of the Institute of Architectural Design and Research Institute of Tsinghua University. Shao Lei is currently Director of the Institute of Housing and Community Studies in the School of Architecture, Tsinghua University.

increase, that is, a net increase of 13 million urban inhabitants every year. Nevertheless, besides the above official statistics, there are 200 million registered as farmers who are no longer engaged in agricultural production — 120 million of them are working in cities and towns, giving rise to the well-known "migrant population" phenomenon.

In the process of unprecedented urban growth, China's cities are facing challenges from all directions, but above all, the challenge of depleting resources. Taking land as an example, since China has very rigid control on the encroachment of farmland, urban growth is confined within limited spaces. This leads to the fast pace of urban renewal and ever-increasing urban density. In 2005, the average density of Chinese cities is 870 persons per square kilometre, and in urban centres of big cities, for example, in Shanghai, the figure reaches to more than 40,000 persons per square kilometre. However, land is only one aspect of the resource challenges Chinese cities are facing. The urban growth is exerting huge demands on water, electricity, petrol and especially non renewable resources.

Cities consume 75% of the global energy. In cites, 33% of the energy are used by buildings, and another 33% are used by transportation to reach these buildings. Obviously, urban planning plays a significant role in developing the pattern of a sustainable city, because it deals with regulating buildings and their locations in the city, as well as the transportation network connecting them.

While trying to accommodate the rising urban population, Chinese cities are experiencing economic and social restructuring, as well as its associated problems, such as environment pollution, water shortage, social segregation, migrant population, affordable housing, urban slums and imbalanced regional development. Taking the development of automobile as an example, there are now 3 million private vehicles on the road in Beijing now, exerting a huge pressure on the road system and energy demand. See Figs. 1 and 2. How to make the rapid urban development comply with sustainable principles is a critical task of urban planners in China.

Understanding Related Actions and Programmes in China

At present in China, there are a number of national programmes related to sustainable urban development. The national governmental institutions involved include the Ministry of Housing and Urban-rural Development, State Environmental Protection Administration, and State Policy and Development Centre. See Table 1.

Source: http://embarq.wri.org/imageupload/.

Fig. 1   Traffic Jams in Xi'an.

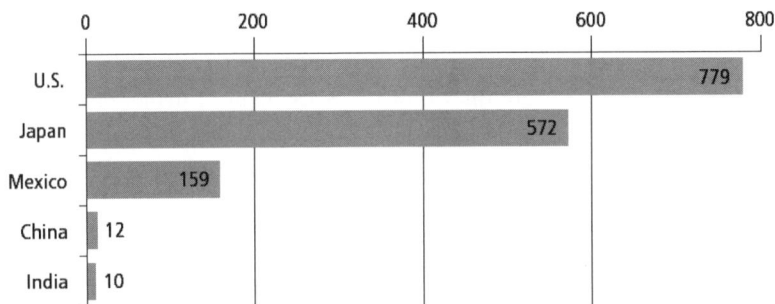

Source: World Bank (2005). Data ranges from 1997-2000.

Source: World Resource Institute (2005). Growing in the Greenhouse: Protecting the Climate by Putting Development First.

Fig. 2   Motor Vehicles per 1,000 People.

MOHURD: Ecological Garden City[1]

Ecological Garden City is a programme administered by the Department of Urban Construction, Ministry of Construction. It was launched in 1992

---

[1]http://www.csjs.com.cn/sys/yllh_detail.aspx?TabaleName=tmp2&id=85.

Table 1   Lists of Some Related National Programmes.

Governmental Institution	Programme Title
MOHURD	Ecological Garden City (Ecological City)
SEPA	Environment Protection Model City
MOHURD	Liveable City Standards
SEPA	Ecological Function Protection Zoning Plan
SPDC	National Development Priority Zoning Plan

as a "Garden City" programme. In 2004, the ecological perspective was added to the programme so the former title was replaced by "Ecological Garden City". It has 19 categories of indices on different aspects of urban planning based on ecological principles such as balanced regional development, natural and cultural heritage, infrastructure, urban amenity and public participation. There are so far 11 pilot ecological garden cities in China.

Related Policies and Standards:

- National Garden City Standards (2000), revised in 2005.
- National Ecological Garden City Standards (2004).

SEPA: Exemplary City in Environment Protection[2]

The Exemplary City in Environment Protection by the State Environment Protection Agency involved a nationwide assessment of urban environment qualities. Based on this assessment, SEPA selects those cities that prove to be the best practioners as "Exemplary City in Environment Protection". So far, there are 500 Chinese cities which have been assessed. Eleven cities have received the title of "Exemplary City in Environment Protection". See Fig. 3. The main focuses of this programme are:

- Urban Air Quality.
- Urban Water Environment.
- Urban Environmental Infrastructures.
- Counter-Pollution Actions.

Related Policies and Standards

- Quantitative Assessment Methods on Urban Environment Comprehensive Harnessing (1988).

---

[2]http://www.chinabaike.com/law/zy/bw/gw/jsb/1349897.html.

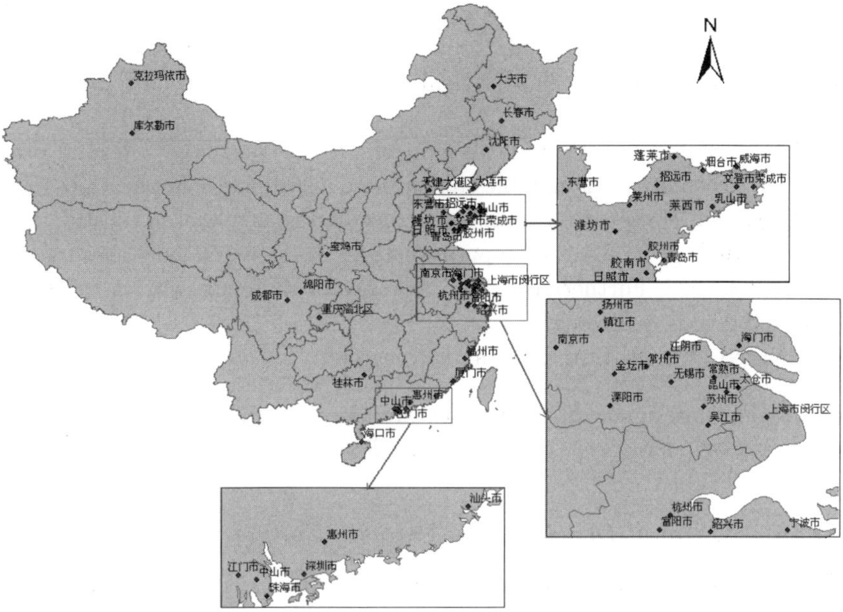

Fig. 3   Exemplary City in Environment Protection.

- Detailed Regulation on Implementing Quantitative Assessment Indexes on Urban Environment Comprehensive Harnessing During the 11th Five-Year Plan (2006).
- Report on National Urban Environment Management and Comprehensive Harnessing (2005).

MOHURD: Liveable City Standards[3]

Liveable City Standards is a research project carried out by the China Urban Science Institute and sponsored by MOHURD. The project was formally approved in 2006, but not yet integrated into present urban planning system. Another reason is the same as in other programmes mentioned above — urban planning is in fact only one aspect of its concerns. The six main criteria of these standards are: urban civilisation, economy, environmental amenity, available resources level, living convenience and public security. The six criteria are further divided into 32 indices. A city which

---

[3]http://news.xinhuanet.com/politics/2007-05/30/content_6175236.htm.

can arrive at a level of 80 points will be recognised as a "liveable city". And in a study conducted in 2006, Beijing was given 63.8 points. In 2007, the newly approved Master Plan of Beijing included "liveable city" as one of its planning goals.

The Liveable City Standards appears to be the most relevant programme to achieve a sustainable city through a systematic application of its index system. However, in terms of its usefulness as a tool for sustainable urban planning, it gives few operational instructions on how these goals can be achieved. Furthermore, the relevance of these six criteria to urban sustainability is questionable.

Related Policies, Standards and Research:

- *Liveable City Scientific Evaluation Standards* (2007).
- *Blue Book on Liveable City: Research Report on Beijing* (2006).

SPDC: National Development Priority Zoning Plan[4]

National Development Priority Zoning Plan is carried out as a national land development plan that takes environmental and resource capacities into consideration. According to this plan, the land mass of China is divided into four categories. It will serve as the basis for the making of the national economic development plan, regional plan and urban plan. Ecological consideration is the main focus of this plan. In those places with high concentration of population and low environmental and resource capacities, the development will be restrained. Those places that are of critical importance to the national ecological balance will be carefully protected.

However, it looks at the land issue in a very broad sense and purely from the perspective of resources. The importance of the distribution of urban functions and the impacts of human behaviours are to a large extent overlooked in this programme.

Related Policies, Standards and Research:

- *National Ecological Environment Construction Plan* (1998).
- *National Ecological Environment Protection Compendium* (2000).
- *The Eleventh Five-Year Plan of National Social and Economic Development* (2006).

---

[4]http://www.gov.cn/zwgk/2007-07/31/content_702099.htm.

- *State Council on National Development Priority Zoning Plan* (2007).
- *Planning Principles on National Critical Ecological Protection Zone* (2007).

Main Characters of Existing National Programmes

(1) They are comprehensive programmes, demanding joint collaboration among different departments of the local government, but not especially concerned with urban planning. Therefore, they give very little information on how urban planning fits into the overall scheme of things.

(2) Most of them are post-evaluation standards instead of in-advance measures. They examine whether a city is sustainable according to certain standards, but give no instructions on how to achieve these standards.

(3) The rationale behind these national programmes is inadequate to cope with the rapid pace of urban development. They examine cities in a static manner rather than regard urban development as a dynamic process.

In an overall sense, though giving descriptions and standards on different criteria to be achieved, these programmes are incapable of providing an action manual for the city authorities to build a sustainable city through a series of planning actions.

Local Practices: Two Cases

After an examination of the national programmes, it is timely to look at how sustainable development is implemented in local daily planning practices. Two projects will be presented here, representing two different contexts and scales of the urban planning problem. Both are government projects. They show that the local governments are the propelling forces behind the making and implementation of urban plans. And on the agendas of both governments, sustainable development are mentioned, and even taken as designated goals, in either the local five-year social and economic development plan (by the local municipality) or the master plan of the city (by the local planning authority). We will examine how the sustainable goals are carried out in practice.

Case 1. Xianlin New Town, Nanjing

Xianlin New Town is a new urban development project in Nanjing. It is situated in the east suburb of Nanjing, and was mainly farmland before urban planning work began in the early 1990s. The development of a new town in this area is the result of two major forces. Firstly, the need to accommodate the increasing urban population and activities of Nanjing. Secondly, the motivation of the local government to release more land to the market to stimulate the local economy. This is a typical situation that urban planners in many Chinese cities are facing.

The master plan of Xianlin New Town was made in the 1990s and it has undergone several major revisions since. According to the master plan, the new town will accommodate universities, hi-tech industry and other urban functions, and at the same time be home to 800,000 residents. The new town is further divided into four districts.

Though constructing an "ecological city" is one of the major goals in the master plan of Xianlin, however, few elements can be identified in the follow up plans and implementation. The most obvious evidences are: the planning of the light-rail route in the area has taken no consideration of the distribution of urban functions and population; the division of urban blocks is too large to make walking a pleasant experience; and the urban functions are distributed over a very large scale which discourages walking and cycling. In other words, transit oriented development (TOD) principles are not realised in the urban plan. On the contrary, the plan encourages the use of private cars instead of mass transportation.

In one of the districts, a conceptual plan was drawn up by an Australian design office through an international competition. Sustainable elements are well integrated into it. The plan delineates four district centres specialising in different functions. Neighbourhoods (urban blocks) are made smaller, so that basic living needs and local activities are within walking distances. The four district centres are connected by a ring road with mass transportation system. And this district ring road is in turn connected to the superior ring road system which connects the entire new town area. With such an urban plan, a lifestyle mainly of walking or cycling is made possible at the local level. Long distance travel is taken care of by mass transportation such as bus rapid transit (BRT) or light rail. Thus, activities are, on one hand, concentrated at district centres, and mixed land-use is encouraged on the other. See Fig. 4.

However, according to the local planning authorities, this plan poses difficulties that are hard to overcome. Further assessment on the feasibility of this plan is to be conducted. In any case, this example indicates that a

Fig. 4   Qilin District Plan, Xianlin New Town, Nanjing.

sustainable urban plan must also take into account the implementation process because the present administrative system, working styles of different governmental offices and even existing regulations may need to be changed.

Case 2. Daming Palace Area Redevelopment, Xi'an

Daming Palace Area is located in the northern suburb of Xi'an. It is right outside the Ming Dynasty city wall and moat. It was the royal palace during the Tang Dynasty. Surrounding the Tang Dynasty Royal Palace which is now a national heritage site, there are about 20 square kilometres of urban area to be redeveloped under this project. In contrast to building a brand new town from scratch as was the previous case, this case represents another major form of urban planning practice in China — urban redevelopment (urban renewal). Usually, urban redevelopment happens where the potential value of the land has not been fully realised, the housing conditions are no longer suitable for living, and/or the local economy demands new stimulus. It usually occurs in a built-up urban area. The old buildings are first brought down, followed by the erection of new replacements, and in most cases, it is accompanied by the upgrading of surrounding urban infrastructure such as roads, pipelines and green spaces. See Fig. 5.

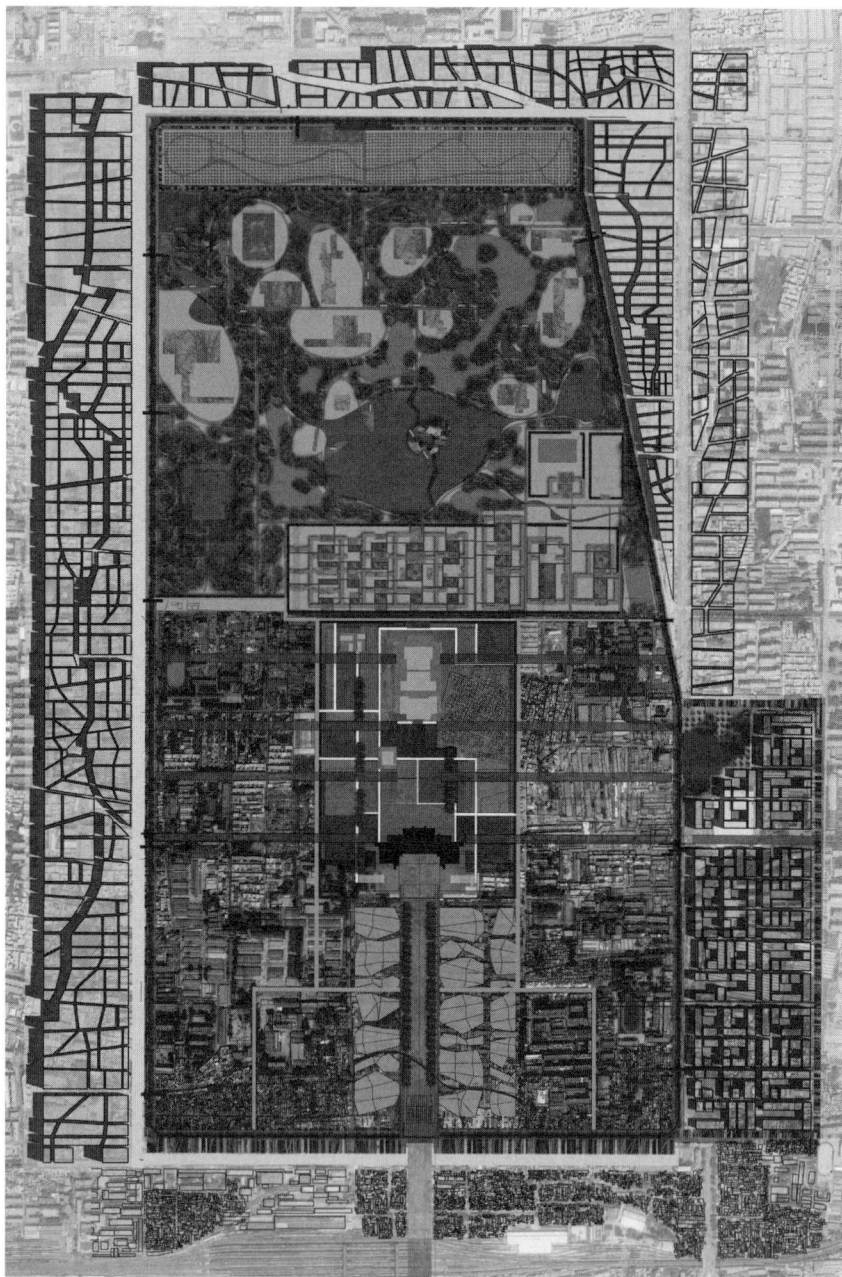

Fig. 5   Daming Palace Project by Team 3+.

Urban redevelopment projects usually face more constraints in implementing a sustainable urban plan due to space limitations. However, in this case in Xi'an, the area is so large that it could be compared to the size of a new town or subcentre of a city. Furthermore, three underground subway lines will pass through this area in the coming decades. Therefore, there is a great opportunity for a TOD model of urban development to be achieved. We can summarise from this case the conditions where sustainable urban planning is possible in urban redevelopment projects:

(1) The area is large enough to encompass various urban activities.
(2) Mass transportation is planned within the area.
(3) Buildings are to be rebuilt or upgraded.

Under such conditions, a sustainable urban plan can be made to organise urban activities in the redevelopment area according to the mass transportation routes and nodes. The relationship between working, living, and other urban functions can be rearranged in a mixed and high-density way, so that shorter trips can be made by walking or cycling, and longer travels are made less frequently and are, in unavoidable cases, taken care of by mass transportation. Therefore, a sustainable urban lifestyle can be encouraged in a designated area.

However, in the Daming Palace redevelopment project, sustainable development is not specifically a goal of the local government. With a narrow-minded focus on stimulating the local economy, especially through the sale of land, the local authority fails to realise that urban redevelopment on such a scale may have fundamental influences on the urban structure and its sustainability for decades to come.

Generally, the implementation of sustainable urban planning at the local level faces several difficulties:

(1) Sustainable urban development requires joint efforts by different government departments; however, the urban planning authorities are incapable of playing this leading role. A centralised coordinating function from the upper level is needed.
(2) The importance of sustainable urban development is already well recognised. It appears on various governmental agenda, policies and urban plans. However, when it comes to practice, it is quite fragmented and incoherent. Good practices need to be highlighted to serve as useful reference.

(3) Though sustainable urban development is set as one of the planning goals, urban planning authorities in practice is still guided by old-fashioned rationales and working methods to produce and implement urban plans. In another words, the present working rationales and methods need to be readjusted to make sustainable urban planning possible.

Strategies and Objectives in Hierarchical Planning System

Urban planning occurs at different levels. It has a hierarchical system in which subordinate plans are in line with superior plans. Ideally, a sustainable urban plan should be conceived at the very beginning of plan-making. Then, following the flow of the work in this hierarchical system, the sustainability concept will eventually penetrate to the lower levels and be realised.

However, the chance of getting involved in the making of a new city from scratch is so rare, and most urban planning work deals with inherited urban conditions in an incremental manner. This, however, does not discount the possibility of realising an eco-city.

Though there are no final conclusions on the standards of sustainable cities, there some common principles widely recognised. They remind us that there are opportunities at different levels of urban planning work where a sustainable city can be achieved, such as:

- TOD urban development.
- Advocating public transportation and encouraging walking and use of bicycles.
- Mixed land-use and high-density.
- Adequate open and green spaces.

Master Plan and District Plan

Main Players: MOHURD, local government, planning authority

Tasks: The master plan decides the spatial arrangement of a city according to its projected social and economic development, including the land use and infrastructure system supporting such a spatial arrangement.

To be integrated into the master plan shall be the ultimate goal of the sustainable city programme under the present planning legal system because most of the fundamental elements of a sustainable city are laid at the master plan level. A master plan usually requires several years to produce and it usually has a duration of 10–20 years. It requires the approval of a higher-level government. When approved, it functions as a law to direct urban development. Usually, once a master plan is made, it should not be changed. However, the rationale behind a master plan has been challenged in recent years because it fails to cope with the rapid and dynamic urban development. As a result, a master plan may need to be revised.

Nevertheless, a master plan is emphasised in sustainable planning because it decides many of the basic elements of sustainability in cities, such as the urban spatial structure, transportation system, infrastructure system, urban development direction and scale, and, most important of all, the basic principles regarding interactions among these elements. Urban sustainability often hinges on establishing a harmonious relationship among these elements. Under the master plan, bigger cities usually produce district plans to perform an intermediary role to direct district development. District plans have the same function as the master plan, but they focus on each district of a city, and give more detailed framework of development for each district.

Strategy: There are two important time points in the master planning process for making a sustainable plan.

(1) The time when a city is making a new master plan. The interval will be 15–20 years.
(2) The time when a city's master plan is under revision. The interval will be 3–5 years.

Obviously, since master plan revision is happening more frequently, it is much easier to be engaged in a revision than in the making of a master plan.

Control Plan

Main Player: Local planning authority

Tasks: Provide detailed planning control on density, height, infrastructure and traffic system of a piece of land to be developed.

A control plan helps to guide the progress on the gound on a daily basis. It is usually carried out by the local planning authority to ensure that the development of a plot complies with the requirements of related urban plans. A control plan is legally binding when it is approved by the planning authority. On sustainable urban development, however, when a control plan is ready, it usually means most of the important elements of a sustainable city have already been decided beforehand and will function as given premises in the making of a control plan. It usually means that it is too late to make any real difference.

Strategy: By continuously and consistently working on different control plans of a defined urban district under a sustainable rationale, the outcome will be a sustainable neighbourhood or district when put together. Of course, this requires a sort of master plan of the district or an action oriented guidance with sustainable principles established beforehand to guide subsequent actions.

Urban Design

Main Players: Public or private design offices, local planning authority

Tasks: Urban design is concerned with the aesthetical aspects of urban forms, such as facades, colour and building volume, and especially the shaping and use of public space.

Before sustainable urban planning was officially recognised as a national standard and acquired a legal status, the most practicable way for sustainable planning to be effective is through urban design.

Urban design is not backed by any statue in the planning system of China. Neither is it required by the legal system of planning, nor is it regulated by any national standards or working manuals. However, it is used by many local municipalities as flexible and additional tools to regulate urban development, so that they can gain more control over private land development and public urban spaces. Therefore, it is a frequently used "backup weapon" to promote locally-based values and requirements on urban development. Integrating sustainable elements into the present legal planning system will take a long process. However, through the wide use of urban design tools, the local authorities will be able to immediately influence urban development.

However, it should be noted that urban design is mainly concerned with the appearance, in other words, the skin of a city. It has no direct influences on basic spatial structures and urban traffic system which are key features that a sustainable city planning requires. Nevertheless, urban design does have its indirect ways of influencing these aspects. Furthermore, when a master plan is already established, it is very hard and time-consuming to make changes to it. But by making a sustainable urban design, it can impose extra requirements on land development so as to channel it in the right direction.

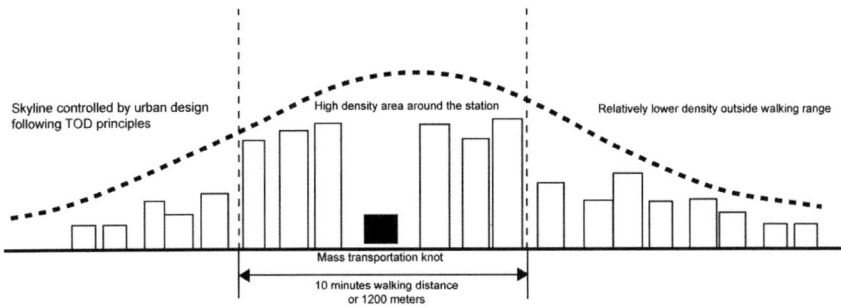

Fig. 6　Controlling Urban Density via Sustainable Urban Design.

Figure 6 shows how the distribution of density of an area around a public transportation knot could be controlled by urban design. Higher density is encouraged in the circle around the station within walking distance, while the density of the area outside walking range is lower. In this way, more urban activities are taking place in a compact urban centre within walking distance; and with the drop in density outside this range, unnecessary transit is reduced. In Fig. 7, urban design can encourage walking and cycling by introducing adequate public spaces within the urban centre, and arranging enough parking spaces on the borders of the urban centre where the main artery roads come in. Through the innovative design of urban spaces with different scales, less use of automobiles is encouraged.

Strategies: There are different levels of urban design: city level, district level and project level.

Usually, at the project level, it will be too late to implement any sustainable elements, unless the scale is large and preferably a public transportation knot is included. However, there are still opportunities at certain occasions such as adding sustainable elements into given urban contexts, for example, designing a pedestrian or cycling system in urban public spaces to increase convenience to pedestrians and discouraging the use of automobiles.

In fact, urban design usually provides more detailed requirements to an urban area than the master plan does. Therefore, seizing the opportunity to come up with the urban design of an area will in the long run channel the local development to sustainable goals. Cooperation with the local planning authority is also a requirement. Without being legally binding, urban design has to be accepted and carried out by the local authority to make any real impact.

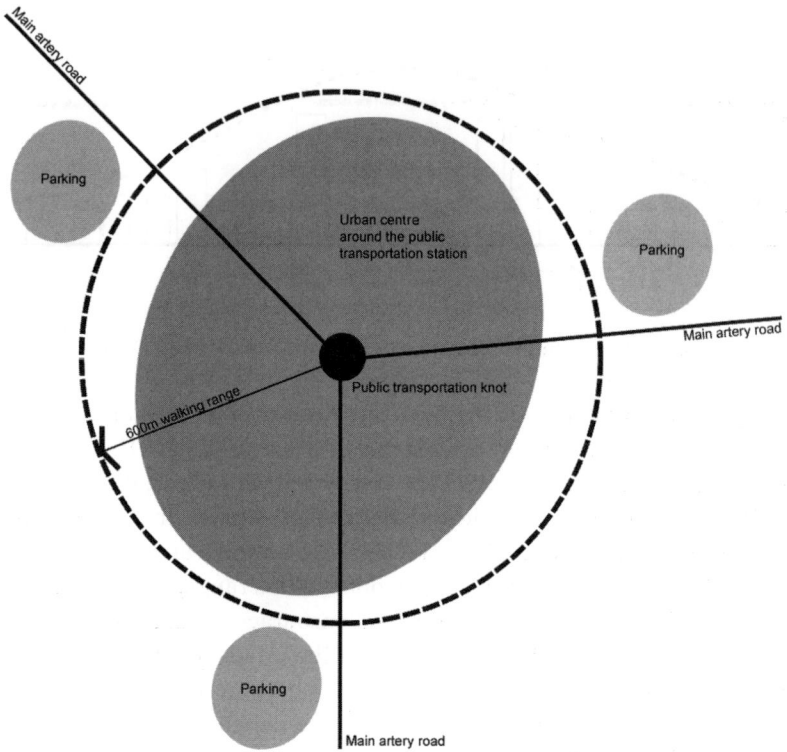

Fig. 7   Urban Centre Spatial Arrangement under TOD Principles.

Special Planning Activities — BRT, Underground System, and New Town

Main Players: Local planning authorities, specialised planning offices on transportation

Tasks: To plan new transportation systems or new expansion of urban areas to meet the needs of urban development.

Strategies: After a master plan is approved by the state government, there are still some occasions where major changes can be applied at least to certain parts of a city.

These occasions include the time when a city is making a city-wide traffic system plan, such as BRT system or underground system, or when a new town area is to be developed to accommodate growth of urban activities and population. Such occasions have become more frequent in Chinese cities because of rapid urban growth.

When a new traffic system is being planned in relation to the existing master plan, certain modifications are inevitable, at least along the peripheral areas the new traffic system covers. Presently, the method of planning an underground system, for example, is to treat it as a completely separate issue. Stations are to be inserted into the existing urban fabric without any changes to the surrounding areas. The underground network and the urban development on top of it are regarded as separate layers. In fact, when an underground route is to be constructed, it is a good opportunity to redistribute land use along the traffic route, so TOD principles could be applied to the affected areas.

New town planning will offer one of the best opportunities to present a systematic set of solutions to a sustainable city, because it will start from the very beginning with basic land use distribution, road system, green spaces and resources. This is the time when the basic pattern of movements and energy-consumption behaviours of the residents of the new town are moulded.

Acknowledgements

In the writing of this paper, the authors would like to acknowledge the auspices of the Energy Foundation research project, *Strategic Report on China's Sustainable City Programme*.

References

Liu, Zhongmei. (2008). "On the Legal Mechanism of Guaranteeing Ecological Carrying Capacity in the Eco-City Construction — A Case Study of Dalian City." *Journal of Liaoning Normal University*, 33(2).

Man, Chengliang and Dong Shanfeng. (2008). "Eco-City of the World — The Planning of Dongtan Eco-City." *Time + Architecture*, February.

Yang, Baojun and Dong Ke. (2008). "Theories and Practices of Eco-City Planning with Master Plan of Sino-Singapore Eco-City in Tianjin as an Example." *China Urban Planning Review*, 32(8).

Ye, Zuda. (2008). "Eco-City: From Concept to Implementation with Shanghai Dongtan and Beijing Changxindian as Cases." *China Urban Planning Review*, 32(8).

Zhou, Ganzhi. (2008). "Some Basic Understandings about Eco-City." *China Urban Planning Review*, 32(8).

CHAPTER 8

Sustainable Living: An Overview from the Malaysian Perspective

Hardev KAUR and Mizan HITAM*

Malaysia has experienced phenomenal economic growth in the last two decades, moving from an agricultural to a manufacturing-based economy. This development, driven by rapid industrialisation, has adversely affected the natural environment. To address this negative impact, the relevant authorities have launched a number of pioneer projects towards sustainable urban living. These include the Petaling Jaya LA21 Programme, Putrajaya Administrative Centre and the Low Carbon Cities Project in the Iskandar Development Region. While these efforts are commendable, they face daunting challenges. These include the complexity of federal-state relations, the lack of community participation and insufficient awareness of the costs and benefits associated with sustainable development. Also, policies, strategies, legislation and enforcement are inadequate and confined to specific sectors.

Introduction

The rate of urbanisation in Malaysia is on the increase, from about 25% in the 1960s to 65% in 2005 and is expected to exceed 70% by 2020 which is relatively a high-level of urbanisation for a Third World country. Rapid urbanisation has had consequences for the distribution of population and exerted huge demands on land, water, housing, transport and employment. The rapid urbanisation process in Malaysia is mainly due to industrialisation in the urban areas. This industrialisation has affected the environment in

*Hardev Kaur is a Senior Lecturer at the Faculty of Administrative Science and Policy, University Technology Mara, Malacca, Malaysia. Mizan Hitam, from the Faculty of Architecture, Planning and Surveying, is currently the Director at University Technology Mara, Melaka, Malaysia.

many ways resulting in flooding, water shortage, poor air quality, inefficient waste disposal, and potential degradation of living and natural environments. The environmental issues are therefore a mixture of problems related to natural resource depletion and exploitation, and the lack of environmental management for sustainable living (Aini *et al.*, 2001). In recent years, air pollution from transportation, industrial manufacturing and open burning, including by neighbouring countries, are causing considerable concern over health impacts (Afroz *et al.*, 2003). The government, in tackling these issues, has undertaken various initiatives and in this paper, it is these initiatives and the attendant problems and challenges that will be addressed.

The Policy and Institutional Framework

Development policies in Malaysia had initially focused on the basic parameters of natural resource exploitation, infrastructure development and poverty alleviation to cater to social and economic growth objectives. During the 1970s, a broader and more cross-sectoral approach to environment and sustainable development was adopted. The concept of protecting the environment, as part of the development planning process, was first given prominence by the Government in the Third Malaysia Plan (1976–1980). A chapter in the Third Malaysia Plan (TMP) 1976–1980 was specifically dedicated to development and environment (Malaysia, 1976) — an unprecedented step, which signalled the recognition of the environment as a component of development planning. In the Third Plan, the overall philosophy was that the objectives of development and environmental conservation should be "kept in balance, so that the benefits of development are not negated by the costs of environmental damage" (Malaysia, 1976: 218). The first two plans had emphasised infrastructure development, economic growth, and social welfare. Environmental provisions were *ad hoc* and sectoral, relating mainly to water and wildlife. Such legislation included the Fisheries Act, the Continental Shelf Act, the Petroleum Mining Act, the Merchant Shipping Ordinance, the Land Conservation Act and the Local Government Act in the 1960s. Later, sectoral legislation included those for Forestry and the Exclusive Economic Zone.

From 1971 to 1976, which was referred to as the first stage in Malaysia's environmental policy, three policy instruments were adapted to enhance environmental quality (Hezri, 2006). First, the necessary legislation was introduced to enhance environmental quality; second, the setting up of relevant government departments to push the green agenda[1] and finally, the passing of Malaysia's development plans that took into account environmental considerations. To facilitate nationwide policy, the National Forestry Council (NFC) was formed at the federal level in 1971 (Sham Sani, 1993). Also, the Protection of Wildlife Act, an important piece of legislation, was enacted in 1972 (amended 1976 and 1988) that empowered the Department of Wildlife and National Parks (DWNP) to manage wildlife reserves on public as well as private land (within protected areas). The Environmental Quality Act (EQA), passed in 1974, focused on pollution control, provided a legal framework at the federal level and is enforceable throughout the nation. This was followed by administrative innovations such as the Division of the Environment (DOE) which was created under the Ministry of Local Government and Housing in 1975, and upgraded to a department in 1983. A ten member Environmental Quality Council was established in the same year to advise the minister; and the DOE was moved in 1976 to the new Ministry of Science, Technology and the Environment (MOSTE, 2002).

The second stage, 1977–1988, saw a series of crises, followed by legal and administrative consolidation, as short-term economic gain vied with long-term conservation strategies, while environmental impacts escalated. Championing environmental issues, civil society organisations began to voice their concerns, both nationally and internationally. This marked the beginning of environmentalism in Malaysia (Consumer's Association of Penang, 1978; Sham Sani, 1993; Singh, 1992).

More international controversies erupted in the following decade: over logging at Baram-Limbang in Sarawak, vehemently opposed by the Eastern Penan tribe since 1982 (Brosius, 1999);[2] dam construction over the Tembeling River, located within the country's then only national park, Taman Negara; and plans to construct a power-generating dam at Bakun in Sarawak (Aiken and Leigh, 1992: 122–129). Malaysia's image abroad started to suffer, as the Government was blamed for deforestation, while the Government, on its part, branded certain environmental NGOs as "thorns"

---

[1] DOE refers to the Division of the Environment while DWNP refers to the Department of Wildlife and National Parks.
[2] Media coverage of the conflict includes *Newsweek*, *Time*, *The Wall Street Journal*, *CNN* and *NBC*. International figures such as Al Gore and Prince Charles sided with the Penan (see Brosius, 1997, 1999). The controversy forced the Malaysian Government to send promotional teams to Europe to protect its logging interests. Later on, it established the Malaysian Timber Council.

in its side (Singh, 1992; Weiss, 2003). In 1987, the Mahathir government detained without trial several NGO officials under the Internal Security Act. Even though the NGOs involved were working on industrial pollution, forestry, and nuclear power issues, their leaders along with other groups in society were accused of creating political instability. All NGO officials were eventually released, but the crackdown has left an indelible impression on Malaysia's NGOs working on politically sensitive issues (Riker, 1994).

It was not until the Sixth Malaysia Plan (1991–1995) that serious efforts to balance environmental with economic goals in the national development planning process were undertaken by the government. The Sixth Malaysia Plan adopted specific environmental and sustainable development goals. The approach was taken further by the Seventh Malaysia Plan (1996–2000), which promulgated the policy objective of integrating environmental considerations within the economic and development planning process. Significantly, the Seventh Malaysian Plan linked these considerations to the continued sustainability of the economic growth of the country. Economic growth remains paramount as a development objective, but it is also recognised as an important means towards sustainable development.

The government also began to actively encourage public and community involvement in environment management with one of the strategic policy thrusts of the Eighth Malaysia Plan (2001–2005) being "empowering local authorities and engaging local communities in addressing environmental problems". During the Eight Malaysia Plan period, the government "continued to enhance collaboration with relevant NGOs that had the necessary expertise and experience to help implement programmes and activities in specific areas".[3] The working relationship between the government and NGOs has been steadily improving over the years with the government recognising the role of NGOs, especially in providing technical advice as well as generating public awareness and supporting community mobilisation. In fact, the implementation of Local Agenda 21 in Malaysia was spearheaded by one of the environmental groups, Environmental Protection Society Malaysia (EPSM).

Malaysia is also currently reviewing its Ninth Malaysia Plan (2006–2010). Issues related to sustainable development such as population

---

[3]Malaysia has a relatively small but active environmental NGO sector with about 15 environmental NGOs and another 10 NGOs with some environmental activities. NGOs range from professional advisory groups to advocacy or community based groups. The most active environmental groups are Environmental Protection Society Malaysia and Sahabat Alam Malaysia.

distribution, urbanisation, internal migration and development are therefore being addressed. To further improve the efficiency and quality of urban services, a National Urbanisation Policy was formulated in 2006. The policy is to drive and coordinate the planning and development of national urbanisation so that it is more efficient and systematic particularly in managing the increase of urban population in 2020. Emphasis will be on balancing the urban social, economic and physical development. The National Urbanisation Policy will be the main pillar of all planning and urban development activities including preparing advancement programmes at state and local authorities' levels.

It is also noted that the environment was given a high priority in Malaysia's overarching long-term policy objective, Vision, 2020. The National Development Policy (the sequel to the New Economic Policy) stated the need to "ensure that in the pursuit of economic development, adequate attention will be given to the protection of the environment and ecology so as to maintain the long-term sustainability of the country's development" (Malaysia, 1991: 5). It also stated that "Nature and natural resources conservation will also be given priority through a responsible and well-balanced exploitation of natural resources which will safeguard the requirements of future generations" (Malaysia, 1991: 39).

The period from 1989 to 2000 reflects international influence on Malaysian environmental concerns, especially the debate around sustainable development. Earlier, Malaysia had participated in global environmental endeavours such as the United Nations Conference on Human Environment (UNCHE) held in Stockholm in 1972, and signed the 26 principles of the Stockholm Declaration and Action Plan. The publication in 1987 of Our Common Future by the World Commission on Environment and Development resulted in the term sustainable development becoming a powerful concept in public and political discussions (WCED, 1987). Malaysia adopted the concept as central to its national interests and arising from this conference, Local Agenda 21 materialised (LA21, Malaysia, 2002).

Malaysia is also a party to a range of international environmental conventions that provide an important orientation to environmental planning and implementation in Malaysia. Important conventions to which Malaysia is a party are: Convention on Biological Diversity (CBD); Ramsar Convention on Wetlands; Montreal Protocol on Reduction of Ozone Depleting Substances; and the UN Framework Convention on Climate Change (UNFCCC). Other conventions to which Malaysia is a party include the Convention on International Trade in Endangered Species (CITES), Basel Convention on transboundary movement of hazardous wastes. It has also pledged a more active role in managing transboundary environmental problems through the Association of the Southeast Asian Nations (ASEAN).

Regional, non-binding multi-lateral arrangements that Malaysia has endorsed include The Jakarta Resolution and The Manila Summit Declaration in 1987 (Law, 2003: 45). Despite shortcomings, these agreements provided a framework for future transboundary problems in the region. After the publication in 1980 of the World Conservation Strategy by the World Conservation Union (IUCN), the Worldwide Fund for Nature, and the United Nations Environment Programme (UNEP) (Hasan, 1992), Malaysian states were initially positive towards conservation, and strategies were prepared for a total of ten states, funded by the Worldwide Fund for Nature Malaysia (WWFM). However, none of the policy prescriptions were ever implemented.[4]

In sum, it can be said that two major factors influenced Malaysia to seriously embrace sustainable development efforts. The first was the country's growing diplomatic influence. Economic success had earned Malaysia the respect and confidence of the developing world, and as a leader of the Group of 77, Malaysia began to be acknowledged as spokesperson of the South (Taib, 1997; Law, 2003). Malaysia, as Chair of G-77, drafted the Langkawi Declaration on Environment and Development, endorsed by the Members, which incorporates concepts of equitable sharing of responsibilities and benefits, and defines the ability of developing countries to respond to environmental challenges. Another recognition of Malaysia's leadership role is evident with the appointment in 1993 of Malaysia as the founding Chair of the United Nations Commission on Sustainable Development (CSD).

The second factor was the allegation of wanton deforestation, voiced by the international community. The plight of the Penan people in Sarawak was a case in point. The federal Government was caught in a dilemma, as on one hand, forestry was under the jurisdiction of the individual states, and on the other hand, the European market threatened to boycott Malaysian timber, putting the industry in jeopardy. In 1988, the European Parliament decided to suspend all European timber imports from Sarawak (Brosius, 1999: 44). The position of Malaysia was fervently defended by then Prime Minister Dr. Mahathir Mohamed, defining the discourse on "environmental justice", and upholding the right to development of the countries in the South, against the "eco-imperialist" position of wealthy countries of the North.

---

[4]Public pressures on high-profile conflicts between conservation and development, such as that over the Tembeling hydroelectric dam, were more instrumental in shaping the growth of conservation in Malaysia.

Funding

Donor Activities

Compared to other Southeast Asian countries, Malaysia receives a relatively small contribution from the international donor community. The Directorate for External Assistance in the Economic Planning Unit (EPU) coordinates the donor programmes. Donors in the environmental and other sectors are coordinated bilaterally, i.e., there is no common forum for donors, but the coordination works well and there are few cases of overlap or donor programmes not in line with government priorities.

Within the funds received, however, environmental and social activities have been accorded priority. The major donor within the environment and natural resource sector is Japan followed by the Danish Cooperation for Environment and Development (DANCED)[5] and the United Nations Development Programme-Global Environment Facility (UNDP-GEF). Japan supports toxic waste management, cleaner production, energy, waste management, forest management and water resource and supply as well as wastewater treatment projects. The Global Environment Facility has channelled funds through UNDP for a major programme in the energy sector as well as smaller projects relating to bio-diversity (conservation and sustainable management of peat swamp forests and marine parks). UNDP is also supporting some projects with its own resources such as work on better environmental planning and management in the highlands. Other donors with activities in Malaysia include Australia, Canada, the European Union, Germany, U.K. and the U.S. The multi-lateral development assistance agencies such as the World Bank and Asian Development Bank have small programmes in Malaysia. DANCED is providing assistance to Malaysia to support the implementation of international environmental conventions. The assistance places priority on the Rio Conventions and more recent instruments such as the Stockholm Convention on Persistent Organic Pollutants (POPs), the Bio-safety Protocol and the Inter-governmental Forum on Forests. Specific projects include enhancing Malaysia's negotiating

---

[5]The DANCED Programme was launched in 1994 as Denmark's contribution to provide new and additional financial resources to development countries to meet the challenges of sustainable development. DANCED has linked the activities and projects of Malaysia's Country Programme first phase which focused on sustainable management of forests and other critical habitats with bio-diversity conservation in the second phase. The linkage is demonstrated by projects related to implementing Malaysia's National Policy on Biological Diversity on the conservation of wetlands, integrated conservation and development in the Perlis State, and establishing a nature education centre in Johor.

capacity and assessing potential impacts (DANCED, 2000). Unlike previous assistance, which had focused on species and habitat conservation, DANCED formulated a more strategic government-to-government intervention (DANCED-EPU, 2001).

Environmental Expenditure

The environment does not have a separate budget line in the budget system. The budget for MOSTE and a proportion of Federal and State Ministries responsible for natural resource management and administration, pollution control, environmental education and training, research and development could be classified as environmental expenditure. In the Seventh Malaysia Plan, the budget for environment-related development expenditure in Malaysia was estimated to be RM 1.9 billion or about 2% of the RM 83 billion in overall development expenditure. The corresponding figures for expenditure in the social sector such as health and education is RM 6.1 billion and about RM 10 billion respectively. No specific estimate was given for the overall environment-related expenditure in the Eight and Ninth Malaysia Plan, but the allocations for forest management, water resources management all got substantial increases.

Sustainable Development Initiatives

In Malaysia, efforts are being made to ensure that large-scale infrastructure projects not only resolve urban problems but are also integrated into the existing urban landscape in ways that enhances the environment and amenities for the urban community. In addition, the ability to integrate land uses and infrastructure has been shown to provide greater opportunities in business and property development. A number of efforts have been taken by the relevant authorities towards sustainable cities in Malaysia. These include the Petaling Jaya LA21 Programme, Putrajaya Administrative Centre and the Low Carbon Cities Project in the Iskandar Development Region. Two of them are located within the Klang Valley in the state of Selangor, which is the fastest-growing region in Malaysia while the carbon city is located in Johor. They are pioneer model projects and represent milestones in the country's sustainable urban development efforts.

Local Agenda 21 — A Community Programme for Sustainable Development

In 1999, the Government of Malaysia and the UNDP embarked on a two year pilot project in Malaysia to establish a LA21 programme. The pilot programme aims at promoting sustainable development at the local level by creating and strengthening participation between local councils, local communities and the private sector. Selangor was the first to draft a sustainable development strategy toward a more developed state by 2005. The Petaling Jaya City Council adopted the Selangor Sustainable Development Strategies and Selangor Agenda 21 as a guide in formulating its action plans, publicity programme, courses, and training for the Petaling Jaya LA21 programme.[6]

The successful implementation of Petaling Jaya LA 21 pilot projects led to current key ecological projects, such as Kelana Jaya Lake rehabilitation scheme, Stream Keepers Handbook project, and Sungei Penchala Rehabilitation programme. The implementation of these projects illustrates the confidence and strong partnership with various stakeholders as well as funding and support from local groups and international agencies, such as the Danish International Development Agency, Canadian International Development Agency, and UNDP-GEF. Specifically, these projects aim at improving the quality of water from the current standard IV to standard IIB that is suitable for recreational purposes. Strong partnership and active participation can be seen from the involvement of the Section 19 Resident Association in monitoring water quality, launching the State Irrigation and Drainage project of On State-One River Pilot Scheme, and launching environmental brigades by the Malaysian Department of Environment. They demonstrate the workability of community-based participation and development.

However, although LA21 is a novel exercise in sustainability, there are still challenges in carrying out the programme. This is because LA21 depends heavily on community or stakeholder participation for its success. In the case of the Petaling Jaya council, there is lack of participation on behalf of the stakeholders in the programme thus inhibiting the sustainable development initiative to a large extent (Petaling Jaya LA21 Report, 2002).

---

[6]Petaling Jaya is Malaysia's earliest satellite new town. It was planned in the 1950s to alleviate the increasing congestion of the capital city, Kuala Lumpur. It has a total area of 51.4 square kilometres and gained the status of a municipality in 1977. It has developed into an important city in the urban conurbation of Kuala Lumpur with a population of about half a million people governed by the Petaling Jaya Municipality. LA 21 was successfully implemented there in 2000.

Putrajaya — Model City for Sustainable Development

Putrajaya is the new administrative seat of the Malaysian Government, following the Government's decision in June 1993 to relocate the federal administrative capital from Kuala Lumpur to the district of Sepang in Selangor. The relocation is part of the decentralisation effort as well as a means to alleviate traffic congestion in Kuala Lumpur and ensure its continued development as Malaysia's premier business hub. Putrajaya is a model city planned with a strong emphasis on environment protection. The city plans to embrace two main themes: city in a garden and intelligent city. The idea for the establishment of the Malaysian Government administrative centre away from Kuala Lumpur started as early as 1993. Among the main rationales for moving the administrative centre away from Kuala Lumpur were to ensure a quality urban living and environment for the new administrative centre, to relieve the pressure on Kuala Lumpur's over-stretched infrastructure, and to resolve the shortage of Government land to cater to increased demand for office space (Siong, 2006). The construction of Putrajaya commenced in October 1996. By 2005, it had about 80,000 inhabitants, with modern and smart public amenities and infrastructure. Putrajaya is equipped with a good inter- and intra-city transport system, including monorail and water taxis, a broadband global multimedia communication platform, and a common utility tunnel for services, hospitals, and schools. About 38% of the land is being developed into parkland. Putrajaya has the largest man-made wetland in Malaysia with a total area of about 160 hectares (ha), which is used for recreational activities as well as scientific and biological research. Putrajaya is the country's largest urban development project on a greenfield site, set to be a model city for sustainable development.

The intention is to build a city that reflects the natural and cultural heritage of the country with the capacity and amenities to meet the challenges of the millennium (Perbadanan Putrajaya and Putrajaya Holdings Sdn Bhd, 1999: 13). The development is in two phases over a period of 15 years [Phase 1 (1996–2000) and Phase 2 (2000–2010)]. Putrajaya Holdings Sdn Bhd, the developer of the township, was incorporated in 1995. Perbadanan Putrajaya was incorporated (1996) as the body to administer and manage Putrajaya (Perbadanan Putrajaya, 1997).

An already completed development within the Putrajaya administrative area is the Putrajaya Lake and Wetlands, which is in the heart of the city and is a critical component of the project. Built to demonstrate the benefits of incorporating the wetlands eco-system into an urban area, Putrajaya Wetlands is next discussed as a best practice in sustainability. The key environment-friendly solution of constructing the wetlands is to treat catchment water before it enters the Putrajaya Lake, thus ensuring that the water in Putrajaya Lake remains clean and unpolluted. The 197 hectare Putrajaya Wetlands is one of the largest freshwater wetlands in the tropics (Perbadanan Putrajaya and Putrajaya Holdings Sdn Bhd, 1999). It is Malaysia's first such project and represents a milestone in its urban development.

Implementation of Putrajaya Wetlands

Central to the development objective of Putrajaya as a model city of sustainable development is the concept of a city in a garden. The planners incorporated nature through greening programmes and created Putrajaya Lake as an integral part of the urban development concept. The 400 hectares Putrajaya Lake, created by damming two rivers, River Chuau and River Bisa, forms the centerpiece and distinctive identity of the new city. Studies of the Putrajaya catchment revealed the presence of increased pollutant levels in water from upstream sources and outside the city's development boundary. Sustaining the long-term urban development of the wetlands is proposed with the aim to create a self-sustaining and balanced eco-system in Putrajaya (Perbadanan Putrajaya and Putrajaya Holdings Sdn Bhd, 1999: 37). The Putrajaya Lake is a constructed wetland with man-made systems that involve altering the existing terrain to simulate natural wetland conditions.

The Putrajaya Wetlands has been constructed to remove pollutants from the catchment before it enters the lake. A series of wetlands is to be constructed to filter and clean the water that enters the lake. As with many other development projects, the Putrajaya Wetlands showcase predominantly Malaysian resources. The Putrajaya wetlands management has also implemented an extensive public education programme to foster greater community awareness and participation in environmental conservation. With the wetlands' construction, Putrajaya Lake and its environs have altered from a terrestrial plantation of palm oil and rubber into a marsh of aquatic plants (in the wetlands itself) and banks of riparian and littoral vegetation (Perbadanan Putrajaya and Putrajaya Holdings Sdn Bhd, 1999: 107). It has become an important part of the green corridor linking Putrajaya to the surrounding forest reserves.

The Putrajaya Wetlands project illustrates the benefits of incorporating wetland eco-systems into urban development. It demonstrates how a country with vision, determination, and planning may draw inspiration from nature to solve an urban problem, which is not just of local but also of global significance. As former Malaysian prime minister, Dr. Mahathir Mohamed said: "We call upon the global community to target at least 30% of the earths' terrestrial area to be greened by the year 2000. The greening of the world will hopefully inspire a new spirit of international cooperation and partnership in which global resources are fairly shared. If successful, we would have solved, at least partially, an important environmental problem" (Perbadanan Putrajaya and Putrajaya Holdings Sdn Bhd, 1999: 11).

Low-Carbon Cities — The Case of the Iskandar Development Region

With more than 3.2 billion people living in the cities for the first time, the world urban population now exceeds the number of people living in rural areas (Sandrasagra, 2007). By the year 2030, it is expected that over 60% of the world's population will be living in towns and cities (UN, 2002). These urban environments are responsible for over 70% of overall carbon emissions. Hence, in order to tackle the issue of carbon emissions, there is a need for global and national strategies for sustainability in urban environments — in both existing and new developments, and from inception to occupation.

As a responsible developing country, Malaysia attaches great importance to the issue of climate change, and has taken several initiatives to reduce carbon emissions and promote energy efficiency. One such approach taken by the government is the idea of introducing low-carbon cities in the South Johor Economic Region (SJER), which is commonly known as the Iskandar Development Region (IDR). IDR is one of the economic growth centres to be developed as an integrated global node of Singapore and Indonesia.[7]

There are three main policies as stated in the master plan for IDR that is known as the Comprehensive Development Plan for South Johor Economic Region, 2006–2025 (hereinafter referred as "CDP"), which have a direct

---

[7]The development region encompasses an area about three times the size of Singapore and two times the size of Seoul Metropolitan Area. IDR covers the entire district of Johor Bahru and several sub-districts (mukim) of Pontian. The IDR covers an area of about 2,216.3 kilometres.

impact on the low-carbon scenario of the IDR development. Among these polices are energy efficient building, sustainable land-use and transportation and natural and green environment.

Energy Efficient Building and Sustainable Neighbourhood Design

In creating liveable communities, energy efficient building and sustainable design guidelines are proposed in the IDR. In order to encourage builders to build energy efficient buildings, the "green building rating" will be used for residential units, and to introduce energy efficient mechanisms on older or existing buildings in the city. Green building is the practice of creating healthier and more resource-efficient models of construction, renovation, operation, maintenance and demolition. Sustainable neighbourhood design will be used and implemented to encourage developers to plan neighbourhood with self-contained facilities to reduce the use of private vehicles and hence reduce fuel consumption and carbon dioxide emission. One of the key thrusts of the IDR is to create liveable communities that encompass quality housing, adequate facilities, quality services and a healthy, safe and lively environment. To this end, the CDP plans not only for the current needs of the population but also for the future, ensuring that inter-generational equity is also sensitively addressed.

Sustainable Land-Use and Transportation

Land-use planning helps to integrate environmentally sustainable development concepts by promoting mixed land-use and public transport (non-motorized vehicles) and compact city development. The use of zoning district systems (base zoning district and special overlay zones) allow appropriate and compatible mixed use development by combining retail/service use with residential or office use in the same building or on the same site which can help to reduce in between space movement. Hence, it can also reduce fuel consumption and carbon dioxide emission. Transit Planning Zones is also introduced in city centres such as within Johor Bahru City Centre and Nusajaya City Centre to promote a combination of commercial and housing on the same site. It allows developments with increased intensity especially the residential component. This aims to support the strategy of encouraging city living and transit oriented development. Transit Planning Zone is an area within a 400 metre radius of rail stations where transit oriented development can be pursued. This form of development will help to promote the use of rail transport. In addition, incentives are also given to encourage sustainable pattern of urban regeneration development through Brownfield development in the existing urban centers of Johor Bahru, Senai and Skudai. It provides a broad range of uses and is intensified in terms of commercial plot ratio and densities to reflect its role as the centre of administration, business, commerce, and employment of IDR and the new growth centre within the Special Economic Corridor (SEC). This high-density development will provide critical mass to support vibrant activity.

Natural and Green Environment

The natural and green environment in IDR covers a total of more than 150,000 hectares of green spaces. This include RAMSAR site (9,483 hectares), Pulai State Park (5,570 hectares), regional park (3,178 hectares), district park (1,514 hectares), town park (941 hectares) and local parks (204 hectares) as well as the agriculture areas. All these green spaces will play an important role as a carbon sink for this region. RAMSAR site is a wetland of international importance which is rare and unique and for conserving bio-diversity. The three RAMSAR sites in IDR are Pulau Kukup, Sungai Pulai and Tanjung Piai, which are Rank 1 Environmental Sensitive Areas (ESA). Other green space accessible to the public include the private open space (POS) such as golf courses. There are also substantial areas in IDR still under the category of agriculture, predominantly palm oil plantations. Some of the areas are classified as Environmental Protection Zone where it requires further environmental control by virtue of their identification as ESAs. In addition, water catchment zones (catchments of Sultan Iskandar Dam) is a Rank 1 ESA and needs to be protected. All activities within the water catchment zone must be controlled and no industrial activities should be allowed.

Challenges in Achieving Sustainable Development

Complex Federal-State Relationship

The implementation of nationwide environmental policies is hampered by federalism. Notwithstanding commitments to sustainable development by the federal Government, wanton environmental destruction is still evident in some of the states. Jomo *et al.* (2004: 226) suggest that, despite the federal Government's "official acknowledgement of the situation, there are few indications that there is political will to directly tackle issues of patronage, low rent capture and forest abuse". There is arguably a degree of indifference on the part of powerful decision-making bodies at the state level vis-à-vis environmental protection, in favour of economic and social development. States continue to invest in economic projects with minimal consideration of the environment. Moreover, the federal system presents a significant challenge to integrated resource management as the Constitution grants each state control over its own land use. Although the federal Government has the authority to acquire state land, states may convert naturally forested areas for agriculture, mining, industry, settlements, or other uses (Hezri, 2006).

The Constitution allocates jurisdiction and competence between the federal and state governments, making institutional coordination and the implementation of policies particularly challenging. While federal government agencies are responsible for formulating and overseeing general environmental policy, state governments have jurisdiction over natural resources, including land, water and forests. The federal-state relationship is further complicated by a provision allowing for the governments to share legislative competence, such as is the case for wildlife protection. However, the Federal Parliament may enact legislation on behalf of the states, provided that they give their consent and that uniformity and harmony in the law and its implementation necessitate such action (DANCED, 2000). The complex relations imposed by the Constitution thus require federal agencies to engage in close consultation — if not directly invite — state governments in the process of drafting laws and policies.

Integration in Theory and Practice

There is as yet no all-government reform agenda for sustainable development. An earlier intent to establish a National Council for the Environment did not materialise. In retrospect, more effective policies for sustainability could have been formulated had the momentum of the pre- and post-United Nations Conference on Environment and Development (UNCED) meetings been sustained by a concrete institutional framework. Most policy changes have been incremental and remain somewhat marginal. Moreover, the regulatory capacity (staffing-level) to address goals formulated in stage one such as environmental conservation and pollution control, has only recently been established.

Lack of a Coherent Institutional Framework

The institutional framework in Malaysia is sectorally-structured; meaning that the administration of natural resources and environmental protection is dealt with, sector-by-sector, by many agencies in various Ministries. Within the Federal government alone, some 20 agencies can be said to have some environment-related function or responsibility. Responsibilities for water, land, agriculture, forestry and wildlife are spread out among the Federal Ministries and various State level agencies. The institutional framework for environmental planning and management is therefore complex, involving both Federal and State agencies. A functional development planning system with a long tradition runs the risk of being monolithic and resistant to change. In the interests of policy integration, there have been proposals in various forums for the incorporation of environmental considerations into all chapters of the Malaysia plans (Hasan,1992). Current practice regards the environment and natural resource management as a separate sector and chapter within the Malaysia plans.

Lack of Community Participation in Sustainable Development Programmes

Programmes such as LA21 have been set up to encourage community participation in achieving sustainable development. In the case of LA21 in Malaysia, there has been a lack of community participation in LA21 programmes at the local level (Petaling Jaya LA21 Report, 2002). More efforts have not been made by the relevant authorities to enhance the role of the stakeholders in the programme. An independent evaluation of the implementation of Agenda 21 in Malaysia for the World Summit of Sustainable Development (WSSD) by a consortium of non-governmental organisations in Malaysia concluded that: "In essence, the words are in the right place but in truth the actions are not. The commitment and focus to implement sustainable development practices is not forthcoming" (MNF for Rio+10, 2003).

The Role of Normative Change

Malaysia's lack of political commitment to sustainable development originates with the ideological stance of former Prime Minister Dr. Mahathir Mohamed, who believed the concept was espoused by some developed countries for "eco-imperialistic" ends. Given the predominance of the executive, this view was pervasive and thwarted proposals for an all-government reform (Brosius, 1999).

Lack of Effective Environmental Planning

A key issue is the lack of effective environmental planning despite the introduction of Environmental Impact Assessment and similar procedures. Policies, strategies, legislation and enforcement are inadequate. The land management system encourages environmental degradation by making conversion from forest and agricultural to urban or industrial land one of the main sources of revenue for developers and local governments alike. There is still insufficient awareness of the long-term costs and problems associated with unsustainable development and environmental degradation.

Environmental management is also relatively new as a political priority. Consequently, sufficient capacity and technical capability within enforcement and other environment-related agencies still need to be built up.

As with many other Asian countries, Malaysia is rapidly urbanising. Beyond meeting the services that are required of all city governments, some key challenges facing Malaysian urban development concern the increased size of cities in terms of both their population and land usage, which, if not properly managed, will have a far-reaching negative environmental impact. Examples include the massive land conversion of palm oil plantations into mixed housing development (a form of unsustainable greenfield development), low-density urban suburbs, illegal hillside development, and encroachment of wetlands, especially in the form of waterfront or riverfront development. There is a growing awareness that these will not remain isolated local issues.

Conclusion

The Malaysian Government has paid increasing attention to protecting the environment as part of its overall effort to seek innovative ways to build sustainable cities. The three initiatives showcase some of those efforts: community participation in Petaling Jaya LA21 Programme, innovative construction of Putrajaya wetlands and the reduction of carbon dioxide emissions in the Iskandar region. They are primarily aimed at making cities better for all who live, work, do business, and play in them. They provide examples of the public-led national processes and approaches that are being implemented at various levels from local to metropolitan and regional to meet existing concerns and challenges.

What is most important is that there is no turning back in regard to sustainable development. Recent efforts of government agencies, especially by the Federal Town and Country Planning Department and local authorities to develop innovative models of city building such as Putrajaya and Low-Carbon cities have led the way in demonstrating the urban possibilities in utilising ecological solutions. Partnership between the different levels of government and inclusiveness appear to be yet another immediate strategic area of policy action. Active and effective participation at the neighbourhood level involving different stakeholders offers new directions for consolidating community-based action. It presents relevant options for achieving not just economic sustainability, but also social justice and equity, which are important in identifying urban solutions tailored as closely as possible to peoples' needs.

References

Afroz, R., M.N. Hassan and N.A. Ibrahim. (2003). "Review of Air Pollution and Health Impacts in Malaysia." *Environmental Research*, 92: 71–77.

Aiken, S.R. and C.H. Leigh. (1992). *Vanishing Rain Forests: The Ecological Transition in Malaysia.* New York: Oxford University Press.

Aini, M.S., A. Fakhrul-Razi and K.S. Suan. (2001). "Water Crisis Management: Satisfaction Level, Effect and Coping of the Consumers." *Water Resources Management*, 15: 31–39.

Brosius, J.P. (1999). "Green Dots, Pink Hearts: Displacing Politics from the Malaysian Rain Forest." *American Anthropologist*, 101: 36–57.

Consumer's Association of Penang. (1978). *The Malaysian Environment in Crisis: Selections from Press Cuttings.* Penang: Consumer's Association of Penang.

Danish Cooperation for Environment and Development (DANCED). (2000). "Malaysia-Danish Country Programme for Environmental Assistance 1998–2000." Danish Environmental Protection Agency, Ministry of Environment and Energy, Copenhagen.

DANCED-EPU. (2001). "Malaysian Danish Country Programme for Cooperation in Environment and Sustainable Development (2002–2006)." Danish Cooperation for Environment and Development, and The Economic Planning Unit, Prime Minister's Department, Kuala Lumpur.

Law, H.D. (2003). "Environmental Governance in Malaysia: Insights and Reflections." Department of Environment, Kuala Lumpur.

Hasan, M.N. (1992). "Environmental Management as a Strategy for Sustainable Development." In *Malaysia's Economic Vision: Issues and Challenges*, H.Y. Teh and K.L. Goh (eds.), pp. 421–437. Kuala Lumpur: Pelanduk Publications.

Hezri, A A. and Mohd. Nordin Hasan. (2006). "Towards Sustainable Development? The Evolution of Environmental Policy in Malaysia." *Natural Resources Forum*, 30: 37–50.

Jomo, K.S., Y.T. Chang and K.J. Khoo. (2004). *Deforesting Malaysia: The Political Economy and Social Ecology of Agricultural Expansion and Commercial Logging.* London: Zed Books and UNRISD.

Ministry of Housing and Local Government. (2002). "Local Agenda 21, Malaysia."

Malaysia. (1991). *The Second Outline Perspective Plan, 1991–2000.* Kuala Lumpur: National Printing Department.

MNF for Rio+10. (2003). *NGO Perspectives for Advancing Sustainable Development in Malaysia. Review of Agenda 21 Implementation in Malaysia.* Kuala Lumpur: Malaysian NGO Forum for Rio+10.

MOSTE. (2002). *National Policy on the Environment.* Kuala Lumpur: Ministry of Science, Technology and the Environment.

Perbadanan Putrajaya. (1997). *"Putrajaya — Review of the Master Plan."*

Perbadanan Putrajaya and Putrajaya Holding. (1999). "Putrajaya Wetlands, Petaling Jaya."

Petaling Jaya Municipal Council (MPPJ). (2002). "Local Agenda 21 Petaling Jaya."

Sandrasagra, Mitre J. (2007). "Climate Change: Cities Getting Serious about CO_2 Emissions." *Inter Press News.* http://www.psnews.net/news.asp?idnews= 37765.

Sham, Sani. (1993). "Economic Development and Environmental Management in Malaysia." *New Zealand Geographer*, 49: 64–68.

Singh, G. (1992). "Case Studies of Environmental Awareness in Malaysia." *Nature and Resources*, 28: 30–37.

Siong, Ho Chin. (2006). "Lessons Learned from Planning of Putrajaya City — Administrative Centre of Malaysia." Seminar UTM-SIT workshop at Shibaura Institute, Japan.

Taib, F.M. (1997). *Malaysia and UNCED, An Analysis of a Diplomatic Process 1989–1992.* London: Kluwer Law International.

UN World Urbanization Prospects. (2002). *The 2001 Revision.* New York: United Nations.

WCED. (1987). *World Commission on Environment and Development: Our Common Future.* New York, NY: Oxford University Press.

Weiss, M.L. (2003). "Malaysian NGOs: History, Legal Frameworks and Characteristics." In M.L. Weiss and S. Hassan (eds.), Social Movements in Malaysia: From Moral Communities to NGOs, 39. London: Routledge Curzon.

CHAPTER 9

Prospects on Ecological Development in Philippine Cities

Marife M. BALLESTEROS*

The Philippine government vision on eco-city development is embodied in the country's Strategy for Sustainable Development Report which was formally adapted in November 1989. This Strategy adheres to the view that economic growth and environmental protection are compatible. It provides eight basic strategies to attain environmental protection and sustainable development. However, while the strategies are excellent, the implementation of ecological initiatives can be found wanting. The challenges to eco-city building as exemplified in the development of the Quezon City Central Business District show that institutions play a key role in the success of ecological initiatives. The poor enforcement of property rights and the inefficient land administration and management in the country have impeded access to land markets and hampered efforts at resource management. Similarly, political considerations at the national and local levels can significantly distort incentive systems.

Introduction

Economic growth has been mainly occurring in cities and this trend is expected to accelerate in the next millennium. However, cities have also been deteriorating as human habitats due to pressures of growth on resources. From the Philippine perspective, the pattern of city growth is similar across all regions. Rapid urbanisation resulted in the conversion of agricultural land to residential, commercial and industrial use. Informal settler communities have proliferated and with poor urban planning

---

*Marife M. Ballesteros is a Senior Research Fellow at the Philippine Institute for Development Studies, a government think-tank based in Manila.

and management, cities are faced with intractable and often interrelated problems of inadequate mass transportation and road systems; pollution, inadequate and inappropriate waste disposal; flooding; inadequate and unsustainable shelter; water shortage; deterioration of sanitation, health and other basic services.

Ecological city development in the country is thus a formidable task. The process of rebuilding and urban renewal is a major undertaking as much as the need for better urban planning and management. The key urban concerns as defined in the Philippine strategy for sustainable development and urban development agenda are the following: 1) traffic and the high cost of moving people; 2) pollution from industrial effluents; 3) solid waste disposal by domestic, commercial and industrial establishments; 4) air pollution from gasoline/diesel fuelled vehicles and industrial establishments; and 5) influx of population to large metropolitan centres.

Addressing these concerns at an integrated level has been difficult mainly due to weak governance at the national and local levels. There are also property rights issues on natural resources which further constraint ecological initiatives. Often actions on wastewater management, solid waste disposal or pollution management take place at the individual or community level. There is an apparent difficulty for an integrated and bigger scale, city or provincial level actions. The reason may not be so much due to the greater resources needed or that several stakeholders are involved but more so to the failure of institutions in the country.

The purpose of this paper is to identify and assess the key institutional issues that hinder the development of ecological cities in the Philippines. While there are several noteworthy ecological projects of government that address specific urban problems mentioned earlier, we present the proposed development of a model urban central business district (CBD) in Metro Manila to illustrate the effects of failure of institutions. The Quezon City CBD (QC-CBD) is an initial effort towards building ecological cities that is intended to address urban concerns — e.g., traffic, pollution, waste management — through physical planning.

The paper is organised as follows. The second section provides an overview of the Philippine strategy on sustainable development. The third section describes the Philippine urban system and ecological problems in cites. The fourth section presents the major urban projects with focus on the development of the QC-CBD. The fifth section is a discussion and analysis of the development challenges faced in the implementation of QC-CBD. The last section concludes the findings of the paper.

Philippine Agenda on Sustainable Development

The Philippines has been pursuing its active involvement in the arena of environment and sustainable development through, among others, the implementation of Agenda 21 which is a collaborative undertaking with the United Nations and other international organisations. Furthermore, the Philippines is also continuing the implementation of its obligations under other international environmental agreements.

The overall strategy and operational framework to implement Agenda 21 and other environment agreements is embodied in the Philippine Strategy for Sustainable Development (PSSD) of 1989 which was crafted through a series of consultations with different sectors of society through the initiative of the Department of Environment and Natural Resources (DENR).

The PSSD stresses the need to view environmental protection and economic growth as mutually compatible. This implies that economic growth can be achieved with adequate protection of the country's biological resources and its diversity, vital eco-system functions, and overall environmental quality. The core strategies to attain this goal are as follows:[1]

Integration of Environmental Considerations in Decision-Making

The basic strategy in sustainable development is for economic and environmental concerns to be addressed simultaneously in the planning/decision-making process. Moreover, policy and plan exercises have to be pursued via a multi-sectoral approach. This is a deliberate shift from the conventional practice characterised as predominantly single sector planning exercises. The importance of pursuing a multi-sectoral approach in policy and plan formulation can never be overstated. For instance, policies that conserve the quality of agricultural land and protect forests improve the long-term prospects for agricultural development. Efficiency in the utilisation of energy and raw materials in industrial processes reduces wastes and can also reduce costs.

Merging environmental and economic considerations in decision-making involves a fundamental re-alignment of the overall objectives of development planning in the light of a new awareness of the environmental implications of

---

[1]This section is mainly based on the PSSD document, www.psdn.org.ph [March 30, 2009].

development activities. This means that the process of development should be viewed from the outset as a multi-purpose undertaking that includes an explicit and defined concern for the quality of the environment. Within such a planning context, it is especially important that analysis and evaluation stress the key role that environmental quality can play in sustainable development.

To effectively implement this desired shift in economic decision-making, the refinement of analytical tools and methodologies is critical. For instance, to accommodate the social and environmental consequences of the misuse of the nation's natural capital in economic calculations, such tools as Natural Resource Accounting, Environmental Impact Assessment (EIA) and Land Use Planning must be properly installed and strengthened.

Natural resource accounting emphasises the productive role of natural resources in the economic system. Natural resource assets must be valued in the same manner as man-made assets. Inasmuch as natural resources are principally the main assets upon which we depend for revenue, employment and foreign exchange, a system of national accounting and analysis must be instituted that recognises them as such.

Like economic analysis and engineering feasibility studies, EIA is a management tool for officials, managers and affected citizens who must make important decisions about major development projects. In recent years, major development undertakings have encountered serious difficulties because insufficient account has been taken of their impacts on the surrounding environment. Some projects have been found to be unsustainable because they caused resource depletion. Others have been abandoned because of public opposition, financial encumbrance due to unforeseen costs, very high liability for damages to natural resources, and the disastrous accidents they have caused.

Given this experience, it is clearly very risky to approve and finance a major project without first taking into account its environmental consequences, as well as, the silting and project design considerations that will minimise, or better still, altogether remove adverse impacts.

At the local/regional level, Land Use Planning is also seen as a basic tool for incorporating environmental considerations in the decision-making process. Optional land-use allocations can be determined using an environmental quality perspective, which take into account ecological principles and the impact of human activities on natural systems as inputs, along with other economic and social demands.

Proper Pricing of Natural Resources

This strategy recognises that to improve resource management, natural resources have to be treated as truly scarce, not as if they were free. This is done by proper pricing based on the cost of replenishment, increasing their supply and providing appropriate substitutes. In essence, this strategy aims to correct the gross underpricing of natural resources (e.g., logs, minerals) that is largely responsible for the wasteful extraction and utilisation of these resources.

The question of who pays for damages to the environment is a key area for policy reform. It has become obvious that natural resources such as timber and minerals are grossly underpriced.[2] They also share with the rest of society very little of the "rents" they get out of exploiting these resources ("rent" represents the surplus after all cost and reasonable profits are paid). The rents from the exploitation of natural resources are huge, and they have gone to only a few. The World Resources Institute, for example, has estimated that for the Philippines, only 20% of the more than P20 billion rents from logs harvested from 1979 and 1982 went to the Philippine government. To attain sustainability, a key area of reform is for government to recover the full economic rent for natural and environmental resources.

A component of this price reform strategy involves charging a price on those environmental resources (e.g., air, water) which have until now been regarded as free resources and which have thus been polluted freely and indiscriminately. At present, polluters continue to view the environment as a mere sink, for which they pay nothing. The Philippines government intends to change this concept. A social price should be assigned to these otherwise free resources. The polluter must then learn to internalise this price within his profit-oriented decision-making process. If there is pollution, the polluter must pay for the consequent social costs. The choice can be made between cutting down on pollution by investing in pollution control devices or cutting down directly on pollutive aspects of an activity. In effect, the polluter regulates his own behaviour within the context of an environmental pricing system. The system is based on the so-called "polluter pays" principle.

Relevant to the successful implementation of such pricing mechanisms is the development of capabilities in environmental economics and the conduct

---

[2]Underpriced means that those given the right to exploit these resources for profit pay very little of the significant damage costs to society.

of measures in this field. In addition, there is a need to set up support funds and incentives for those willing to shift from pollutive or destructive technologies to those that are environmentally protective.

Property Rights Reform

Natural resources have a tendency to be exploited as free resources by individuals even though they are in effect scarce resources. This is the case for "open access" resources in which there are strong tendencies for misuse and depletion. It is difficult for an individual producer such as a shifting cultivator or an artisanal fisherman to conserve an open access resource and unilaterally regulate his exploitative efforts, since from his perception anything that he conserves will only be taken up by others. This is the famous "tragedy of the commons".

The Philippines government plans to achieve self-regulation in the exploitation of natural resources by assigning secure access rights perhaps even private ownership over these resources to responsible individuals and communities. Through secure access rights, the individual or community establishes a lasting tie with the resource and a long-term stake in its protection for sustained productivity.

Among the creative and secure instruments being developed are forest stewardship contracts, small-holder timber concessions, artificial reef licenses, community forests, community fishing grounds and mining cooperatives to ensure equitable access and tenurial security in the utilisation of natural resources. It has to be noted, however, that an essential condition for transferring control over resources or distributing resource rights is for recipient individuals or communities to demonstrate the capacity for the sustainable development of such resources.

Property rights reform in the area of land administration is also undertaken. Land information is an important resource and efficient land information system is needed for an effective management of land resources and property rights enforcement.

Establishment of an Integrated Protected Areas System

This strategy stresses the importance of the preservation of the variety of genes, species, and eco-systems. Eco-systems are composed of species, and species are composed of genes and all these are linked to one another. The stability of eco-systems ultimately depends on the diversity of genes and species. Unfortunately, this is not generally recognised in the country.

The establishment of protected areas for the conservation of wildlife and unique eco-systems for the purpose of conserving genetic resources for scientific, educational, cultural and historical values are contained in several laws. As an initial step towards protected areas, the Philippines government will implement a re-assessment of the status of parks and equivalent reserves. This will serve as the basis for developing rehabilitative strategies for degraded parks and at the same time identify new areas where conservation of genetic resources and preservation of bio-diversity can be pursued.

Rehabilitation of Degraded Eco-systems

Rehabilitation of degraded eco-systems is a significant strategy given the massive destruction of eco-systems that has already occurred. Under such conditions, nature's regenerative capacity is not enough. Deliberate rehabilitative efforts are needed.

Rehabilitation must keep pace with the continuous degradation caused by the increasing demands for both raw materials and products that come from natural resources. As the pressures on these resources continue to intensify, the greater the need for the country's commitment and capability for rehabilitative action. A concerted action of a magnitude never tried before in the reforestation of denuded watersheds, mangrove replantation, clean-up and control of pollution and revival of biologically dead rivers, and seagrass transplantation is a priority area to be vigorously undertaken.

Natural eco-systems, however, will continue to be threatened unless a more comprehensive programme on eco-systems rehabilitation is undertaken. Rehabilitation has to be linked to eco-systems protection programmes and to policy reforms and institutional strengthening that decisively deal with the socio-economic roots of eco-system degradation.

Strengthening of Residuals Management in Industry (Pollution Control)

The most commonly applied instrument for pollution control is "end-of-pipe" control systems that treat or attempt to limit waste products with standards and limits on the permissible emissions rate. Residuals management, however, looks at the pollution problem within a more comprehensive framework of materials policy which includes resource recovery, recycling, and appropriate by product design that save on materials and energy.

The move to be undertaken is towards adopting recent innovations in industrial process designs which are aimed at reducing waste streams, especially as increasing restrictions on disposal becomes more necessary. Reformulating products, developing saleable by-products from residuals, and re-designing or combining processes are some innovations that have often been found to reduce wastes and costs as well. The use of bio-gas digesters to recover methane from piggery or distillery wastes is another example of pollution reduction through technological innovations.

Resource recovery is also a strategy that can be adopted in the country and may prove highly economical because materials and energy costs are quite high relative to labour costs. Paper, glass, metals, plastics, oils and other materials could be recovered from waste streams and recycled by networks of workers.

In addition to and in support of technological innovations is the strengthening of enforcement of appropriate pollution control laws. Other policy instruments such as the use of economic incentives to encourage pollutive firms to install pollution control facilities and collective actions such as the installation of central collection and treatment facilities for wastewater are needed to supplement current enforcement efforts. These are especially important given the relatively small capital base of enterprises involved. More conciliatory forms of pollution regulation involving persuasion and information dissemination aimed at altering polluter as well as end-consumer behaviour are among the schemes to be implemented to effect positive change in business attitudes towards the environment.

Integration of Population Concerns and Social Welfare in Development Planning

Population is the critical factor in sustainable development. Population and the values espoused determine the speed at which productivity can be increased or conversely the pressures on land and natural resources brought to bear by the process of development. For a developing country like the Philippines, it is important that the population factor — in all its dimensions — is turned into a real asset for building a strong industrial base, for multiplying productive forms of livelihood, and for preserving and improving fragile eco-systems and the overall natural resource environment.

The country's population programme will not be limited to controlling numbers but will include improvements in health, education and values formation. It must be implemented as part of a comprehensive socio-economic programme at the regional and community levels. The population programme will be based on methods that are consistent with the cultural and religious norms of the population. Within our traditional rural society the benefits of additional labour will always outweigh the benefits of reducing family size. It is for this reason that our population policies recognise the limitations of promoting fertility control in isolation from other incentives.

Managing population distribution and mobility is being considered to limit the rapid and often uncontrolled population growth in urban areas. Promotion of programmes and policies that lead to balanced regional development are important. The development potential of all regions is assessed and programmes to increase opportunities for livelihood will be implemented to encourage migration towards less densely populated and less environmentally sensitive areas.

Inducing Growth in the Rural Areas

Economic recovery and long-term stability depend on increasing incomes and employment in the rural areas, where a majority of our people reside. The rural poor are linked very closely to natural resources. Their actions have a direct impact on natural resources. Conversely, any change in the actual and potential productivity of these resources has serious repercussions on their present and future welfare, even on their very survival. The sheer number of rural poor already in place right on or beside fragile ecosystems makes them a formidable force either for environmental destruction or protection.

Attention on rural development is given importance, as it has already been established that poverty forces the rural poor to be destroyers rather than caring towards the very resources that can liberate them from poverty. The economic, social and political potentials of the countryside will be harnessed to alleviate poverty and uplift the conditions of the rural poor.

Promotion of Environmental Education

Environmental education as conceived in the PSSD has two major objectives. The first is to enable citizens to understand and appreciate the complex nature of the environment, as well as the role played by a properly managed environment in economic development and to develop social values that are strongly supportive of environmental protection and which will create the commitment and political will to deal with difficult issues. A well-informed and motivated citizenry will provide the mass base necessary for the continued protection of the environment.

Decisions are ultimately a political responsibility, but the likelihood of the best choices being made is greatly enhanced when there is widespread knowledge and understanding of all aspects of the issues at hand. This could be achieved by integrating environmental concepts in the elementary and secondary schools. This will equip people with the basic capability to make up their own minds in an informed way and may even prompt them to do something positive to help protect the environment.

The second objective is to develop the local knowledge base about the local environment and natural resources through the development and promotion of tertiary and graduate courses in ecology, environmental science, resource management and resource economics. Research and development in these areas will be promoted.

Strengthening of Citizens' Participation and Constituency Building

Lessons from both failures and successes in environmental and developmental efforts have shown that citizens' participation is an important decisive factor. Absence or lack of it has caused failures. Its active presence has resulted not only in efforts meeting immediate targets but also in the assured sustainability of positive trends that have been initiated.

People have the inherent capacity to improve themselves and their community. Problems confronting them can be solved through their own efforts. In cases where the poverty of their situation and the difficulties they face are too serious for them to deal with, initial assistance from government and non-government institutions may be needed. Their active participation in planning and implementation is important so they have less dependence on external support.

In promoting the active participation of the citizenry for sustainable development, non-government organisations (NGOs) can be the central vehicle in mobilising people to participate. NGOs have certain advantages. They have less bureaucratic red tape and can thus move fast. They have already established strong direct links with the grassroots. Their members are the very citizens whose participation is needed and who see their NGO membership as a citizen's responsibility. They are thus imbued with the needed commitment and drive to deal with difficult sustainable development issues. A strategy in this regard is to develop a network among NGOs as well as NGOs and governmental organisations which will work on community organising, public information campaigns, research/situation assessment, environmental surveillance and monitoring, science and appropriate technology and the like.

While the PSSD's underlying themes are leaning towards rural development, the core strategies recognise rural-urban interdependence.

The Philippine Urban Eco-system

The Philippines is one of the fastest urbanising countries in Asia. In 1980, 37.2% of its population was urban. By 2005, total urban population reached 53 million, representing over 60% of the country's total population. It is estimated that by 2030, 75% of its total population will be urban with three out of every four individuals living in towns and cities less than 20 years from today (Fig. 1).

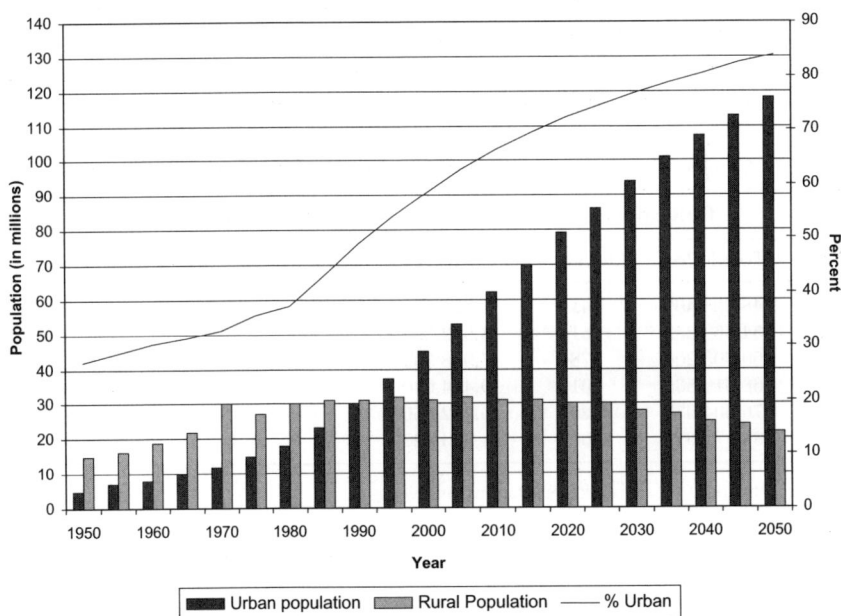

Source: UN World Urbanisation Prospects, The 2007 Revision.

Fig. 1 Urban and Rural Population Growth.

The distribution of population across regions shows the dominance of the Metro Manila region. Metro Manila has been 100% urban since the 1960s, comprising 11.5 million individuals as of 2007 or 13% of total Philippine population. The population in the metropolitan area is growing at an annual rate of 2.1% higher than the national average growth rate. The primacy of Metro Manila as a settlement area is also reflected in its population density. There are more than 18,000 people per square kilometre in the city, three times that of the city-state of Singapore and more than 60 times the national average (Table 1).

Metro Manila continues to dominate the urban hierarchy and domestic economy. It represents the largest concentration of consumers in Southeast Asia (i.e., in concentration not purchasing power). By 2015, it is expected to become the 15th largest city in the world.[3]

However, with greater concentration, critical problems of large urban areas emerge. One of these problems has to do with traffic and the high cost of moving people. In Metro Manila, for instance, there were more than 1.5 million registered vehicles in 2006, representing close to 30% of the total number of registered vehicles in the country. In the meantime, no new high capacity transit facilities (e.g., LRT, MRT, BRT) have been added to the system since the 1990s and road construction has been limited and, generally, has not kept pace with the number of vehicles. For this reason, traffic congestion has become chronic in Metro Manila. As

Table 1   Comparative Population Growth and Density, Philippines and Metro Manila.

	Philippines		Metro Manila		
Year	Total Pop	Density	Population	% Share of Total Pop	Density
1980	48,098,460	141	5,926,000	12	9,565
1985	54,668,332	161	6,942,204	13	11,206
1990	60,703,206	178	7,948,392	13	12,830
1995	68,616,536	201	9,454,040	14	15,260
2000	76,504,077	225	9,932,560	13	16,032
2007	88,574,614	260	11,553,427	13	18,650

Source: Philippine Yearbook (NSO), various years.

---

[3]Webster, Douglas, Arturo Corpuz and Christopher Pablo (2002). "Towards a National Urban Development Framework for the Philippines: Strategic Consideration." Report prepared for the National Economic Development Authority (NEDA), p. 20 and http://www.un.org/esa/population/publications/wup2001/wup2001dh.pdf [January 21 2009].

observed in another study,[4] traffic in Metro Manila moves at an average of 12 kph at peak hours, much slower when compared to such cities as Jakarta (26 kph), Shanghai (25 kph) and Bangkok (21 kph). Overall, efforts to improve transportation systems have been insufficient and sporadic. For instance, the effective urban-industrial heartland of Luzon has remained essentially unchanged since the late 1970s. Recent road extensions and improvements have extended commercial traffic, but these have been more exceptions rather than the rule. These conditions have increased the cost of domestic transportation and limited opportunities for urban growth and regional development.

Another major problem in Metro Manila is air pollution emitted by transport vehicles (60%) and stationary industrial sources (40%). High volume sample measurements of total suspended particulates (TSP) indicate that annual averages can exceed 250 milligrams per cubic meter (mg/m^3), exceeding the U.S. annual average TSP air quality standard by over 200%. Furthermore, jeepney, bus and taxi commuters are exposed to excessive concentrations of Respirable Suspended Particles (RSP) in the order of $1,000 \, mg/m^3$, while millions of Metro Manila residents are exposed to ambient concentrations of RSP in the order of $100 \, mg/m^3$.

Sulfur dioxide (SO_2) does not appear to be a major problem in Metro Manila. There is relatively less concentration of heavy industry near urban centres and consequently the levels of SO_2 measured in Manila are all well below 0.05 parts per million (ppm) on an annual average basis. However, since most of the major vehicles in Metro Manila are diesel-fuelled, the exposure to SO_2 by people directly exposed to traffic exhaust is higher.

The supply of potable water in urban areas is likewise lamentable. In 2004, only about 58% of households in urban areas had access to drinking water.[5] Nationally, just over 20% of urban households have piped water. The situation in urban areas has, however, improved in recent years. Piped water system coverage has increased from 44% in 1993 to 51% in 2003.[6]

The percentage of urban households with connections to wastewater facilities is even smaller. In 2004, only about 7% of urban households were

---

[4]Webster, Douglas, Arturo Corpuz and Christopher Pablo (2002). "Towards a National Urban Development Framework for the Philippines: Strategic Consideration." Prepared for World Bank-NEDA.

[5]http://www.who.int [April 1, 2009].

[6]http://www.who.int [April 1, 2009] and United Nations International Childrens Fund, 2006.

linked to a central sewerage collection system.[7] The overwhelming majority of the urban population relies on septic tanks which are often improperly constructed, or otherwise poorly maintained. In many cases as well, industrial establishments in urban areas have no wastewater treatment resulting in water pollution problems in many parts of the country.

Water pollution is very evident in Metro Manila. It has been reported as early as the 1990s that all four water bodies in the metropolis (Pasig-Marikina, Navotas-Malabon-Tullaban-Tenejeros, Manila Bay, and Laguna Lake) are polluted and considered "biologically" dead except for the upstream portion of Marikina River.

The water pollution is caused by the general public and, to a lesser extent, by the industrial sector. All metropolitan areas in the Philippines have no efficient sewage collection and treatment except for some affluent subdivisions with residents who can afford an expensive sewage treatment facility. Only about 12% of Metro Manila's population is served by a sewerage collection system. The balance of unserved areas contributes about 70% of all the bio-degradable organic pollutants that flow into the different river systems in Metro Manila. Untreated or partially treated industrial wastewater is also being discharged into rivers, lakes, or esteros. These wastes account for the other 30% of the organic pollutants that have all but killed Metro Manila's water systems.

Municipal solid wastes or garbage usually finds its way into the river system through open canals and culverts and end up in the river system and exert additional oxygen demand. The disposal and proliferation of toxic and hazardous wastes from industries also adds to this problem. This is especially true in Metro Manila where 69% of the country's 15,000 industrial firms are located. Most of the toxic substances are apparently discharged without treatment into natural water bodies and coastal waters.

Another pervasive problem in urban areas is solid waste management. While solid waste collection is generally more efficient in urban areas than in rural areas, waste generation also tends to be higher in urban areas (0.5–0.7 kilogramme per capita vs. 0.3 kilogramme in rural areas). An extremely inadequate solid waste management programme contributes to a very serious environmental problem in Metro Manila. On a daily basis in 2008, about 7,000 tonnes of solid wastes are generated in the capital region (National Solid Waste Management Commission). Of these, only

---

[7]http://www.who.int [April 1, 2009].

about 700 tonnes per day are recycled or composted. The balance of around 6,000 tonnes are either: 1) hauled to the city's dump sites; 2) dumped into creeks, canals and rivers; 3) burned thereby contributing to air pollution: or 4) otherwise left on streets, creating considerable health hazards. The most immediate consequence is the lamentable situation of decay and stench. There are no sufficient funds to finance a systematic and integrated solid waste management system.

Significant Projects for Ecological Cities

The Philippine government projects on ecological cities gives top priority to improving water and air quality and solid waste management in urban areas specifically Metro Manila. Some of these key projects are as follows.

River Revival Project

The DENR, in cooperation with other government agencies, the private sector and non-governmental organisations, is undertaking a rivers revival programme, foremost of which is the *"Ilog Ko, Irog Ko"* project aimed at lowering the pollution load of the Navotas-Malabon-Tenejeros-Tullahan River System. The DENR, being the lead agency, has committed to lower the industrial pollution load by 60% from 32,777 kilogrammes. Bio-chemical Oxygen Demand (BOD) per day to about 23,200 kilogrammes BOD per day. To date, the DENR has lowered the industry load by about 7%. The Metropolitan Waterworks and Sewerage System (MWSS) is committed to implement a basin-wide septic tank cleaning programme that will lower the sewage load from a load of about 26,608 kilograms BOD per day to about 9,978 kilograms BOD per day. The National Housing Authority (NHA) is also committed to remove all the squatter shanties lined along the 26 kilometre waterway and relocate them within the basin, thus lowering the pollution load. The Department of Public Works and Highways (DPWH) is committed to dredge the 26 kilometre waterway and build (2) parallel roads along the waterway.

The cost to implement these programmes is about US$25.75 million spread over a three year period. The installation of a sewerage collection and a marine outfall will increase the total cost to US$236.8 million. It is expected that the river system will be fully rehabilitated and the entire 26 kilometre waterway will be capable of sustaining marine life.

Another component of the river revival programme is the Manila Bay Clean-Up Project. This will focus on six major river network systems which

empty their wastes into Manila Bay. The six major river network systems
are:

— Navotas-Malabon-Tenejerns-Tullahan River System,
— Pasig-San Juan-Marikina River System,
— Las Pinas-Zapote River System,
— Paranaque River,
— Laguna Lake Basin, and
— Meycauayan River.

The clean-up of Manila Bay will entail the clean-up of the individual
sink systems. Among the projects lined up for lowering the pollution load of
each of these sources are the following: 1) septic tank cleaning and sewerage
collection and treatment for domestic sewage; 2) individual or combined
wastewater treatment plants for industrial firms; 3) dredging of rivers to
remove accumulated debris; and 4) transfer of squatter families along the
river banks.

Air Pollution Control Project

The current efforts for air quality management in urban regions are particularly addressed to the Metropolitan Manila area where most of vehicles and industrial firms are located. Other urban growth centres, however, have already started and are stepping up the air pollution control
programme.

Vehicle exhaust emission is the most pressing air pollution problem.
The short-term activities being implemented to alleviate the situation
are stepped up efforts to enforce the anti-smoke belching law and educational campaigns to raise the level of awareness and knowledge of
motorists and the general public on the air pollution problem. The long-
term policy options for air quality management programme for Metro
Manila to minimise vehicular pollution cover a wide range of concerns
such as:

— Incentives for low-pollutant vehicles and additional tax for pollutive
  vehicles.
— Promotion of "environment-friendly" fuel additives and appropriate pol-
  lution control devices.
— Regulation of importation of second hand cars.
— Development of an efficient mass transportation system.

Emissions from industries and power plants are also a major concern as economic development progresses. Major policy options being considered to minimise the air pollution efforts from these sectors include the following:

— Providing disincentives for pollutive industries that are located in Metro Manila and other urban centers.
— Strict implementation of land-use plans and zoning regulations.
— Promotion of energy conservation and energy efficient production processes.
— Adoption of low or non-waste technologies.

This programme include acquisition of monitoring equipment and manpower training to beef up the monitoring and enforcement capabilities of the environmental agencies.

Solid Waste Management Project

The Department of Interior and Local Governments (DILG) in cooperation with the DENR has undertaken a Local Solid Waste Management Project starting 2004. The aim is to delegate to all Local Government Units (the authority to implement solid waste management programme at the community or *barangay* level).[8] The programme encourages innovative community practices on solid waste management such as waste segregation, waste recycling, waste recovery, efficient garbage collection and stringent enforcement of laws, rules and ordinances on solid waste management. Furthermore, local governments are required to provide an inventory of sites to serve as sanitary landfills in lieu of operating open dumps. Engineering designs are now being prepared and reviewed based on the Environmental Impact Assessment made.

Quezon City Central Business District (QC-CBD) Project[9]

Unlike the other three Projects, the QC-CBD is intended to address urban concerns such as traffic, pollution and waste management through urban physical planning that considers various aspect of ecological development.

---

[8] "Barangay" is the smallest political unit in the Philippines.
[9] This section is taken mainly from the Report on the Preparation of a Comprehensive Framework for the Development of a Central Business District in Quezon City, August 2006, pp. 1–2 and 2–4.

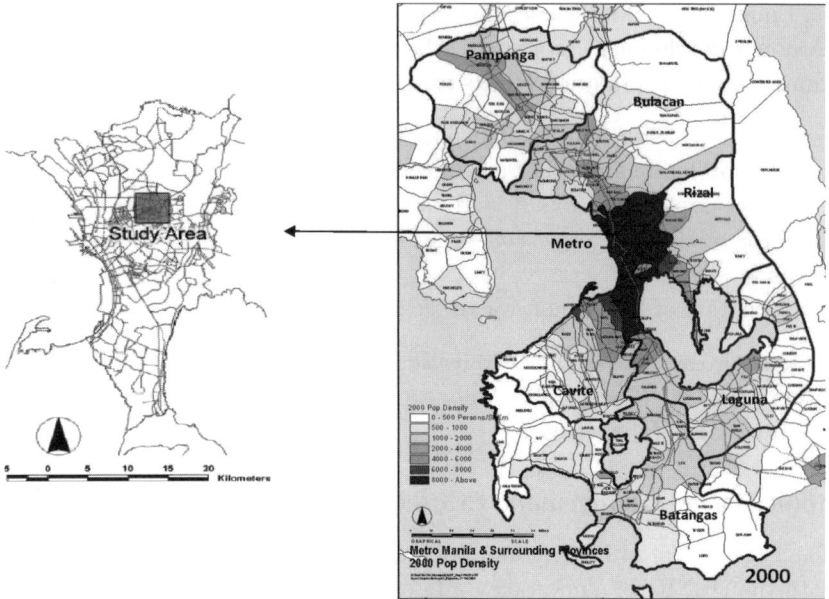

Source: Corpuz (2006b) Figure.

Fig. 2   Mega Manila, 2000.

Quezon City is the largest city of Metro Manila covering an area of over 16,112 hectares. The City has the largest area of urban open space and serves as a transport hub, being the gateway to Metro Manila, both from the north (i.e., provinces of Bulacan and Pampanga) and from the east (i.e., province of Rizal). The development of the Quezon City CBD is critical to the connectivity of the metro centre to the metro suburbs (Fig. 2).

Metro Manila and its expanded region will continue to be the primary market and the main attraction for investments in the country in the coming decades. Thus, it is important that the central city, Metro Manila is well connected to the subcentres to provide access and circulation of different modes of transport and to absorb a high proportion of employment and residential growth.

The CBD is proposed to be developed along the major transport lines. The site is a 250-hectare area composed of the North Triangle and the East Triangle. Despite its prime location and large economic potential, the area is currently under-developed. Large portions of the land are either vacant or under-utilised (Fig. 3). Informal settlers clustered in several parts of the area occupying about 23 hectares. The rest of the area is occupied by the Parks

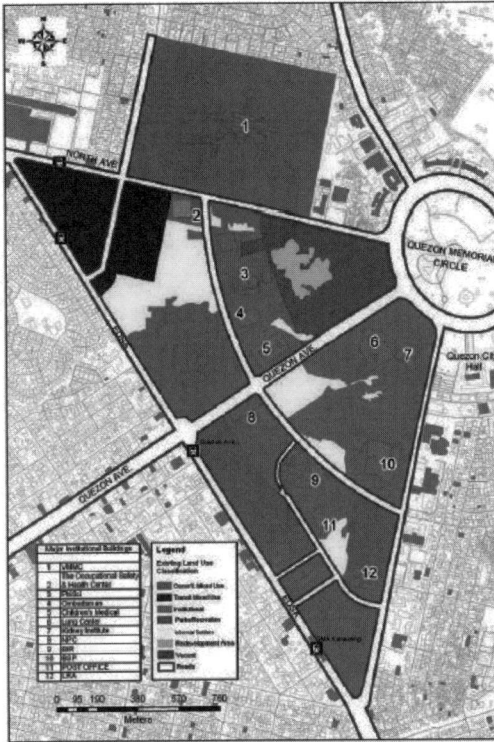

EXISTING LAND USE	GROSS AREA	%	LEGEND
Commercial Mixed Use	0.00	0%	
Institutional	156.47	62%	
Transit Mixed Use	21.06	8%	
Parks/Recreation	22.30	9%	
Informal settlers	23.18	9%	
Redevelopment (Housing)	0.00	0%	
Vacant	17.62	7%	
Roads	10.01	4%	
Total	250.64	100%	

Source: Comprehensive Concept Plan for QC-CBD.

Fig. 3   Map of CBD Area.

and Wildlife centre as well as government and medical institutions including educational facilities. Although 79% of the total CBD area appears to be occupied, a significant portion of the area is open unutilised space. Only 33% of the area identified for institutional, transit and informal house uses

Marife M. Ballesteros

| **External Linkages and Internal Integration** | **Enhancing Development Opportunities and Unlocking Values** | **Establishing District Themes** |

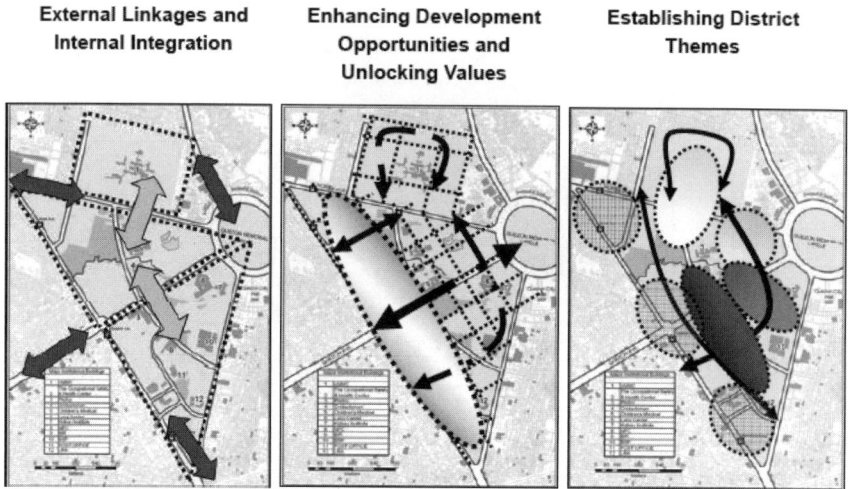

Source: Comprehensive Framework QC-CBD 2008.

Fig. 4   Urban Design Concept.

is physically occupied by structures. This leaves about 155.4 hectares that could be immediately available for CBD development.

The proposed CBD is a development strategy that will lead to a vibrant, environment-friendly CBD characterised by the following (Fig. 4): 1) external linkages and internal integration; 2) enhanced development opportunities and unlocking values; and 3) established district themes.

The external linkage provides for a well-developed and efficient road and transport system which will link Metro Manila to the suburbs as well as an internal transit system to link three main areas comprising the CBD. New road networks will be created to improve internal access and circulation. And, to encourage people to utilise public transport, efficient and convenient "door to door" transit is planned. The transit system would also allow for walkable areas and opportunities to introduce additional greenery to the CBD.

The area occupied by the CBD provides unique development opportunities. It will unlock the higher value development potentials of the area as well as those areas previously difficult to access. The improved housing for informal settlers translates into significant social impact not only in terms of better health conditions, but also improved water and sanitation facilities. The development would be an opportunity to test different approaches to water conservation in an urban setting. Likewise, with the improved road network, the use of eco-friendly technology such as fuel-cell, electric hybrid and compressed natural gas transits would be highly feasible.

The size of the CBD and the unique features of the existing land-use (e.g., large park areas, clustering of specialised health, government, academic institutions, clustering of media and recreational institutions) provides an opportunity to divide the area into development themes. Although the overall land-use is mixed-use, specific land uses are emphasised to establish neighbourhood character and identity. Districts of high- and low-densities are envisioned to distinguish areas which are most active both in daytime and nighttime (office and retail and recreational centres) from those areas with residential focus or mixed used with cultural, recreational and health focus.

Challenges to Ecological Initiatives: QC-CBD Experience

The discussion on this section focuses on the challenges to ecological initiatives in urban areas. Given the participation of the author on the QC-CBD Project, the analysis is based mainly on the Quezon City Project.

The QC-CBD is an important undertaking not only because of its business potential but also its social and ecological impact. The vision is to build a park community from street plans to entire neighbourhood layouts that is more sociable, civic and inclusive. The success of the QC-CBD will create greater consciousness of ecological effects that can influence the development of other metro areas in the country.

The implementation of the QC-CBD development is still at its preparatory stage. This stage is critical because it involves several major activities that will identify the key decision-makers, the political process at play, how incentives are defined through the property rights system and the distribution of gains among key players. The preparatory stage presents important lessons and reveals major challenges on ecological initiatives.

It is useful to point out that there are several constraints to the development of the QC-CBD. These constraints can be grouped into three main issues: 1) property rights; 2) informal settlements; and 3) governance structure.

Property Rights Constraints

As shown in Fig. 5 and Table 2, the government is the single largest owner of the area. Over 95% of the land area is owned by government

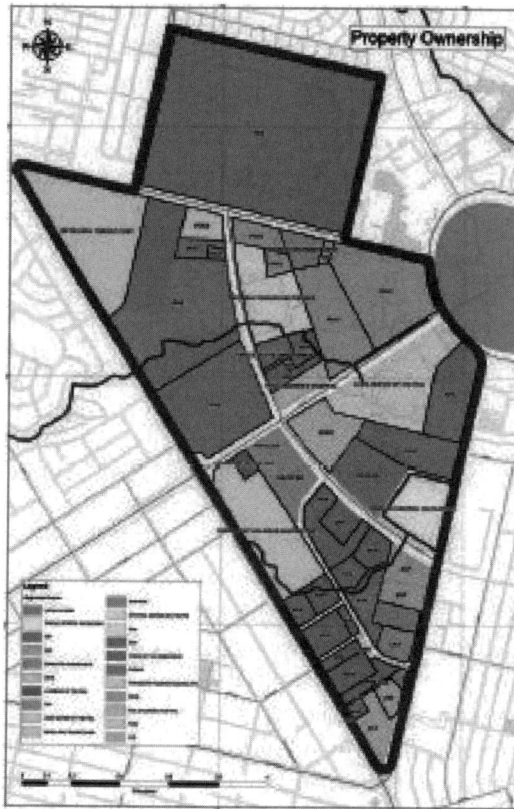

Source: Comprehensive Concept Plan for QC-CBD.

Fig. 5   Land Ownership Map.

Table 2   Landownership Area Distribution.

Owner/Occupant	Land Area (ha)	%
Government Corporation	202.9	80.9
National Government Agency	31.2	12.1
Private Sector	11.9	4.7
No Data	4.9	2.0
Total	250.9	100

or government-controlled corporations with the National Housing Authority (NHA) as the biggest single landowner. NHA alone owns 42.1% of the total area. The other portions of government land are titled to numerous government agencies. Only a small area (11.9 hectares) is privately owned.

Since ownership is mainly government, it would have been easy to consolidate these properties for re-development. However, this has not been the case because the bulk of the land parcels are legally encumbered. It is estimated that around 97 hectares or 41% of the CBD area is encumbered. The encumbrances include cases of multiple ownerships, presidential proclamations providing for transfer of usufruct rights to other government agencies and mortgage guarantees (Table 3). Multiple land ownership and existing encumbrances limit the availability and configuration of land immediately available for development.

The cases related to land ownership have been pending in courts for the last 12 years. On the other hand, the issuance of presidential proclamation has added to the issues on the rightful property custodian of government lands. Based on legal procedures, the issuance of another presidential proclamation over use of government land supersedes existing proclamation on the same land. However, this can be problematic when there are existing contracts undertaken by the government agency with a third party based on previous proclamations. Also, when land is proclaimed as housing for informal settlers, the government essentially transfers usufruct rights to the informal settlers. Presidential Proclamations are President's discretion but it cannot bind the government unless the issuance of rights goes through an approval process by appropriate government agency. Often, Proclamations are used as tools for "political gimmickry" thus many Proclamations are issued but not acted upon.

Encumbrances also include existing lease contracts that have yet to expire in the next 20 years. Although lease contract is consistent with the development process, the bargaining cost tends to increase substantially when potential economic gains are huge. For instance, the current lessee of about 38 hectares of land in the North triangle has not utilised the land at all for the last ten years. Almost 80% of this rented land is vacant or occupied by informal settlers while 20% is used as terminals for buses plying provincial routes. However, the company has no intention to end lease contract and should government terminate contract for re-development purposes, the compensation requested for termination is way above the lease rent that it currently pays to government.

Another property rights constraint is that some portion of the CBD area are still public land. The North Triangle includes the 23-hectare Parks and Wildlife centre which is a public land and thus cannot be disposable. The law requires a legislative process to convert public lands into alienable and disposable (A&D) lands. The process can be tedious and

Marife M. Ballesteros

Table 3   List of Encumbrances on Government Properties.

Encumbrance	Cases	Owner	Occupant	Sq m
Notice of Levy on Execution	NPV vs. Home of David Realty	NPC	NPC	9,722
	Petition for declaration to nullify *ab initio* the purported copy of Decree No. 17431	NHA	PDEA	42,226 11,355
	Plaintiffs vs. BSP, for forcible entry with application for writ of injunction	BSP	BSP	22,770
	NHA vs. Lung Centre of the Philippine Plaintiffs vs. NHA, for title annulment etc.	Lung Centre	Lung Centre	17,231 121,463
	Plaintiffs vs. NHA, for ownership/possession of real property, immunity to eviction, annulment of titles	NHA	Bureau of Fire Protection	4,000
Lease Contract	Lease: Robinsons, San Jose Builders	NHA	Vacant	13,700
	Lease: Robinsons, San Jose Builders	NHA	Informal Settlers, Terminal, NHA	257,602
	Lease: Robinsons, San Jose Builders acknowledgement of lease until it expires on 2020	NHA	Manila Seedling	143,996
Ninth Mortgage Supplement	Between MRT Corp and BPI as on Shore collateral agent	MRTC	LRT depot	160,461
Mortgage	In favour of LBP to guarantee Php 400M	Ombudsman	Ombudsman	10,000
	In favour of NHA to guarantee Php 32M	NHA	Vacant	2,000
Amendment to Proc. 915, MO 127	Transferring to Supreme Court land to expand Court of Tax Appeals	NHA	Vacant/informal settlers	11,772
	Future NEA site	NEA	NEA	2,602
Amendment to Proc	Transferring to Department of National Defence (DND)	NHA	VMMC	540,000

(Continued)

Table 3   (*Continued*)

Encumbrance	Cases	Owner	Occupant	Sq m
Encroachment	NHA vs. Manila Seedling Bank	NHA	Manila Seedling	70,000
Claim on Ownership of Elliptical Road	State vs. Subido Family	GOP	Vacant	

Source: Comprehensive Concept Plan for QC-CBD and updated information.

affected by rent seeking activities of legislators. Moreover, public ownership restricts freehold disposition which is critical in the development of the CBD because leasehold will not be able to attract high quality residential developments that are recognised pre-requisites of CBD office and other commercial developments.

The Philippine land administration and management is weak in various aspects: legal and policy framework, land administration infrastructure and land taxation. A major weakness of Philippine land policy is the failure to clearly identify society's preferences regarding land-use. The transcending importance of efficient land-use to society is well understood but the political economy of establishing social preferences regarding land-use is the problematic part. Thus, there have been significant problems in land-use and allocation which to a large extent is due to weaknesses and inconsistency in the legal and policy framework governing land-use and management.

The land information system in the country is also inefficient. Land information is scanty and its accuracy doubtful. Access to land information can be extremely difficult both for government and the public. Government has no clear policy on data sharing and linking of essential land records in government land agencies. It is difficult to link these records because of the following: 1) poor segregation of functions among land agencies; 2) land records are often regarded as primarily for internal agency use only rather than for the purpose of policy coordination and the general public; 3) absence of national standards on recording, surveying, mapping to allow integration of information across land agencies; and 4) poor overall management of land records.

The absence of a standard valuation methodology in the country also affected the process of CBD development. Accurate and reliable information on property values is not available. So far, there is no reliable database and methodology in the country to establish the true market values of private and public lands. Available data on land values show that values change depending on the purposes for which it is used. Government agencies use different valuation methods and there is no clear pattern of differences in land values used by the registry of deeds, the Bureau of Internal Revenue (BIR), or the local government unit.

These problems in land administration have in effect delayed implementation of the CBD project. The government has yet to sort through the various property rights issues and to understand the legal implications before appropriate actions can be undertaken.

Informal Settlements

The presence of several informal settler communities in the CBD area prevents the development of the land they occupy and affects the commercial viability of adjacent areas. There are close to 12,700 families in the CBD area spread out over eight communities occupying over 23 hectares or 9% of total CBD area. These families reside in predominantly makeshift houses with densities as high as 4,000 persons per hectare. They occupy potentially prime land that could be utilised for high valued activities.

One of the key policy concerns in the country is that of informal settlements. While the Constitution upholds private ownership, legislators have enacted laws that are tolerant of squatting. Thus, occupation and possession as a mode of acquisition have become common not only on public lands but also private and patrimonial properties. Land markets are, thus, constrained by the presence of a third party that have no legal claims over possession and enjoyment of the land but only *quasi-legal* or *de facto* rights over use of the land. The presence of squatters has increased transaction cost in the land market. Evicting them is no easy task. The law entitles squatters to a due process before eviction and demolition can be undertaken. Litigation, however, is a slow and tedious process. On the average, resolution of squatting cases takes years. Carrying out a court order is even more difficult. Thus, the practice has been to bargain with informal settlers by providing them with options for relocation. Government at the national and local levels usually adopts the humane approach to resettlement. It generally adheres to the policy of maximum tolerance when dealing with informal settlers. The reasons behind this approach are legal and political. Informal settlements are the vote-rich areas and are considered by politicians to represent the disadvantaged sector of society.

Resettlement is a costly undertaking not only in terms of the money involved but the considerable time needed to undertake the process. Considerable delays are expected on these cases. The Urban Development and Housing Act (UDHA) which recognises the rights of informal settlers in the occupation of land requires an adequate resettlement area for displaced families. The law also supports preference for on-site or in-city relocation as opposed to off-site arrangements.

The political and legal aspects are the key considerations in formulating a resettlement strategy plan. There are major resettlement experiences which can be adopted for the QC-CBD. From this experience, it is shown that the process alone can be tedious considering the size of informal settlements in the CBD area.

The preparatory process for resettlement in the CBD can last from three to five years. During this period, the major activities include the following. First, undertake actual census, tagging and situation mapping analysis to determine the actual number of households affected. Usually, when major resettlements projects are to be undertaken, the number of informal settlers in the affected area balloons, thus, the need for census at the initial stage. The census will also determine the socio-economic status of the families so that appropriate financing programme can be provided. Second, develop consensus for the resettlement plan. Often, the needs and expectations of affected settlers are diverse. Different resettlement packages thus have to be prepared from which household can make choices based on their needs and capacities. Third, select relocation sites that are affordable and accessible to economic centres. This can take time, since consideration include not only the land cost but also expected development cost. Also, one has to work within bureaucratic guidelines on land procurement. So far, the NHA which is the primary agency to clear the area of informal settlers has yet to start the consensus building process with informal settlers.

The other important consideration is fund sourcing. The full cost of relocation for the CBD area would amount to P2.55 to P3.61 billion pesos (Table 4). Assuming that both on-site and off-site strategy for relocation will be provided, the total subsidy (i.e., total cost less total loans) would amount to P1.02 to P2.09 billion. Properties in the CBD that are affected by informal settlements are those owned by NHA. However, NHA assets are primarily in the form of land and thus have to identify resources or deals with the private sector to raise funds for resettlement. Indeed, when a large number of informal settlers are involved, the difficult task is to balance the cost implications, land availability and social responsiveness of the Project.

Table 4   Summary of Resettlement Scenario Costs (PhP billion).

Type of Cost	A: Total Families = 12,700			B: Total Families = 10,500		
	Scenario 1a MRB Onsite/ Offsite	Scenario 2a MRB Onsite/ H&L Offsite	Scenario 3a H&L Onsite/ Offsite	Scenario 1b MRB Onsite/ Offsite	Scenario 2b MRB Onsite/ H&L Offsite	Scenario 3b H&L Onsite/ Offsite
Onsite cost	1.33	1.33	0.29	1.33	1.33	0.29
Offsite cost	1.22	1.87	3.32	0.71	1.09	2.65
Total cost	2.55	3.20	3.61	2.04	2.42	2.94
Total subsidy	1.02	1.68	2.09	0.78	1.16	1.68

Notes:

a. Densities and unit costs are based on NHA and Habitat models.

b. Offsite does not distinguish between in-city or near city locations.

c. Total subsidy = total cost – total loans.

Source: Comprehensive Concept Plan for QC-CBD.

Governance Structure

Given the nature of land ownership in the area, the Project would necessarily require direct intervention from the national government. It was however, the Local Government of Quezon City that initiated the preparation of the comprehensive framework for the CBD which is now adopted by the national government as its basic guide for development. The local government of Quezon City does not own any land in the proposed CBD, but is a major stakeholder under the local government code. The development of the CBD would have major implications in zoning ordinances and other local ordinances to support the framework. Also, the Project would translate into significant financial and economic gains in terms of increase revenues for the City, higher value of land assets, improved housing of residents and better environment impact.

The QC-CBD is earmarked as one of the priority projects for implementation in the next two years. The Project is now under the management of a TriDev (Tripartite) Commission organised through Executive Orders of the President of the Philippines. The Commission has the representation of the President, the CBD's biggest landowner, the NHA, the single biggest landowner and the local government which has jurisdiction over the land use of the properties in the CBD.

The powers of the Tridev Commission are as follows: 1) oversee the preparation of the Master Development Plan based on the concept plan; 2) manage, control and direct the implementation of the Master Development Plan; and 3) formulate deal structures and agreements with property owners.

However, it is now obvious that the Commission does not have the flexibility to sanction, command resources and enter into financing deals. TriDev would be helpless to sanction developers should they not enforce the policies of the Commission. The continuity and consistency of policies may also become an issue since Tridev representatives can change overtime. A major concern is the inability of a Commission to enter into finance contracts with local or international investors. This could substantially constraint development considering the necessary basic infrastructure and resettlement activities that have to initially undertaken.

The Quezon City local government recommended transforming the Commission into a special purpose vehicle that may be called the Quezon City Development Authority (QCDA) which will have the attributes and powers of a corporation. The corporation will be the vehicle to facilitate the implementation and fulfilment of the detailed comprehensive Master Plan. As a corporation, it can require control over the implementation of the development plan. It will also open avenues for leverage financing and other finance options. The QCDA proposal is patterned after the state-owned Bases Conversion Development Authority (BCDA) which managed the development of the Fort Bonifacio CBD in Makati City and the construction of express interchange connecting Metro Manila to Northern provinces.

A comparison of implementation through a Commission vs. that of a Corporation is presented in Table 5. Despite the apparent merits of the QCDA model, it does not appear to be the appropriate structure for the QC-CBD development. A major hindrance is the different interests of government agencies with whom specific properties have been assigned. Under the BCDA model, government has been successful in the consolidation of properties since the entire land is under one government entity. The QCDA proposal was met with strong opposition from the agency landowners and while the national government can exercise its powers over these agencies, it chose to respect the property rights of these agencies. This condition to uphold the existing property rights in the area has been clearly stated in the provisions of the executive orders creating the Tridev Commission.

The protection of property rights of government entities and institutions are setting the development process at a very slow pace due to the difficult act of finding consensus among the concerned government institutions. NHA would rather oversee and manage the disposition of its properties and enter into agreements or contracts on its own. The government hospitals on the other hand would agree to a development that is in line with their own plans.

Based on the different interests and objectives of stakeholders, the proposed consolidation of these lands may not be feasible. It has also been argued that creation of another state-owned corporation can be complicated and could add to the national government fiscal burdens. Thus, the most likely scenario is to develop the QC-CBD under an individual scheme. Under this scheme, the risk of the CBD resulting into "pockets" of development is plausible. Moreover, this scheme places a heavy burden on the local government both as regulator and provider of basic services. As regulator, the local government has to ensure that individualised projects deviate minimally from the CBD Master Plan. Also, the local government of Quezon City has to make investments to build the enabling infrastructure, namely,

Table 5   Proposed Governance Structure for QC-CBD.

	Governance by Tri-Dev Commission	**Governance by QCDA Corporation**
Nature	Tri-Dev Commission is a policy-making body which determines the master plan, policies and objectives for the CBD	QCDA is a government corporation with all the attributes and powers of a corporation; determines the master plan, policies and objectives for the CBD
Mode of creation	Presidential Proclamation	Corporation Code, but incorporation shall be mandated in an Executive Order
Composition	Office of the President (OP), NHA, Quezon City as members	Office of the President (OP), NHA/landowners, Quezon City as shareholders
Allocation of resources	Mainly coordination efforts with no commitment to allocate resources	Presence of OP enhances coordination of the national government institutions required for the development of the CBD (e.g., DPWH for road network; DOTC for LRT/MRT access and transit circulation) QC to make available to QCDA its resources as local government to facilitate land consolidation and approval of development and other permits to ensure compliance with overall Master Plan for CBD
Governance	Tri-Dev may enter into a MOA with investors; however, Tri-Dev may be helpless to sanction investors if the latter does not enforce the policies of Tri-Dev	Direct control and management by QCDA of investor companies as shareholder/investor with proprietary rights to the CBD
	Investors deal with 3 separate parties in terms of policy and implementation issues; continuity and consistency of policies may become an issue	Negotiations with Third parties (private investors, utility and service providers) will be coordinated through QCDA

(*Continued*)

Table 5 (*Continued*)

	Governance by Tri-Dev Commission	Governance by QCDA Corporation
Financing	Entirely private sector	Funds to be provided by OP to be invested as equity contribution in QCDA
	Government loses proprietary interest on land under a joint venture with private sector	Funding to be provided by QC as equity contribution in QCDA for development of common infrastructure and utilities in a manner that will make the CBD as integrated development
		Corporate vehicle allows deferment of payment of consideration for the land while landowner continues to retain proprietary interest indirectly
		Valuable asset base will allow corporate vehicle to attract financing from institutional investors
Returns	Lower risk but lower returns to government	Equitable risk/return sharing mechanism among various landowners to the extent of their respective interests
		Allows easier transferability of the land at lesser cost since land is represented by shares in TPDC

internal road networks to ensure an integrated development. The public nature of roads implies that returns to investments will be indirect through increase revenues for the City. On the other hand, if the local government leaves it to the private sector to internalise infrastructure development in their projects, there is a tendency for the private sector to contain the externality effects which can further hinder the implementation of plans.

With the advance of decentralisation in the country, the local government plays a central role in urban planning and management. The local government can provide an alternative option when the political system at the national government is hampered by different conflicting interests. The governance structure that will implement the CBD Plan is critical. It requires political will at the national or local level. National government support of local level initiatives is also necessary for implementation since most resources are within the control of the national government.

Conclusions

The Philippine Strategy for Sustainable Development provides an excellent vision that supports ecological city development. The basic tenet of this strategy is that environmental protection and economic growth are mutually compatible. However, for most part, government action on ecological city is reactive rather than proactive. Thus, major government projects for ecological development are in large urban areas where ecological problems are most significant. This is partly because only in recent years has sustainable development been accorded a key part in the development agenda.

In particular, Metro Manila is the recipient of most of these ecological projects. Metro Manila is the capital region in the country and the region alone supports almost one-third of the country's population and domestic economy. The region has the largest concentration of consumers in Southeast Asia and by 2015, it is expected to become the 15th largest city in the world.

Part of the reason for the ecological deterioration of Metro Manila is poor urban planning. Urban renewal in several parts of the Metro region has to be undertaken to abate environmental deterioration of the city. The development of the QC-CBD is a major ecological initiative that aims to address the concerns of traffic, pollution and waste disposal through urban physical planning. The comprehensive conceptual framework for the CBD development is consistent with the basic strategy of creating a balance between economic growth and environment. Although the "CBD" concept seems business oriented, the social and environmental implications are of utmost importance due to its potential impact in improving urban connectivity both within Metro Manila and regional areas, providing housing to informal settlers, encouraging "walkability" and use of ecology-friendly transport technology.

However, this project has been faced with several issues which have magnified some institutional failures in the country particularly with regards to property rights, informal settlements and governance. The poor enforcement of property rights and the inefficient land administration and management in the country have impeded access to land markets and hampered efforts at resource management. Similarly, political considerations at the national and local levels can significantly distort incentive systems.

The constraints of poor institutions are not only confined to projects such as the QC-CBD but also to other ecological initiatives. For instance, the poor enforcement of property rights and rent-seeking activities are also major concerns in water management.[10] In the case of the QC-CBD, the presence of institutional constraints would imply providing other options for development. If total land consolidation is not possible, an individual lot development model can be considered where owners manage their own land while the local government provide development controls using both regulations and incentives. With the advance of decentralisation in the country, the local governments play a central role in building eco-cities. The local governments can provide an alternative mechanism when national government decisions are hampered by weak institutions. We thus need to strengthen local institutions and local government capacities.

References

Coase, R. (2002). "Why Economics Will Change." *ISNIE Newsletter*, 4(1), 1–7.

Corpuz, A. (2006). "Population and Settlements 2." *Provincial Development and Physical Framework Guidebook*. Powerpoint presentation.

———. (2006). "Centrographic Measures of the Growth of Metro Manila with Comparisons to the Metropolitan Areas of Bangkok and Jakarta." 31st Conference, Federation of Asian Economic Associations, Singapore.

Dijk, M.P. van. (2007). "Ecological Cities in China, What Are We Heading for, Just More Ecological Urban Water Systems?" A Contribution to the Switch Annual Conference in Tel Aviv, November 26–27.

Francisco, H. (2004). "Water Allocation Mechanisms and Environmental Service Payments." In *Winning the Water War*, Rola, Francisco and Liguton (eds.). Manila: Philippine Institute for Development Studies.

Housing and Urban Development Coordinating Council (HUDCC) and the Philippine Institute for Development Studies. "National Urban Development and Housing Framework." 2008–2010. draft.

Llanto, G. and M. Ballesteros. (2003). "Land Issues in Poverty Reduction Strategies and the Development Agenda: The Philippines." *Land Reform Bulletin (Special Edition)*. FAO and the World Bank.

Peirce, N. (2009). "The 'Humane Metropolis' — Are We Ready?" The Humane Metropolis Web Site. www.humanemetropolis.org/articles/2007-04-01-Peirce.html [February 2, 2009].

---

[10]Francisco, Herminia (2004). "Water Allocation Mechanisms and Environmental Service Payments." *Winning the Water War*, pp. 133–151. Tabios, III Guillermo Q. and Cristina David (2004). "Competing Uses of Water: Cases of Angat Reservoir, Laguna Lake and Groundwater Systems of Batangas City and Cebu City." *Winning the Water War*, pp. 105–131.

Philippine Sustainable Development Network. (2009). www.psdn.org.ph/agenda21/pssd.html [March 30, 2009].

Platt, R.H. (2009). "Epilogue." The Humane Metropolis Web Site. www.humanemetropolis.org/book/ [February 2, 2009].

_____. (2004). "Toward Ecological Cities: Adapting to the 21st Century Metropolis." *Environment*, 46(5): 12–27.

Quezon City Government and the World Bank. (2006). "Preparation of a Comprehensive Framework for the Development of a Central Business District in Quezon City. Final Report." August.

Soderbaum, P. (2000). "Ecological Economics, Political Economics for Social and Environment Development." The Earthscan Web Site. www.earthscan.co.uk/?TabId=1242&v=451002 [February 2, 2009].

Tabios, G. and C. David. (2004). "Competing Uses of Water." In *Winning the Water War*, Rola, Francisco and Liguton (eds.). Manila: Philippine Institute for Development Studies.

United Nations Population Division. (2009). "World Urbanization Prospects: The 2001 Revision." The United Nations website. www.un.org/esa/population/publications/wup2001/wup2001dh.pdf [January 2009].

Webster, D., A. Corpuz and C. Pablo. (2002). "Towards a National Urban Development Framework for the Philippines: Strategic Consideration." Prepared for World Bank-NEDA.

World Health Organization. (2009). www.who.int.

Biographies of Authors
(in Order of Paper Presentation)

Hidefumi IMURA is a Professor for environmental systems analysis and planning in the Graduate School of Environmental Studies at Nagoya University. After receiving a Ph.D. (1974) in applied physics at the University of Tokyo, he joined the Japan Environment Agency, and subsequently worked for the Ministry of Foreign Affairs and the Yokohama Municipal Government. He has a wide range of expertise covering domestic and international environmental policy issues, environmental technologies, economics, and information in East Asian countries. He was a lead author of Working Group III of the Third Assessment Report of IPCC. He is one of the leading researchers on environmental issues in China. He was the Co-Chairman of the Task Forces on "Financial Mechanisms for Environmental Protection" and "Ecological Compensation" of the China Council on International Cooperation for Environment and Development (2002–2006). He is conducting a study on economic development and water resources supply and demand in the Yellow River Basin.

William S.W. LIM graduated from the Architectural Association (AA) London and continued his graduate study at the Department of City and Regional Planning, Harvard University. Lim is President of AA Asia and Chairman of Asian Urban Lab. He was conferred a Doctor of Architecture Honoris Causa by RMIT University in 2002. Currently, Lim writes and lectures on a wide range of subjects relating to architecture, urbanism and culture in Asia as well as on current issues relating to the postmodern, glocality and social justice.

LYE Liang Fook is a Research Fellow in the East Asian Institute, National University of Singapore. His research interests include China's central-local relations, propaganda and the media (particularly newspaper media groups), leadership changes and political stability in China and China-ASEAN relations. He was part of a team that completed a study on the Suzhou Industrial Park, a flagship project between China and Singapore. He has also written about the Sino-Singapore Tianjin Eco-city project. He was formerly with the Singapore Ministry of Foreign Affairs.

CHEN Gang is a Research Fellow in the East Asian Institute, National University of Singapore. He studied international relations and obtained his Ph.D. degree at the China Foreign Affairs University. He is the single author of the book *The Kyoto Protocol and International Cooperation against Climate Change* (Beijing: Xinhua Press, 2008) and Politics of China's Environmental Protection: Problems and Progress (Singapore: World Scientific, 2009). His research papers have appeared in refereed journals such as *The Chinese Journal of International Politics, The Journal of East Asian Affairs, American Studies Quarterly, Journal of China Foreign Affairs University* and *the International Forum.* His research interests include China's domestic politics and foreign policy, environmental governance, international relations and transnational cooperation against climate change.

POW Choon-Piew is an Assistant Professor in the Department of Geography at the National University of Singapore. Broadly trained as an urban/social geographer, he has an abiding interest in urban development issues with a focus on Asia, in particular, cities in China and Southeast Asia. His most recent research examines how the development of commodity housing enclaves in Shanghai has transformed the social and spatial organisation of the city leading to the formation of exclusive "middle-class" residential enclaves and the marginalisation of urban poor and migrant workers. Another research project that he is currently undertaking looks at the planning discourses and practices revolving around the idea of urban sustainability and the formation of the "eco-city".

Harvey NEO is an Assistant Professor in the Department of Geography at the National University of Singapore (NUS). Broadly trained as a political/economic geographer, he received his Ph.D. from Clark University (Massachusetts, U.S.). His research interests include the political economy of the livestock industry, geographies of food, nature/society issues and eco-cities. He has published in these areas in journals such as *Geoforum, Area and Asia Pacific Viewpoint.* At NUS, he teaches "Nature and Society" and "Eco-Development in Southeast Asia".

Rujiroj ANAMBUTR is a Senior Lecturer and Chairman of the Masters Programme in Landscape Architecture in the Department of Urban Design and Planning, Faculty of Architecture, Silpakorn University, Thailand. He is currently an appointed member of the board of the Architect Council of Thailand (ACT), a governing body responsible for professional practices, promotion, and ethics of all architecture professions including Architecture, Landscape Architecture, Urban Design and Interior Architecture. He is also serving as an expert member on the Environmental Impact Assessment Report Committee for Community Service Projects, for the Office of Natural Resources and Environment Policy and Planning. He has extensive experience as team leader on several planning, design and research of cities and urban area projects.

Suraya A. AFIFF holds a Ph.D. degree in Environmental Science, Policy, and Management from the University of California, Berkeley, the U.S. Currently, she teaches environmental politics at the Anthropology Graduate Programme at the University of Indonesia apart from her involvement with **KARSA** (the Learning Circle on the Reformation of Village Institution and the Agrarian Reform), Yogyakarta, Indonesia.

WANG Tao graduated from the Department of Architecture of Xi'an Jiaotong University in 1994. From 1998 to 2000, he studied for a Master's degree in urban planning in the School of Architecture of Tsinghua Univeristy and started his Ph.D. study in 2000 at Faculty of Architecture and Fine Arts, Norwegian University of Science and Technology. Wang received his Ph.D. at the end of 2004 with his thesis on the social housing development in China. WANG Tao works as an executive editor-in-chief of Community Design magazine by Tsinghua University. He concurrently heads the R&D Section of the Institute of Architectural Design and Research Institute of Tsinghua University. His main research fields are urban housing, urban renewal and sustainable urban planning. He was the independent consultant for Energy Foundation on Sustainable Chinese Cities Programme, and is now a member of the Special Commission for Human Settlements under the Chinese Society for Sustainable Development.

SHAO Lei (B.A, D.Eng.) has held full time appointments in the School of Architecture, Tsinghua University. He was appointed Assistant Professor in 2003 and Associate Professor of Urban Planning and Design in 2008. From 2006–2007, he was a visiting scholar in the Graduate School of Design, Harvard University and visiting instructor in the Department of Architecture, Massachusetts Institute of Technology. He is currently Director of the

Institute of Housing and Community Studies in the School of Architecture, Tsinghua University. As an architect and urban planner, he has presided over a number of projects and research programmes including the Conservation Planning of Xiangfan Historical and Cultural City, Hubei Province (2005–2006); the Urban Design of the Old City, Heze, Shandong Province (2004); the Study on Community Problems in Shichahai Area, Beijing Old City, UNESCO Programme (2003–2004); the Study of Public Facilities of Large Residential Areas in Beijing, Research Programme of Beijing Municipal Planning Committee (2003–2006).

Hardev KAUR is a Senior Lecturer in the Faculty of Administrative Science and Policy Studies at University Technology Mara and is presently based at the branch campus in Malacca. She has just completed her Ph.D. thesis on community participation in Local Agenda 21 with specific reference to the Petaling Jaya and Miri City Councils. She has also presented papers on governance, public and community participation and Local Agenda 21 at a number of seminars and workshops.

Datuk Dr. Mizan HITAM, from the Faculty of Architecture, Planning and Surveying, is currently the Director at the Mara University of Technology, Melaka campus. He obtained his Ph.D. from the University of Newcastle upon Tyne, the UK in 1997 and a Master's degree from Ohio State University, Columbus, the U.S. in 1988. His area of specialisation is in Town and Country Planning, Urban Development Policy and Housing and Land Development, and Islamic Arts and Architecture.

Marife M. BALLESTEROS is a Senior Research Fellow in the Philippine Institute for Development Studies, a government think-tank based in Manila. She has a doctorate degree in Development Economics from Nijmegen University (Netherlands). She is adviser to the Housing and Urban Development Coordinating Council (HUDCC) and the Philippine Senate on urban development and housing policies. In particular, she assisted in crafting national policies and programmes on housing finance, community infrastructure programmes, rental housing regulations, land administration reforms, the national urban development and housing framework, and the national land-use code. She is also on the technical advisory committee for the Comprehensive Rehabilitation of the Municipality of Bacolor and for the development of the Quezon City Central Business District. She is concurrently a member of the Southeast Asia Urban Environment Management Network (SEA-UEM) where she serves as resource person on urban environment issues.

Index